Secure Communications and Asymmetric Cryptosystems

AAAS Selected Symposia Series

Published by Westview Press, Inc.
5500 Central Avenue, Boulder, Colorado

for the

American Association for the Advancement of Science
1776 Massachusetts Avenue, N.W., Washington, D.C.

Secure Communications and Asymmetric Cryptosystems

Edited by Gustavus J. Simmons

Routledge
Taylor & Francis Group
LONDON AND NEW YORK

First published 1982 by Westview Press

Published 2019 by Routledge
52 Vanderbilt Avenue, New York, NY 10017
2 Park Square, Milton Park, Abingdon, Oxon OX14 4RN

Routledge is an imprint of the Taylor & Francis Group, an informa business

Library of Congress Catalog Card Number 82-60126

ISBN 13: 978-0-367-28688-0 (hbk)

About the Book

Secure message transmission is of extreme importance in today's information-based society: military, diplomatic, and corporate data transmissions must be safeguarded; so also must the account of every individual who has an automatic-teller bank account or whose purchases are subject to point-of-sale, direct account debiting. The only known way to keep all such transactions secret and authentic is by way of cryptographic techniques. But most cryptosystems in use today are not fool-proof--their "symmetric" nature allows them to be compromised if either the sender's or the receiver's "key" (decoding algorithm) falls into the wrong hands.

This book reports on the enormous amount of work that has been done in the past three years on an exciting new concept, "asymmetric" cryptography. In asymmetric systems, the information held by the transmitter and by the receiver is not only different, but also is related by a "computationally complex" problem that makes it infeasible to derive one key from the other. Using these systems, it is possible to communicate secretly and to "sign' messages--or "fingerprint" the transmitter for the receiver--even though the transmitter--or the receiver--has been compromised. It is also possible to communicate in privacy over open channels without prior exchange of secret keys. Moreover, messages can be authenticated when the message content cannot, or should not, be concealed from an opponent. For example, weapons monitoring devices in an opponent's territory can transmit messages of guaranteed accuracy, and the opponent can check the accuracy of the message without being able to alter it. These new capabilities portend revolutionary applications of vast commercial and social importance.

About the Series

The *AAAS Selected Symposia Series* was begun in 1977 to provide a means for more permanently recording and more widely disseminating some of the valuable material which is discussed at the AAAS Annual National Meetings. The volumes in this *Series* are based on symposia held at the Meetings which address topics of current and continuing significance, both within and among the sciences, and in the areas in which science and technology impact on public policy. The *Series* format is designed to provide for rapid dissemination of information, so the papers are not typeset but are reproduced directly from the camera-copy submitted by the authors. The papers are organized and edited by the symposium arrangers who then become the editors of the various volumes. Most papers published in this *Series* are original contributions which have not been previously published, although in some cases additional papers from other sources have been added by an editor to provide a more comprehensive view of a particular topic. Symposia may be reports of new research or reviews of established work, particularly work of an interdisciplinary nature, since the AAAS Annual Meetings typically embrace the full range of the sciences and their societal implications.

WILLIAM D. CAREY
Executive Officer
American Association for the Advancement of Science

Contents

About the Editor and Authors

Gustavus J. Simmons *is manager of the Applied Mathematics Department at Sandia National Laboratories, Albuquerque, New Mexico. His research has been primarily in the areas of combinatorics and graph theory and in information theory and cryptography, especially as applied to message authentication and systems design.*

Leonard M. Adleman *is professor of mathematics at Massachusetts Institute of Technology and professor of computer science at the University of Southern California. A specialist in computational complexity with particular emphasis on number theoretic problems, he has also done research on both theoretical and applied aspects of cryptography.*

Whitfield Diffie, *currently manager of secure systems research at Bell Northern Research, has been doing research for more than fifteen years in symbolic mathematical manipulation, proof of correctness, and cryptography. His pioneering work has earned him several awards, including the IEEE Fink Award and the IEEE Information Theory Society Best Paper Award.*

Martin E. Hellman *is professor of electrical engineering at Stanford University. He has been a leader in the study of cryptanalysis and the development of the concept of public key encryption systems, and his work has earned him the IEEE Fink Award and the IEEE Information Theory Society Best Paper Award.*

Ralph C. Merkle *is manager of scientific languages at Elxsi International in Sunnyvale, California. His research has focused on public key cryptosystems, public key distribution systems, and digital signatures.*

Ronald L. Rivest *is associate professor of computer science at Massachusetts Institute of Technology. His areas of specialization include complexity theory, design automation, and cryptography.*

Adi Shamir *is professor of applied mathematics, Weizmann Institute, Rehovet, Israel. His specialties include combinatorics, algorithms, cryptography, and semantics.*

Hugh C. Williams *is professor of computer science at the University of Manitoba, Winnipeg. He has published on computational number theory, and on extensions and security of the RSA cryptosystem.*

Gustavus J. Simmons

1. Introduction

The principal subject of the symposium on which this volume is in part based is the problem of achieving secure communication of digital messages over publicly exposed communications channels -- by which is meant not only providing for the privacy or secrecy of the messages, but also of insuring their integrity against either forgery or alteration. As might be inferred from the title, both those papers presented at the symposium and those selected from the recent literature for inclusion in this volume treat various aspects of this problem (of secure digital communications) using asymmetric (read also "public key" or "two key") cryptographic systems. In this introduction we shall first try to make clear the importance of the problem -- both to the individual and to business -- and then to introduce the reader to the unavoidable specialized technical vocabulary used in the field. Finally, a Baedeker to the collected papers will be provided in the hope that the collection will give a cohesive overview of the current state of the art in this important area of communications science.

On first hearing that the subject is the security of digital communications, the reaction of many people is that the problem doesn't concern them personally -- that while it

This article sponsored by the U. S. Department of Energy under Contract DE-AC04-76DP00789.

may be an important military or government problem or perhaps even a significant problem for large corporations, they have no immediate stake in its solution. Nothing could be further from the truth; but the explanation for this widespread opinion is that those secure digital communications systems we come in contact with are transparent (by which we mean invisible) by design to the users. For example, automated remote bank tellers are in common usage. To make a cash withdrawal, the customer punches in on a keypad (digital) information identifying himself (his PIN -- personal identification number) and presents a magnetically recorded message on his passcard to authorize withdrawal of funds from his account. He depends (probably without having consciously thought through all the subtle aspects of what this dependence implies) on the system's security features to prevent other parties -- including employees at the bank who may have access to all of the information about his account filed in the computer's memory -- from impersonating him and creating fraudulent withdrawal requests on his account that would be accepted and honored as authentic requests made by him. Similarly, in what appears to be the precursor of another major change in retailing -- rivaled only by the introduction and acceptance of credit cards -- a number of large department stores have set up direct debiting of the customer's account. Again, a digitized message from the point-of-sale is forwarded to a central computer where it is checked for authenticity and a charge made to the customer's account for the merchandise that is being transferred to (presumably) his possession. While it is true that there may be legal limitations to the liability that he can be assessed as a result of the system accepting a forged or altered order in his name -- he is still dependent on the security of the digital communications to insure him from this risk.

There are few invasions of privacy that cause people to become as incensed as having their mail opened and read -- whether by an individual or by a government agency -- even though there is little or no physical security provided by an envelope whose sanctity they expect to be honored. Postmaster General Bolger has recently pointed out that it will shortly be physically impossible for the post office to provide communication by shipping pieces of paper back and forth between the communicants, and that the exponentially increasing communications load will force the introduction of electronic mail sometime in the 80's. Two pilot experiments, one in the U.S. and one in France, have already demonstrated the feasibility of this and the experience with computer networks, such as the ARPA net in the U.S. and the Davies net in Great Britain has laid foundations for the protocols needed for handling message forwarding in large network systems. Electronic mail during transmission over public channels such as a COMSAT data link -- if unsecured -- is mail without an envelope, i.e., open to the view of even the casually interested interloper. While it is true that people have tolerated the lack of privacy for their mail under special circumstances, such as the V-mail of WWII or in telegrams and telexes -- where they have frequently devised private codes to regain some degree of privacy, it is very doubtful that mail without an envelope would be an acceptable replacement for the present service. One of the problems is that a satellite down link is publicly accessible, and that simple and easily obtained equipment can monitor the packet switching information attached to each communication to sort out and monitor messages of particular interest to the eavesdropper. Cryptographic techniques -- not necessarily the two key techniques focussed on here -- are the only means of providing an envelope for electronic mail.

Rather than continue listing instances in which we have a personal stake in the security of digital communications, we conclude that an ever increasing fraction of our day-by-day affairs are being transacted by means of digital messages communicated on our account. In many instances these communications are interpreted to incur liabilities that we are ultimately responsible for, while in others they represent data about us -- business records, credit records, legal data, medical files, etc. -- that if altered in an undetected way could have disastrous consequences. The bottom line is that there must be some way of insuring the user, in proportion to the sensitivity of the communication, of the privacy and integrity of the communications system; i.e., that he cannot be impersonated so that fraudulent messages would be accepted as authentic and that his communications will be concealed from unintended recipients. As was noted at the outset -- this was the principal subject of this symposium -- and of the papers collected here. The only means we know of for achieving secure digital communications is to use cryptographic techniques to conceal some essential part of the communication from unauthorized recipients.

Unfortunately, the tutorial paper given by L. Adleman at the AAAS symposium was not available for inclusion here. However, the first part of the papers by G. J. Simmons (Chapter 10) and by W. Diffie (Chapter 3) provide an introduction to the subject of cryptology. A thumbnail introduction is given here to acquaint the reader with at least the essential concepts and vocabulary of the field.

Put in the simplest terms possible, a cryptosystem is an invertible recipe (algorithm) shared in secret by the transmitter and the intended receiver that converts messages whose content is to be concealed into other messages called *ciphers* whose content has the appearance of random noise to anyone not in possession of the recipe. These derived messages are then transmitted over the public communications channel instead of the originals. The recipe, while invertible to anyone in possession of the secret information so that they can recover the original message, is designed to be inscrutable to anyone not in possession of the secret information. The message whose content is to be concealed, is called *plaintext* even though it may be a random-like number itself, such as computer files, data telemetry records, market activity reports, seismic signals, etc. The name is an anachronism from a time when messages were mainly texts in a natural language. The transformed message is the *ciphertext* (or cipher). The process of creating ciphertext from plaintext is called *encryption* (conversely, *decryption*). The essential part of this process -- the secret shared by the authorized users -- is referred to in a poorly specified way as the *key*. Several of the papers in this volume give precise definitions for their intended usage of this term, but roughly speaking the key is that information known only to the authorized users of the system on which the concealment recipe depends. One of the reasons that this definition, though intuitively satisfactory, may not be sufficiently precise for mathematical analysis is that while in some instances the secret "information" is easily identified as such because it is a number or a register fill, etc., in others it is intimately tied to the hardware design and therefore requires an information theoretic specification of the number of bits of equivocation (information) that it represents to an outsider (not in possession of the key). Using this operational description of cryptosystems, we can distinguish between the existing symmetric (one key) systems and the newer technology that is of concern here of asymmetric (public key or two key systems) cryptosystems. With the single exception of a cryptosystem known as a one time key or one time pad (defined precisely in several of the papers), the cryptosecurity of all cryptosystems depends on the computational (infeasibility) difficulty of anyone working backward from a knowledge of only the ciphertext (but not of the key) to recover the plaintext. What is meant by computational infeasibility (not impossibility!) is that while it is possible in principle for a cryptanalyst to invert the system, it is not possible in practice since the number of elementary computer operations required to do so is so large that legions of giant computers would require centuries for the task. In addition, any currently acceptable cryptosystem must satisfy the far more stringent requirement that the key not be recoverable (i.e., that its recovery be a computationally infeasible problem) by anyone having plaintext and ciphertext pairs -- but not the key. The generic classification of cryptosystems as symmetric (one key) or asymmetric (public key or two key) is dependent on how the information used by the transmitter and receiver is shared. Through the end of 1979, all of the publicly known cryptosystems were *symmetric* (i.e., alike from either the transmitter's or receiver's point of view) in the sense that either the same key was held in secret by both communicants, or else that each held one from a pair of related keys where either key was easily derivable from the other. Recall that the secret encryption recipe was defined to be invertible: in some instances reapplying the same process used to encrypt the plaintext to the ciphertext recovers the original plaintext. A very famous example of such an involutory system is Vernam stream ciphering of binary encoded signals using a key stream and an exclusive OR operation (later papers define all of these terms precisely for those readers not familiar with them already). In other instances the decryption key is a simply derived inverse to the encryption key -- for example, the inverse linear transformation to a linear transformation used to effect the encryption in some circa WWII systems. In an *asymmetric* cryptosystem the keys held by the transmitter and receiver are not only different, but in addition it is computationally infeasible to compute at least one of them from a knowledge of the other (and of plaintext-ciphertext pairs). Obviously, in a symmetric cryptosystem if either the receiver's or the transmitter's key is compromised, further secure communications are impossible with that key. This means that in a symmetric cryptosystem both the transmitter's and the receiver's key must be securely stored (and usually physically protected) if secure communications are to be possible. In an asymmetric cryptosystem however, one of the keys (clearly it must be one from which the other key cannot be derived) can be publicly exposed. In fact, for a variety of secure communications it is deliberately exposed in a public directory of keys (hence the name *public key* cryptosystem). If the exposed key is at the receiver, the transmitter can still authenticate messages but cannot insure their secrecy -- while if the exposed key is at the transmitter, the receiver can be certain of the secrecy from parties other than the transmitter and himself -- but not of the identity of the transmitter, i.e., of the authenticity of the communication.

The concept of having the keys in a cryptosystem be separated by a computationally infeasible problem was the discovery of W. Diffie and M. Hellman and independently of R. Merkle in 1976. The first two papers, by these authors, in the selected papers section of this volume mark the beginning of a major new line of development for the science (art?) of secure communications. The following two papers, by R. Merkle and M. Hellman and by R. Rivest, A. Shamir and L. Adleman describe the first public key systems proposed which are still the main contenders for practical applications. The paper by G. Simmons is a comparative study of one key versus two key cryptography in which the problem of authentication without secrecy (discussed at length in the paper presented at this symposium) is first described. The final paper by R. Merkle in the selected papers section is indicative of the rapid maturing of the field of asymmetric encryption from a preoccupation with finding candidate public key algorithms, to the systems questions surrounding the use of such techniques to obtain secure communications. Procedures and policies (usually referred to collectively as protocols) are as important to accomplishing a particular secure communications objective as the encryption algorithm. As an indication of this, three out of the five papers presented at this symposium (those by W. Diffie, R. Merkle and by G. J. Simmons) are primarily concerned with specific protocols.

It is appropriate that W. Diffie, who as the coinventor of public key cryptography had the first word to say on the subject, should have the last word to say in this volume in his paper Cryptographic Technology: Fifteen Year Forecast.

Part 1

The Contemporary (1981) Scene

Hugh C. Williams

2. Computationally "Hard" Problems as a Source for Cryptosystems

Introduction

A cryptosystem is used for hiding or obscuring the content of a series of messages in such a way that only the intended recipients can determine the meaning of these messages. To anyone else they appear to be meaningless gibberish from which (ideally) no information concerning the actual message contents can be derived. Most modern cryptosystems have basically two main components; the first of these is the *algorithm* -- a prearranged set of procedures -- and the second is the *key*. The message or *plaintext* M is transformed or *encrypted* by the sender into *ciphertext* $C = E_{K_1}(M)$ by using his encryption algorithm in conjunction with his encryption key K_1. The recipient of this ciphertext C applies his decryption algorithm D and decryption key K_2 to *decrypt* C and recover the original message $M = D_{K_2}(C)$.

It is generally assumed that the general algorithms for encryption and decryption are known to everyone but that K_1 and K_2 are secret. Further, for conventional or *symmetric* cryptosystems, K_1 and K_2 can easily be derived one from the other; thus, anyone with knowledge of K_1 or K_2 can determine M from C. That is, both K_1 and K_2 act as keys to unlock the meaning of C. It must be stressed here that both the sender and recipient of a message must know K_1 in order to communicate; consequently, it is essential that K_1 be exchanged between them over a secure channel. The actual process by which K_1 is produced is in itself an important problem. It should certainly be as random as possible in order to prevent the possibility of easy determination.

As an example of the above consider the following simple cryptosystem. We will use as plaintext the sentence

This cipher can be broken.

Key K_1: The word COMPUTERS is the key for this system.

Algorithm:

1. Put the key word into its numerical form 143598267 by replacing each of its letters by a number indicating the proximity of that letter to the beginning of the alphabet relative to the other letters of the key word.
2. Under the numerical key arrange the plaintext into an array with as many columns as there are letters in the key word.

```
C O M P U T E R S
1 4 3 5 9 8 2 6 7
T H I S C I P H E
R C A N B E B R O
K E N
```

3. Replace each letter in the plaintext by that letter which is a distance k from it in the alphabet. Here k is the key word digit at the top of the column in which the plaintext letter appears.

Ciphertext: ULLXL QRNLS GDSKM DXVLI Q

Notice that if anyone knows K_1, he can decrypt any ciphertext produced by using this system. This is a particular example of what is called a polyalphabetic substitution cipher. For more information on such classical cryptosystems see Kahn [11] and Shulman [29].

We illustrate the ideas discussed above in Figure 1.

Naturally, the security of any cryptosystem is of paramount importance. We say that a cryptosystem is *unconditionally secure* if a *cryptanalyst* (an unauthorized individual who is attempting to intercept messages) cannot determine how to decipher messages regardless of how much ciphertext and computer power he has available to him. An example of such a system is the *one-time pad* [11, p. 403]. Unfortunately, such a system requires as much key K_1 as message and we have the problem of transmitting K_1 by a secure means. If we have a cryptosystem in which the encryption and decryption algorithms are inexpensive and yet the task of a cryptanalyst is computationally infeasible, we say that such a cryptosystem is *computationally secure*. A task is said to be *computationally infeasible* if it can be achieved using only a finite amount of computation and yet the amount of computation required would exhaust the physical computing resources available to the universe.

Currently, much work is being done on the problem of developing cryptosystems which are computationally secure and for which it is not necessary to have a secure means of distributing the key K_1 used in the encryption operation. The purpose of this paper is to describe how computationally difficult problems have been used in the development of systems which are believed to possess these properties.

In much of this work we will assume that the messages M are numbers rather than a sequence of characters. It is easy to see that any sequence of characters can be readily coded into numbers. For example, one could simply assign the numbers 01, 02, 03, ···, 26 to the letters A, B, C, ···, Z, respectively, and then assign other numbers to the special characters such as punctuation marks and blanks. Thus, the

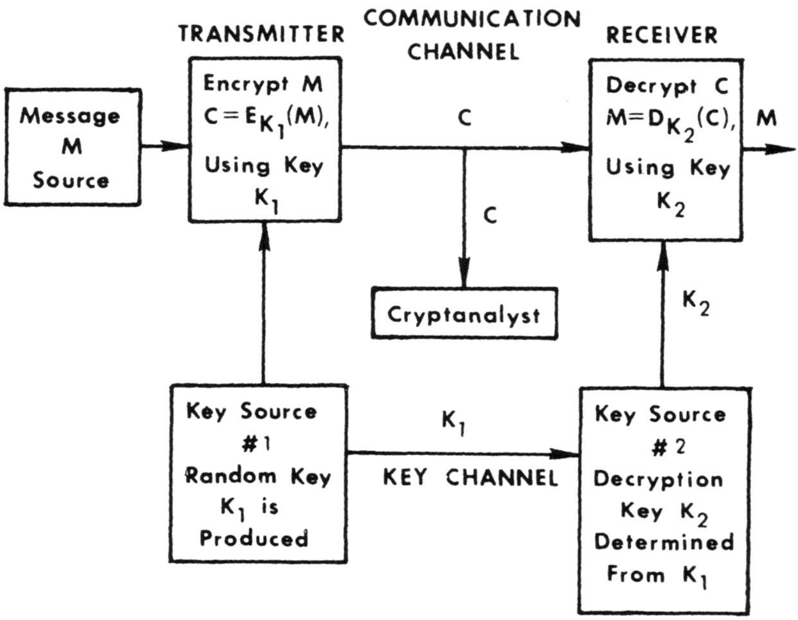

Figure 1. The key channel must be secure.

word "encrypt' would be numerically coded as 05140318251620. There are, of course, many other ways in which this can be done. We will also assume, on occasion, that our numerical messages are less than some quantity. If they are not, they can be *blocked* into smaller sections, each of which is less than the required amount.

One Way Functions and Public Key Cryptosystems

A *one way* function F is a function such that

1. F(x) is easy to compute for any given x in the domain of F.
2. Given almost any y such that y = F(x) for some x, it is computationally infeasible to find x.

Some examples of possible one way functions are given in Pohlig and Hellman [19] and Purdy [20]. They can be very useful for protecting the password file of a computer. In most computer systems each user A is issued his own password P_A. When A wishes to use the computer he provides P_A to the machine and it determines, by checking whether or not P_A is in the password file, if A can have access to the system. This is not very secure, as almost anyone with access to the system might be able to discover P_A from the password file and then impersonate A.

If, instead of having P_A stored in the computer system, we have $F(P_A)$, the computer can still validate any potential user by computing $F(P_A)$ from the submitted P_A and comparing it to the entries in its stored list. However, in this case, anyone with access to this list cannot determine P_A since he cannot invert F. One way functions are also useful in solving problems of key distribution (Diffie and Hellman [4]) and key exchange authentication (Arazi [2]).

In cryptography one way functions by themselves are not very useful; the recipient of some ciphertext C = F(M) cannot

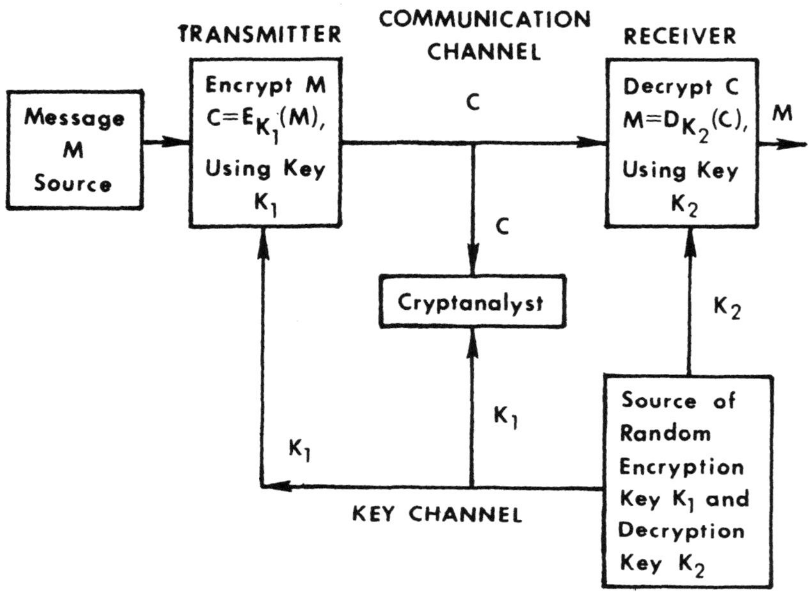

Figure 2. Public key (asymmetric) cryptosystem. Knowledge of K_1 and C provides the cryptanalyst with too little information for him to determine M. Thus, the key channel need not be secure.

invert F to find M. If we modify the idea of a one way function to that of a trapdoor one way function, we can develop a cryptographic system. A one way *trapdoor* function is a function F such that

1. F(x) is easy to compute for any x in the domain of F.
2. Given almost any y such that y = F(x), for some x, it is computationally infeasible to find x unless certain special information used in the design of F is known. If this information is known, it is easy to find x.

Let $F_{K_1}(x)$ be a trapdoor one way function such that a quantity K_1 is needed for the evaluation of $F_{K_1}(x)$. Suppose further that K_2 is the special information needed to invert $F_{K_1}(x)$; that is, if $y = F_{K_1}(x)$, there exists a function $G(w,K_2)$, which can be easily evaluated for any w, such that $x = G(y,K_2)$. If we define $E_{K_1}(M)$ to be $F_{K_1}(M)$ and $D_{K_2}(C)$ to be $G(C,K_2)$, we have a *Public key (Asymmetric) Encryption* system [4]. This is a cryptosystem which has the following properties:

1. Given K_1 and K_2, $E_{K_1}(M)$ and $D_{K_2}(C)$ are easy to compute.
2. $D_{K_2}(E_{K_1}(M)) = M$.
3. Unless K_2 is known, it is computationally infeasible to determine M from knowledge of K_1, E_{K_1} and $C = E_{K_1}(M)$.

An individual who wishes to receive secure messages need only make his encryption algorithm E_{K_1} and key K_1 publicly known, while keeping his decryption key K_2 secret. Anyone can send him ciphertext but, since only he knows K_2, only he can decrypt this correspondence. We illustrate this type of cryptosystem in Figure 2.

One other problem which has become important in modern communication systems is that of *authentication*. This problem is handled by making use of *signatures*. A signature is a simple means by which the recipient of a message can authenticate the identity of the sender. A signature should have two properties:

a. Only the sender should be able to produce his signature.

b. Anyone should be able to verify the validity of a signature.

If

4. $E_{K_1}(D_{K_2}(M)) = M$,

we say that the public key system described above is also a signature system.

Suppose that A has a public key encryption scheme which is also a signature system. For brevity we will make a change in our notation and denote A's scheme by E_A (encryption algorithm including key) and D_A (decryption algorithm including key). If A wishes to sign a message and send it to B he can send M and $D_A(M)$. B can verify that A has sent M by checking that $E_A(D_A(M)) = M$. Since only A knows D_A, only he could send $D_A(M)$. For more information on this problem of authentication see [2], Rabin [21], and Merkle [16], [17].

We see now that the problem of creating a secure public key cryptosystem can be reduced to the problem of creating trapdoor one way functions. This leads us to a relatively new area of computer science and mathematics called Complexity Theory.

Some Naive Complexity Theory

For many years mathematicians have been aware that certain problems are very difficult to solve. For example, consider the following two problems.

1. Factoring Problem. Given a composite integer N and an integer $m \leq N$, find an integer a such that

$1 < a \leq m$ and $N = ab$, where b is an integer. For example, if $m = 1000$ and $N = 2^{32} + 1 = 4{,}294{,}967{,}297$, we find that $N = 641 \cdot 6700417$.

2. Knapsack Problem. Given a set of k rods of varying lengths $a_1, a_2, a_3, \cdots, a_k$, find a subset of these rods that exactly fills a knapsack of length $S < a_1 + a_2 + a_3 + \cdots + a_k$. For example, suppose $k = 4$, $a_1 = 29$, $a_2 = 31$, $a_3 = 42$, $a_4 = 6$ and $S = 77$. We see that $S = a_1 + a_3 + a_4$.

The subject of Complexity Theory attempts to deal with two important aspects of any given problem. These are

a. The most efficient method of obtaining a solution of the problem.

b. The number of operations needed to perform this task.

In order to prevent even a rather naive view of this interesting and important discipline, we require several definitions and concepts. For a more rigorous presentation of the material discussed here see Garey and Johnson [7].

We use the term *instance* of a problem to mean a particular case of a general problem. For example, factoring $2^{32} + 1$ with $m = 1000$ is a particular instance of the general factoring problem. The term *input length* is used to describe the number n of symbols used to characterize a particular instance of a problem. That is, n can be thought of as the length of the bit string of input that would be supplied to a computer before it could begin to search for a solution to this instance of the problem.

We say that a function f(n) is O(g(n)) if there exists a constant C such that

$$f(n) \leq c|g(n)|$$

for all $n \geq 0$. A polynomial time algorithm is defined to be an algorithm which solves any instance of a particular problem in a length of time which is $O(p(n))$ for some polynomial function p of the input length n. Any algorithm whose time requirements are not so bounded is called an *exponential time* algorithm. By P (polynomial) we denote the class of all problems which can be solved by polynomial time algorithms. As an example, consider the simple problem of finding the product or quotient of two integers a and b. Here $n = \log_2 a + \log_2 b$ and the time needed to multiply or divide is proportional to $(\log_2 a)(\log_2 b) = O(n^2)$; thus, this is a problem in P.

In Table 1 below, let f(n) denote the length of time needed by an algorithm to solve a problem.

Table 1.

f(n)	type	n=1	n=2	n=5	n=10	n=20	n=50
n	polynomial	1	2	5	20	20	50
n^2	polynomial	1	4	25	100	400	2500
n^3	polynomial	1	8	125	1000	8000	125000
2^n	exponential	2	4	32	1024	1048576	1.1258×10^{15}
$n!$	exponential	1	2	120	3628800	2.4329×10^{18}	3.0414×10^{64}

For small values of n, a given polynomial function can exceed a given exponential function; however, as n increases, an exponential function will ultimately overtake and greatly exceed any polynomial function. Because of this rapid rate of exponential functions, computer scientists regard problems which are not in P as computationally hard or *intractable*.

Let NP (*nondeterministic polynomial*) denote the class which consists of all problems such that any guess at a solution of any instance of a problem in the class can be checked for validity in a period of time which is $O(p(x))$. For example, the factoring problem is in NP because any guess at a factor of N can be checked by trial division and division is a problem in P. Also, any guess at a solution of a particular instance of the knapsack problem can be checked by addition, a problem in P; thus, the knapsack problem is in NP.

It is a simple matter to see that P is a subclass of NP; one of the important unsolved questions in Complexity Theory is whether P = NP. If this is not the case, then there must exist problems for which no really efficient method of solution can ever be developed. Naturally, this is of great concern to people interested in developing public key cryptosystems.

A very remarkable result concerning this question has been the discovery of a special subclass of problems in NP, called the *NP-complete* or NPC problems. If any problem in NPC can be shown to be in P also, then P = NP. The knapsack problem is one of several problems which have been shown to be in NPC. If anyone could develop a polynomial algorithm for solving this problem, then polynomial algorithms exist which will solve all the problems in NP. These NPC problems are therefore the hardest problems in NP. It is currently believed that all NPC problems are computationally intractable. Indeed, a proof that a problem is in NPC is often considered to be a sufficiently strong argument for giving up trying to devise an efficient algorithm for solving it.

The class of problems denoted by Co-NP is made up of problems which are the complements of the problems in NP. For example, the complement of the knapsack problem is the problem of showing, for a given knapsack of length S, that it is not possible to find, from among the given set of rods, a subset which will exactly fill the knapsack. If, in the instance of the knapsack problem given above, we have S = 76, we see by exhausting all the possibilities that no set selected from among a_1, a_2, a_3, a_4 will exactly fill S. Notice that, in order to show that an instance of an NP problem has a solution, it is sufficient to exhibit the solution. It can easily be verified as such. However, in order to verify a guess at a solution of the complementary problem, it might be necessary to conduct an exhaustive search.

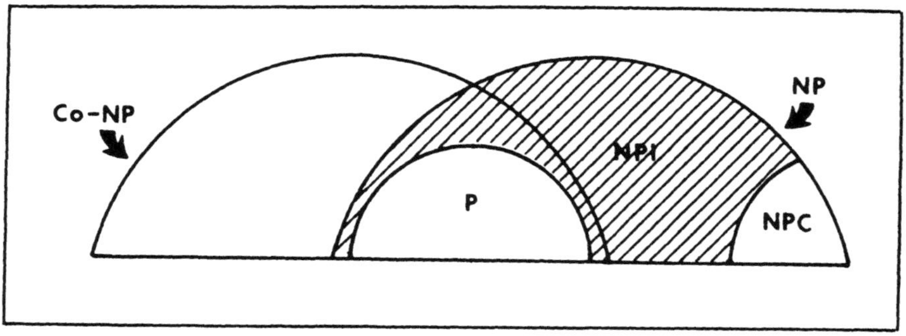

Figure 3. Classification of problems. We assume here that NP $\neq$ P, Co − NP $\neq$ NP. It may or may not be true that P = Co − NP $\cap$ NP.

Because it does not seem to be possible to provide a simple means of verifying any guess at a solution of every instance of some problems in Co-NP, it is currently believed (but not yet proved) that Co-NP $\neq$ NP. It is known that if there exists a problem in NPC such that its complement is in NP, then NP = Co-NP. Thus, if a problem and its complement can both be shown to be in NP, it is felt that it cannot be in NPC. Brassard and Adleman, Rivest and Miller [see 3] have independently shown that the factoring problem and its complement are in NP; thus, this problem is probably not in NPC. The class P is a subclass of both NP and Co-NP but it is not known whether or not P = Co-NP $\cap$ NP. This is a very important question to those interested in factoring. In connection with this we mention that if P $\neq$ NP, there must exist a class of problems, denoted by NPI (nondeterministic polynomial *intermediate*) which is made up of problems which are in NP but not in P or NPC. It could be that factoring is a problem in this class. In Figure 3 we illustrate, by means of a Venn diagram, the classification of the different types of problems discussed here.

Despite the fact that there are still a number of important unanswered questions in complexity theory, we see that we have, at least, a means of identifying what the hard problems must be, if there are any at all. Naturally, it would be desirable to base encryption techniques on these problems. We will describe how this has been attempted in the following sections; but, before we do this, it is important to mention several caveats with regard to this complexity theory approach.

Attacks on Cryptosystems

The idea of using computationally intractable problems in the design of cryptosystems seems to be very attractive;

however, Shamir [27] has pointed out that there are a number of difficulties associated with doing this.

1. Complexity theory deals with the worst possible case of any problem. It could be that only one or a few instances of a problem are truly intractable. A cryptosystem based on such a problem would only occasionally be secure.
2. Complexity theorists assume that only a certain amount of information is available for the solution of a particular instance of a problem. Cryptanalysts frequently have much more information at their disposal, such as corresponding plaintext and ciphertext. The existence of this extra information is not taken into account in analyzing the complexity of problems.
3. Given any particular difficult problem, it is not always possible to convert it into a cryptosystem.

Also, Even and Yacobi [6] have provided evidence which suggests that the problem of breaking any public key cryptosystem is <u>not</u> as hard as an NPC problem. Thus, at the moment, the state of complexity theory is inadequate to demonstrate the computational infeasibility of any cryptosystem. The only method currently available for *certifying* the security of any cryptosystem is to expose it to a concentrated but unsuccessful attack under conditions favorable to the cryptanalyst.

There are several types of attack which can be mounted on any particular cryptosystem.

<u>Ciphertext Only Attack</u>

The cryptanalyst has at his disposal a large quantity of ciphertext and possibly some knowledge of the plaintext. For example, he would know that in English the letter E occurs 13% of the time. Clearly any ciphertext that succumbs to this attack is useless.

Known Plaintext Attack

In such an attack the cryptanalyst has a quantity of plaintext and corresponding ciphertext and must determine the decryption key. This kind of attack is often mounted when data which has become declassified is made available to the cryptanalyst. For example, diplomatic proposals or timed press releases often fall into this category of data.

Chosen Text Attack

It this type of attack the cryptanalyst has access to corresponding plaintext and ciphertext of his own choosing and attempts to determine the decryption key. There are two types of such attack.

1. Chosen plaintext attack. The cryptanalyst selects his plaintext and obtains the corresponding ciphertext. This sort of information could be obtained by an individual if he were to submit a certain sensitive proposal (such as a diplomatic proposal) and, when it was sent elsewhere for discussion, intercept it in its encrypted form.
2. Chosen ciphertext attack. The cryptanalyst selects a certain quantity of ciphertext and obtains, by a ruse or from a third party, the decrypted form of this text.

Clearly, the attack most favorable to the cryptanalyst is the chosen text attack and, for any system to be considered secure, it must be able to resist such an attack. Certainly, a public key system must be invulnerable to a chosen plaintext attack, as the encryption key is available to anyone.

Although there are difficulties associated with the use of complexity theory to certify the security of cryptosystems, we still are able to use this theory to provide us with a source of possible trapdoor one way functions. As we mentioned above, it is not often easy to convert a hard problem to such a function; nevertheless, this has been done for some problems. In doing this use is made of *modular arithmetic*.

Mathematicians write the expression

$$a \equiv b \pmod{m}$$

(a is congruent to b modulo m) to denote the fact that the integer m divides exactly the difference of the integers a and b. For example,

$$32 \equiv -4 \pmod{12} \quad .$$

Note that if the remainder on dividing a by m is b, then $a \equiv b \pmod{m}$. As another example we have

$$\begin{array}{r} 23 \\ 21753\,\overline{)512491} \\ \underline{43506} \\ 77431 \\ \underline{65259} \\ 12172 \end{array} \quad ;$$

hence,

$$512491 \equiv 12172 \pmod{21753} \quad .$$

In fact, the remainder on dividing a by m is the only number b which is congruent to a modulo m such that $0 \leq b < m$. One very important consequence of the definition of congruence is that if p(x) is any polynomial function of x with integer coefficients, then $p(a) \equiv p(b) \pmod{m}$ whenever $a \equiv b \pmod{m}$.

In the next sections we will see how modular arithmetic is used to convert the two problems enunciated in the preceding section to public key cryptosystems. In fact, except for the scheme described by McEliece (see [15] and Sloane [31]), all known possible public key techniques are based on these two problems.

The RSA Public Key Cryptosystem

Shortly after the publication of Diffie and Hellman's seminal paper [4] on public key cryptosystems, Rivest, Shamir and Adleman [23] (for whom the RSA system is named) discovered a very elegant candidate for such a scheme. Their technique makes use of the following simple number theoretic result: if $R = pq$, where p, q are distinct primes, and $\phi(R) = (p-1)(q-1)$, then

$$X^{\phi(R)} \equiv 1 \pmod{R} \quad ,$$

for any X which is not divisible by either p or q.

The designer of an RSA cryptosystem selects at random two large (about 100 digits) primes p and q and calculates $R = pq$. He also selects at random a value e ($< R$) such that the greatest common divisor of e and $\phi(R)$ (denoted here by $(e,\phi(R))$) is 1. He then solves the congruence

$$de \equiv 1 \pmod{\phi(R)} \quad ,$$

for d such that $0 < d < R$. There is a simple procedure for doing this, based on the Euclidean algorithm, which requires $O(\log R)$ operations. For this scheme the public encryption key is $K_1 = \{e,R\}$ and the secret decryption key is $K_2 = d$.

If some individual wishes to send a secure message M (such that $(M,R) = 1$ and $M < R$) to the designer of this system, he sends

$$C = E_{K_1}(M) \equiv M^e \pmod{R} \quad ,$$

where $0 < C < R$. The designer calculates

$$D(C) \equiv C^d \equiv M^{ed} = M^{1+k\phi(R)} \equiv M \pmod{R} \quad .$$

Since $M < R$, it can now be uniquely determined.

It might appear that the problem of calculating $M^e \pmod{R}$ for large e is very time consuming. In fact, there is a very simple and fast method for doing this which takes $O(\log_2 e)$ steps to complete. Briefly, it is done by performing a sequence of squaring and multiplication by M operations as indicated by the binary representation of e (see [23]).

Consider the following simple example. Here we put $p = 11$, $q = 19$, $R = 209$, $e = 17$. We find that $\phi(R) = 10 \cdot 18$ and

$$17d \equiv 1 \pmod{180}$$

for $d = 53$. If $M = 5$, then

$$C \equiv 5^{17} \equiv (((5^2)^2)^2)^2 \cdot 5 \equiv 80 \pmod{209} \quad \text{and} \quad C = 80 \ .$$

To decrypt C, we calculate

$$80^{53} \equiv ((((80^2 \cdot 80)^2)^2 \cdot 80)^2)^2 \cdot 80 \equiv 5 \pmod{209} \ .$$

The security of this scheme depends very much on the difficulty of factoring R. If a cryptanalyst can factor R, he can easily calculate d and be able to decrypt all ciphertext. There are a large number of different factoring methods currently known (see Guy [9]), but the most powerful of these techniques (Dixon [5] and Schroeppel) still require about

$$e^{\sqrt{\log N \log \log N}}$$

operations to factor N. Thus, a very fast computer (one multiprecise operation per 10^{-6} seconds) might require 3.8×10^9 years to factor a 200 digit number [23].

It must be stressed here that many numbers which are very large can be factored relatively easily when their prime factors have certain special forms. As an extreme example of this, we mention that it is known that the truly immense number

$$2^{2^{4724}} + 1$$

has $29 \cdot 2^{4727} + 1$ as a factor. Hence, great care must be taken by the designer of this type of cryptosystem when he selects his primes p and q. This problem has been discussed in [23], Rivest [24] and Williams and Schmid [32].

Although it is true that anyone who can factor R can decrypt messages sent under this scheme, it is not known whether the act of decrypting these messages is equivalent in difficulty to factoring R. Simmons and Norris [30] and Herlestam [10] have attacked this cryptosystem by using the fact that if some P can be found such that

$$C^P = (E_{K_1}(M))^P \equiv 1 \pmod{R} \quad ,$$

then M can be found without having to factor R. But in [32] it is shown that

a. the chance of finding such a value of P by a random search is very very small for large, properly selected values of p and q;

b. a fast method of finding P can almost certainly be converted into a fast method of factoring R.

Thus, it seems that, if the system designer has selected his value of R carefully, revealing its value and that of e gives too little information to a cryptanalyst for him to deduce d. For this reason it is felt that the RSA scheme is a valid public key cryptosystem.

In summary, we point out that this system has several important and desirable properties.

1. It seems to be very secure (so far).
2. The key size is small.
3. It is also a signature scheme.

Unfortunately, it also possesses some disadvantages.

1. The processes of encryption and decryption are expensive. Approximately one second is needed per 6000 bits of information on a special purpose piece

of hardware constructed at M.I.T. (L. Adleman, personal communication).

2. Determination of suitable keys is somewhat expensive.
3. Reblocking of the message or two different R values are required when the system is used for signatures.

We conclude this section by mentioning that some other cryptosystems have been developed which also use the difficulty of factoring as their means of providing security. One of these, the Lu-Lee (COMSAT) system [14], has been broken by Adleman and Rivest [1] and others (see [8]). Rabin [22] and Williams [33] have presented public key cryptosystems for which it can be shown that decryption is equivalent in difficulty to factoring. In view of this it would seem that these systems are superior to the RSA system; however, because of the constructive nature of the proofs of their security, both of these schemes are susceptible to a selected ciphertext attack [33]. This difficulty can be overcome by setting up the system very carefully, but the resulting schemes are somewhat cumbersome. It would be very desirable to have a nonconstructive proof of the equivalence of the problem of breaking the RSA system and the problem of factoring; at the moment, this seems very far from being achieved.

The Merkle-Hellman Trapdoor Knapsack

We have already mentioned that the knapsack problem is one of the most difficult problems in NP; nevertheless, there are instances of this problem which are very easy to solve. For example, if the rod lengths were $1,2,4,8,16,\cdots,2^n$. Then the problem of determining the correct rods to fit into a knapsack of length S is simply the problem of developing the binary representation of S. We can generalize this idea by considering the set of rods A', which we represent as

$$a' = (a_1', a_2', a_3', \cdots, a_k') \quad ,$$

where a_i' is the length of the i-th rod and

$$a_2' > a_1' \quad ,$$

$$a_3' > a_1' + a_2' \quad ,$$

$$a_4' > a_1' + a_2' + a_3' \quad ,$$

$$\cdots\cdots\cdots\cdot$$

$$a_i' > a_1' + a_2' + a_3' + \cdots + a_{i-1}' \quad ,$$

$$\cdots\cdots\cdots\cdots\cdots\cdots$$

$$a_k' > a_1' + a_2' + a_3' + \cdots + a_{k-1}' \quad .$$

If S' is the length of the knapsack, our problem is to find $X = (x_1, x_2, x_3, \cdots, x_k)$, where $x_i = 0$ or 1, such that

$$S' = a_1'x_1 + a_2'x_2 + a_3'x_3 + \cdots + a_k'x_k = A' \cdot X \quad .$$

This, however, is also an easy problem. For we note that x_k here can be one if and only if $S' \geq a_k'$. Having deduced x_k, we then have to solve the knapsack problem of representing $S' - a_k'x_k$, using $a_1', a_2', \cdots, a_{k-1}'$. If we repeat the above reasoning, we find that $x_i = 1$ if and only if

$$a_i' \leq S - a_k'x_k - a_{k-1}'x_{k-1} - \cdots - a_{i-1}'x_{i-1} \quad .$$

For example, if $A' = (5,7,17,31)$ and $S' = 53$, we see that $53 > 31$; hence, $x_4 = 1$. Also, $53 - 31 = 22 > 17$ and $x_3 = 1$; $53 - 30 - 17 = 5 < 7$ and $x_2 = 0$; $53 - 30 - 17 - 0 = 5$ and $x_1 = 1$. We have $X = (1,0,1,1)$ and

$$53 = 5 + 17 + 31 \quad .$$

We can convert the easy knapsack problem above into a

much harder knapsack problem by selecting at random a pair of integers w and m such that $(m,w) = 1$ and $m > a_1' + a_2' + a_3' + \cdots + a_k'$. We calculate

$$a_i \equiv wa_i' \pmod{m} \quad ,$$

where $0 < a_i < m$ $(i = 1,2,3,\cdots,k)$ and put $A = (a_1,a_2,a_3,\cdots, a_k)$. To solve the knapsack problem with A instead of A' is very difficult if m and w are not known. If they are known, we can calculate an integer w^{-1} such that

$$ww^{-1} \equiv 1 \pmod{m}$$

(see preceding section). To find X such that $S = A \cdot X$ for some S, we simply note that

$$Sw^{-1} \equiv w^{-1}A \cdot X \pmod{m}$$

or

$$S' = A' \cdot X \quad ,$$

where $S' \equiv w^{-1}S \pmod{m}$ and $0 < S' < m$. Since S' and A' are now known, we can evaluate X easily.

For example, if $m = 61$ and $w = 25$, $A = (3,53,59,43)$, and $S = 105$, we have $w^{-1} = 22$ and $S' \equiv 22 \cdot 105 \equiv 53 \pmod{61}$. Thus, $S' = 53$ and since

$$27 \cdot 3 \equiv 5, \;\; 22 \cdot 53 \equiv 7, \;\; 22 \cdot 59 \equiv 17, \; 22 \cdot 43 \equiv 31 \pmod{61} \quad ,$$

we have

$$A' = (5,7,17,31) \quad .$$

From the previous example we get $X = (1,0,1,1)$.

Merkle and Hellman [18] have used these ideas in the development of a cryptosystem based on this trapdoor knapsack. The designer of such a system should select

1. $k = 200$[†],
2. a_i' chosen randomly from the integers between $(2^{i-1} - 1)2^{200} + 1$ and $2^{i-1} \cdot 2^{200}$,
3. m and w chosen randomly from the integers between $2^{401} - 1$ and $2^{402} - 1$.

He calculates

$$a_i \equiv wa_i' \pmod{m} \qquad (0 < a_i < m)$$

and makes

$$A = (a_1, a_2, a_3, \cdots, a_k)$$

public. If someone wishes to send a secure 200 bit binary coded message M to the designer, he evaluates $S = A \cdot M$ and transmits S as his ciphertext. (For example, if M were the binary message 1011 and $A = (3,53,59,43)$, then $S = 105$). To decrypt S the designer calculates

$$S' \equiv A' \cdot M$$

for M.

This is a very attractive scheme which is based on a problem which is among the hardest problems in NP. However, Shamir and Zippel [28] have shown that, if a cryptanalyst should get possession of the value of m only, he can then recover w and $A' = (a_1', a_2', \cdots, a_k')$ and therefore be able to decrypt all traffic sent to the designer. Also, Hellman and Merkle (see Merkle [16]) have noted that if either w^{-1} or some elements of A' are known to a cryptanalyst, he can probably break the system.

All of these difficulties can be overcome by *iterating* this scheme. That is, the designer selects two (or more) pairs (m_1, w_1) and (m_2, w_2) at random and then calculates A by

† Actually, Hellman and Merkle recommended $k = 100$, but we shall see below that $k = 200$ is a better choice.

putting

$$b_i \equiv w_1 a_i' \pmod{m_1}$$

$$a_i \equiv w_2 b_i \pmod{m_2} \qquad (0 < a_i < m_2) \quad .$$

Now $S' \equiv w_1^{-1} T \pmod{m_1}$, where $T \equiv w_2^{-1} S \pmod{m_2}$ and $0 < S' < m_1$.

It should also be pointed out that Schroeppel and Shamir [25] have developed a general purpose algorithm that makes use of $O(2^{k/4})$ computer memory positions to solve the knapsack problem in a time interval of $O(2^{k/2})$. Thus, they recommend that in order to have a secure knapsack system, the value of k should be about 200.

We now list some of the desirable properties of this knapsack scheme.

1. The system seems to be secure (so far) in its iterated form with $k \geq 200$.
2. Even for the iterated version, the processes of encryption and decryption are very rapid.
3. Keys can be generated quickly.

As with the RSA system, there are some difficulties.

1. The key size is very large (over 40,000 bits).
2. It is often difficult to produce signatures using this scheme.

Some other cryptosystems have also been developed which are based on the knapsack problem. The Graham-Shamir system (see [28] and Lempel [12]) is a simple variant of the Merkle-Hellman knapsack. Leung and Vacon [13] have presented a cryptosystem, designed around the knapsack problem, which seems to be very secure. Unfortunately, when this system is being used, it is necessary to transmit 100 times more ciphertext than corresponding message text. We also mention that Shamir [26] has developed a signature scheme around the knapsack problem. This scheme, while requiring a large key, is still very simple and fast; however, it cannot be used as a cryptosystem.

In this section and the last we have seen that many possible public key cryptosystems have been developed. Even though all of them have certain disadvantages, if they are as secure as is currently believed, several of them could be used for the very important task of exchanging the secret keys needed by certified conventional cryptosystems. The exchanging of these keys need not take place very often but must be done in an environment of extreme security.

Conclusion

In spite of the number of proposed public key cryptosystems, it must be stressed here that we are still a long way from demonstrating that any of them is provably secure. Since the problem of factoring is so old, it might be felt that a scheme which is as difficult to break as it is difficult to factor a certain large number is, in a sense, certified in its security. However, it could be that in the future someone might develop a method that can be used to factor numbers of a certain (but now unknown) type. In a directory of public keys for cryptosystems based on the factoring problem there could be several schemes whose security would be compromised by this discovery. At the moment we simply have no way of knowing whether this could occur. Also, it should not be forgotten that there is the possibility that no such thing as a provably secure public key cryptosystem exists. This would certainly seem to be the case if it were ever proved that $P = NP \cap Co\text{-}NP$ [6].

The simple elegance and beauty of several of these recent public key encryption schemes should not be allowed to lull us into a feeling of complacency. The work that needs to be done in this new and exciting area of research has really just begun. What is needed are new measures of complexity especially tailored to the problem of cryptanalysis. When we can certify the security of cryptosystems according to such measures of cryptocomplexity, the problem of secure communications will be solved. Until this is done we can never free ourselves of the disturbing feeling that some clever individual may discover a method which will allow him to read over our shoulders.

References

[1] L. M. Adleman and R. L. Rivest, "How to break the Lu-Lee (COMSAT) public-key cryptosystem," Preprint (1979).

[2] B. Arazi, "Maximizing the domain of messages to be signed digitally," Preprint (1980).

[3] G. Brassard, "A note on the complexity of cryptography," IEEE Trans. Inform. Theory, IT-25 (1979), 232-233.

[4] W. Diffie and M. E. Hellman, "New directions in cryptography," IEEE Trans. Inform. Theory, IT-22 (1976), 644-654. (see pp. 143-180, this volume.)

[5] J. D. Dixon, "Asymptotically fast factorization of integers," Math. Comp., 36 (1981), 255-260.

[6] S. Even and Y. Yacobi, "On the cryptocomplexity of a public-key system," Preprint (1979).

[7] M. R. Garey and D. S. Johnson, Computers and Intractability, W. H. Freeman, San Francisco, CA (1979).

[8] J. M. Goethals and C. Couvreur, "A cryptanalytic attack on the Lu-Lee (COMSAT) public-key cryptosystem," MBLE Research Laboratory Report R424, Brussels (1980).

[9] R. K. Guy, "How to factor a number," Congressus Numerantium XVI Proc. Fifth Manitoba Conference on Numerical Math., Winnipeg (1976), 49-89.

[10] T. Herlestam, "Critical remarks on some public-key cryptosystems," BIT, 18 (1978), 493-496.

[11] D. Kahn, The Code Breakers, the Story of Secret Writing, MacMillan, New York (1967).

[12] A. Lempel, "Cryptology in transition: a survey," Comput. Surv. 11 (1979), 285-304.

[13] S. K. Leung and G. Vacon, "A method for private communication over a public channel, " Preprint (1979).

[14] S. C. Lu and L. N. Lee, "A simple and effective public-key cryptosystem," COMSAT Technical Review, 9 (1979), 15-24.

[15] R. J. McEliece, "A public-key cryptosystem based on algebraic coding theory," Deep Space Network Progress Report 42-44, Jet Propulsion Labs, Pasadena, CA (1978), 114-116.

[16] R. C. Merkle, "Secrecy, authentication, and public-key systems," Technical Report No. 1979-1, Information Systems Library, Stanford Electronics Laboratories, Stanford, CA (1979).

[17] R. C. Merkle, "A certified digital signature," Preprint (1979).

[18] R. C. Merkle and M. E. Hellman, "Hiding information and signatures in trapdoor knapsacks," IEEE Trans. Inform. Theory, IT-24 (1978), 525-530. (See pp. 197-215, this volume.)

[19] S. C. Pohlig and M. E. Hellman, "An improved algorithm for computing logarithms over GF(p) and its cryptographic significance," IEEE Trans. Inform. Theory, IT-24 (1978), 106-110.

[20] G. B. Purdy, "A high security log-in procedure," Comm. ACM, 17 (1974), 442-445.

[21] M. O. Rabin, "Digitalized signatures," Foundations of Secure Computation, R. Lipton and R. DeMillo, Eds., Academic Press, New York (1978), 155-166.

[22] M. O. Rabin, "Digitalized signatures and public-key functions as intractable as factorization," Tech. Rpt. MIT/LCS/TR212, MIT Lab. Comput. Sci., Cambridge, MA (1979).

[23] R. Rivest, A. Shamir, and L. Adleman, "A method for obtaining digital signatures and public-key cryptosystems," Comm. ACM, 21 (1978), 120-126. (See pp. 217-239, this volume.)

[24] R. Rivest, "Remarks on a proposed cryptanalytic attack on the MIT public-key cryptosystem," Cryptologia, 2 (1978), 62-65.

[25] R. Schroeppel and A. Shamir, "A $T \cdot S^2 = O(2^n)$ time/space tradeoff for certain NP-complete problems," to appear as MIT Lab. Comput. Sci. Rpt.

[26] A. Shamir, "A fast signature scheme," Tech. Rpt. MIT/LCS/TM-107, MIT Lab. Comput. Sci., Cambridge, MA (1979).

[27] A. Shamir, "On the cryptocomplexity of knapsack systems," Tech. Rpt. MIT/LCS/TM-129, MIT Lab. Comput. Sci., Cambridge, MA (1979).

[28] A. Shamir and R. E. Zippel, "On the security of the Merkle-Hellman cryptographic scheme," Tech. Rpt. MIT/LCS/TM-119, MIT Lab. Comput. Sci., Cambridge, MA (1978).

[29] D. Shulman, An Annotated Bibliography of Cryptography, Garland Publishing, New York and London (1976).

[30] G. J. Simmons and M. J. Norris, "Preliminary comments on the MIT public-key cryptosystem," Cryptologia, 1 (1977), 406-414.

[31] N. J. A. Sloane, "Error-correcting codes and cryptography," The Mathematical Gardner, Wadsworth, Belmont, CA (1981), 346-382.

[32] H. C. Williams and B. K. Schmid, "Some remarks concerning the MIT public-key cryptosystem," BIT, 19 (1979), 525-538.

[33] H. C. Williams, "A modification of the RSA public-key encryption procedure," IEEE Trans. Inform. Theory, IT-26 (1980), 726-729.

Whitfield Diffie

3. Conventional Versus Public Key Cryptosystems

Introduction

During the 1970s, cryptography has emerged from a little known aspect of military, diplomatic, and intelligence activities to become a much discussed aspect of data communication and storage. This increased concern with communication security in academic and commercial laboratories, as well as new areas of the federal government, has lead to two major cryptographic developments.

In 1975, the National Bureau of Standards, published a proposed standard algorithm for data protection and this algorithm was adopted in 1977, after two years of public controversy over its security, as Federal Information Processing Standard 46, the Data Encryption Standard (DES) [9]. Both the publication of the standard and the controversy over its adoption have drawn the attention of the technical community and lead to a much wider awareness of modern cryptographic principles and practices.

The second development, public key cryptography [2], is almost exactly the same age as DES; the concept was discovered in the spring of 1975 and the first paper on the subject appeared in June 1976 [3]. The term "public key cryptography" refers to new kinds of cryptographic systems in which some of

This paper is a summation of the author's thoughts during the summer and fall of 1978 and was first presented as an invited lecture at the International Communications Conference in Boston, June, 1979.

the keying material can be made public in such a way as to permit both freer and more secure communication. Since the discovery of the public key concept, two major approaches, drawn from different areas of mathematics, have been found for implementing it and the field has developed into such a thriving area of research that it has on occasion been treated as a competing product by the advocates of DES.

A public key cryptosystem is one in which the conversion of plaintext to ciphertext to plaintext are done using different keys. Furthermore, given one of the keys, it is just as difficult to discover the other as it would be to discover the plaintext given only a sample of the ciphertext. This separation of the keys for encryption and decrypting makes it possible to disclose one (the public key) while retaining the other (the secret key).

Because the public key can be revealed without compromising the secret key, the process of providing suitable keys to the sender and receiver of a secret message ("key distribution") can be carried out with less reliance on third parties. Public key cryptosystems also make possible a new form of authentication called a "digital signature." A message that has been encrypted with a secret key could only have been created by the holder of that secret key, but the identity of the creator can be verified by anyone who has the corresponding public key. This property (creatable by only one person but recognizable by many) allows the digital signature to play much the same role in electronic communication that a written signature plays in paper communication.

Public key systems at present, however, also have their drawbacks. The computational methods used to achieve the novel properties are drawn from areas of mathematics previously untapped by cryptography. In consequence, public key systems fail to enjoy the confidence placed in conventional techniques. The current public key systems are also computationally less efficient than their conventional rivals. This limits their usefulness and often requires that they be used in combination with conventional techniques. In consequence of these shortcomings and perhaps of over enthusiastic initial claims by the developers of public key cryptography, some critics have gone so far as to suggest that public keys offer little or no benefit.

In the following chapters, we will attempt to give a brief tutorial introduction to the issues involved and attempt to present a balanced view of the relative merits of conventional and public key cryptography, both at present and in the future.

Conventional Cryptographic Systems

Data in usable and understandable form, whether accounting information, human speech, or a computer program is called *plaintext*. The process by which the plaintext is transformed into an unintelligible or ciphertext form is called *encryption* or *enciphering* and that by which the ciphertext is returned to plaintext is called *decryption* or *deciphering*.

The facilities for making this change from plaintext to ciphertext and back, whether a set of instructions, a program, or a piece of electronic equipment, are called a *cryptographic system, cryptosystem,* or merely *system.*

Cryptosystems are divided into two parts called respectively the *general system* and the *specific key* or just *key*. The general system is closely analogous to an ordinary lock in that it may be adapted by the use of different keys to provide security for a variety of different people.

Example: The Data Encryption Standard

In 1975, the National Bureau of Standards proposed a cryptographic algorithm designed by IBM as the Data Encryption Standard (DES) -- a single cryptographic mechanism

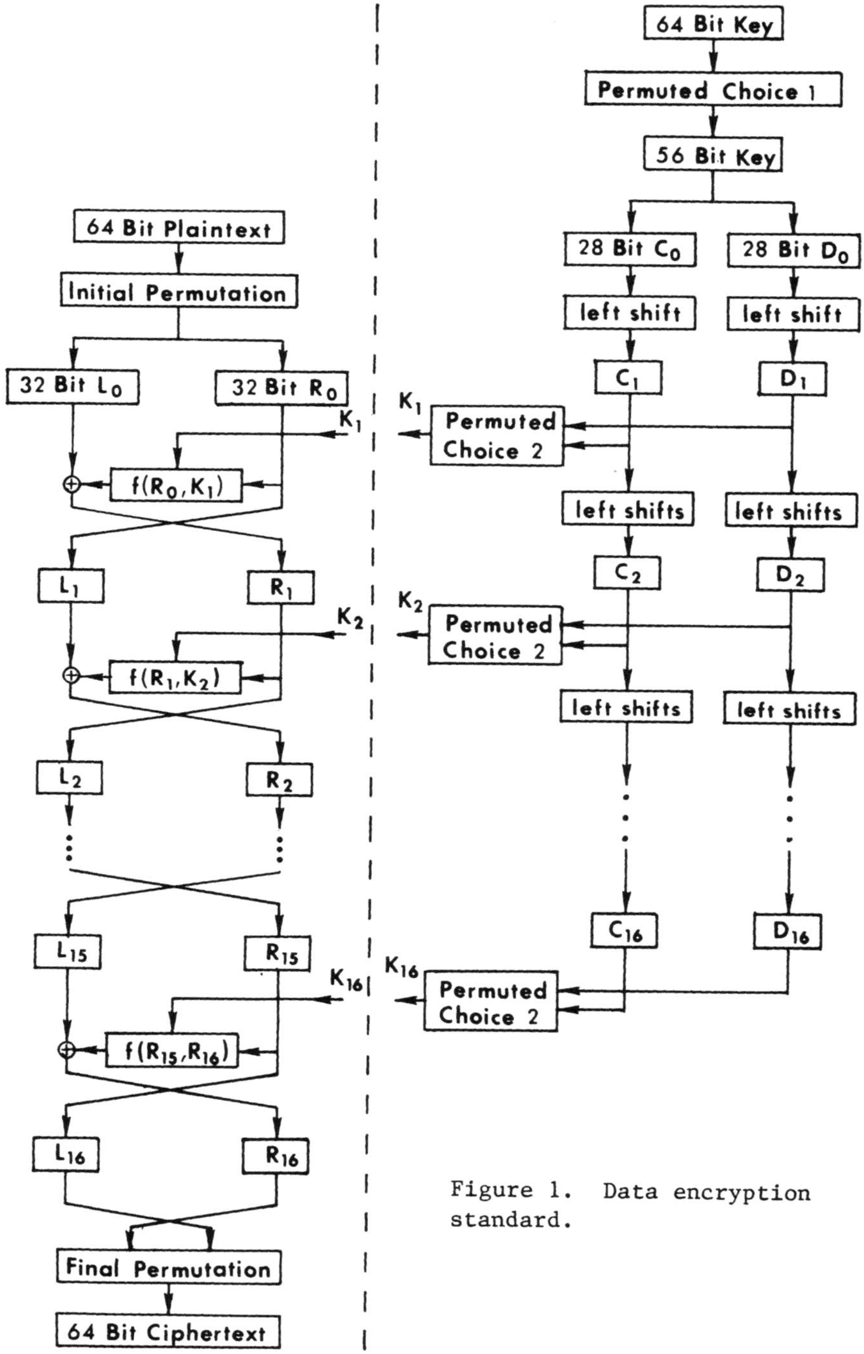

Figure 1. Data encryption standard.

intended for widespread use in commercial and nonmilitary governmental applications. This algorithm was adopted in 1977 and promulgated in Federal Information Processing Standards Publication No. 46 [9].

The DES is a primitive element which can be used in several ways as a building block in finished cryptographic systems. In its basic form it takes 64 bits of input and transforms these under the control of a 56 bit key to produce a 64 bit output.

The figures show the flow of information in DES. After an initial rearrangement of the input bits, the plaintext is subjected to sixteen rounds of a complex nonlinear transformation.

As shown on the left side of Figure 1, this transformation encrypts the left half of its input by XORing it with a function, Figure 2, of 48 bits of the key and the right half of its input. The right half itself is carried through unchanged to become the left half of the input to the next round.

The f function initially expands its 32 bit input from eight groups of four bits each to eight groups of six bits by copying the first bit of each group to be the last bit of the expanded form of the preceding group and copying the fourth bit of each group to be first bit of the expanded form of the succeeding group. The new first bit for group 1 is taken from the end of group 8 and, similarly, the last bit of group 8 is taken from the beginning of group 1. If the original eight four bit groups were:

$$(1,2,3,4)(5,6,7,8) \cdots (29,30,31,32)$$

then the resulting sequence of six bit groups would be:

$$(32,1,2,3,4,5)(4,5,6,7,8,9) \cdots (28,29,30,31,32,1) \ .$$

These 48 bits are now XORed with 48 bits selected from the

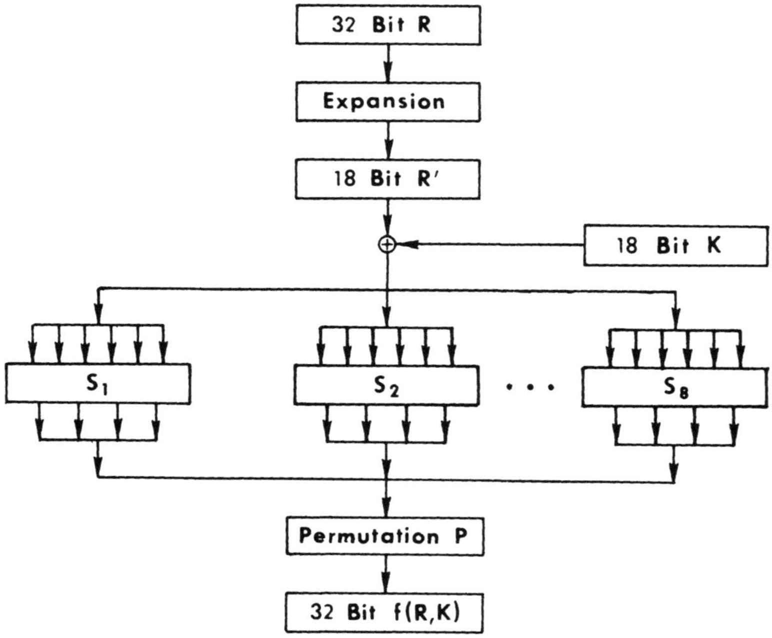

Figure 2. f(R,K) Flowchart.

key according to a complex schedule indicated on the right side of Figure 1. The left and right halves of the 56 bit key are stored in two 28 bit registers. At each round these registers are circularly shifted left by either one or two bits (varying in a prearranged fashion from round to round). Twenty-four bits selected from the left half, and 24 bits selected from the right half then form the left and right halves of the 48 bit key for that round.

The 48 bits resulting from expansion are contracted back to 32 by the eight S-boxes, each of which accepts six bits of input and generates four bits of output. Each S-box contains four invertible transformations which operate on four bit groups. The first and sixth bits of each group (the bits that were copied from adjacent groups) select one of these four transformations to operate on the center four bits. The 32 bit output of the S-boxes is then subjected to a fixed permutation designed to redistribute the outputs of each S-box to the inputs of different S-boxes in the following round.

Examination of this process shows that its effects are reversed when it is "run backwards." The decryption is done by performing the sixteenth round first, followed by the fifteenth, and ending with the first.

A piece of hardware to implement the DES can be built with a few thousand logic gates, the major part of which are taken up by two thousand bits of read-only memory in the S-boxes. Each round requires two XORs and eight table lookups, and the speed of implementation varies substantially with the amount of computation done in parallel.

Since its adoption, several companies have introduced products using the standard. These range from single LSI chips to complete communication security systems. Current LSI implementations range in speed from 640 bits per second (Intel) to 10 million bits per second (Fairchild).

Public Key Systems

A public key cryptosystem is a cryptographic system in which each encryption process is governed by not one but two keys. The two keys are inverses of each other, that is to say anything encrypted with one can be decrypted with the other and vice versa. The important additional property of a public key cryptosystem is that given one of the keys, it is extremely difficult to find the other. This allows one of the keys to be made public while its inverse is kept secret, giving the systems their name. Public key cryptosystems have two very important properties.

- Because it is not necessary to keep both of the keys secret, one can be made readily available, published in a phonebook for example. Anyone wanting to transmit a confidential message can encrypt it in the "public key" of the addressee with assurance that only the addressee will be able to read it.

- Just as a message encrypted in a public key can be produced by anyone but can only be read by the holder of the corresponding secret key, a message encrypted in a secret key can be read by anyone, using the corresponding public key, but could only have been produced by the holder of the secret key. This gives it the fundamental property of a signature.

A public key distribution system is a mechanism which allows two people who have never had any prior secure contact to establish a secure channel "out of thin air." Public key distribution systems do not provide any signature mechanism but, at present, some are faster and more compact than public key cryptosystems which makes them better for many applications.

<u>Example: Public Key Distribution System</u>

The first practical public key distribution system [2] makes use of the apparent difficulty of computing logarithms over a finite (Galois) field GF(q) with a prime number q of elements (the numbers $\{0,1,\cdots,q-1\}$ under arithmetic mod q). Let

$$Y = \alpha^X \bmod q, \quad \text{for} \quad 1 < X < q - 1 \quad ,$$

where α is a fixed primitive element of GF(q) (that is the powers of α range over the nonzero elements $1,2,\cdots,q-1$ of GF(q)), then X is referred to as the logarithm of Y to the base α, over GF(q):

$$X = \log_\alpha Y \quad \text{over} \quad GF(q), \quad \text{for} \quad 1 < Y < q - 1 \quad .$$

Calculation of Y from X is easy, taking at most $2 * \log_2 q$ multiplications. For example

$$\alpha^{18} = (((\alpha^2)^2)^2 * \alpha^2 \quad .$$

Computing X from Y, on the other hand can be much more difficult [11] and, using the best known algorithm, has computational complexity similar to finding the factors of a number close to q [1].

Each user generates an independent random number X_i chosen uniformly from the set of integers $\{1,2,\cdots,q-1\}$. He keeps X_i secret but places

$$Y_i = \alpha^{X_i} \bmod q$$

in a public file with his name and address. When users i and j wish to communicate privately they use

$$K_{ij} = \alpha^{X_i X_j} \bmod q$$

as their key. User i computes K_{ij} by obtaining Y_j from the public file and letting

$$\begin{aligned} K_{ij} &= Y_j^{X_i} \bmod q \\ &= (\alpha^{X_j})^{X_i} \bmod q \\ &= \alpha^{X_j X_i} = \alpha^{X_i X_j} \bmod q \quad . \end{aligned}$$

User j obtains K_{ij} in a similar fashion

$$K_{ij} = Y_i^{X_j} \bmod q \quad .$$

Another user must compute K_{ij} from Y_i and Y_j, for example by computing

$$K_{ij}^{(\log_\alpha Y_j)} = Y_i \bmod q \quad .$$

If logarithms over GF(q) are easily computed, the system can be broken, but at present neither a threateningly fast method of doing this computation nor a way to bypass the logarithm and compute K_{ij} from Y_i and Y_j without first obtaining either X_i or X_j is known.

If q is a prime slightly less than w, all quantities are representable as w bit numbers. Exponentiation then takes at most 2 × w multiplications over GF(q), while computing the logarithm requires $q^{1/2} = 2^{w/2}$ operations, using the best currently known algorithm. The cryptanalytic effort therefore grows exponentially relative to encryption or decryption. If w = 200, at most 400 multiplications are required to compute Y_i from X_i, or K_{ij} from X_i and X_j, yet taking logarithms over GF(q) is thought to require 2^{100} or approximately 10^{30} operations.

This system can be implemented efficiently with respect to both speed and storage, and a variation in which q is not prime is the basis for an experimental local secure network at the Mitre Corporation [16].

Example: The RSA System

The RSA system [13], named after the initials of its inventors, Rivest, Shamir, and Adleman, is drawn from number theory. It is based on the fact that multiplying large (e.g., 100 digit) prime numbers is computationally easy, but that factoring the product of two such numbers appears to be computationally infeasible. A block of plaintext is encrypted by exponentiation in a finite arithmetic structure. The exponent in this operation together with the product of the primes comprise the public key. The inverse operation can be performed only by those who know the pair of primes (the secret key).

A user A selects two very large prime numbers, P and Q at random, and multiplies them together to obtain a number N. The number N is made public, but its factors, P and Q, are kept secret. Using P and Q, A can compute the Euler totient function $\varphi(N)$ (the number of integers less than N and relatively prime to N) as

$$\varphi(N) = (P-1)(Q-1)$$

he then chooses another number E at random from the interval 2 through $\varphi(N) - 1$. This number is also made public. A missage block M is an integer between 0 and N-1 and can be stored in roughly 700 bits. Enciphering is carried out on M using the public information E and N, as

$$C = M^E \bmod N$$

where C represents the enciphered block.

Using the secret number $\varphi(N)$ user A can easily [5, Vol. 2, p. 315, ex. 15] calculate a number D such that

$$ED = 1 \pmod{\varphi(N)} \quad .$$

(If E has a common factor with $\varphi(N)$ then D does not exist, but the algorithm will indicate this and another E can be chosen.) Equivalently, $E_D = \varphi(N) + 1$. Then, because

$$X^{k \neq \varphi(N)+1} = X \bmod N$$

for all integers X between 0 and N - 1 and for all integers k, deciphering is easily accomplished by raising C to the D-th power

$$C^D \; M^{ED} = M^{\varphi(N)+1} = M \bmod N \quad .$$

As a very small example, suppose P = 17 and Q = 31 are chosen so that N = PQ = 527 and $\varphi = (P-1)(Q-1) = 480$. If E = 7 is chosen then D = 343. (7X343 = 2401 = 5X480 + 1.) If M = 2 then

$$C = P^E = 2^7 \bmod 527 = 128 \quad .$$

Note that only the public key (E,N) is needed to encipher M. To decipher, the private key D is needed to compute

$$
\begin{aligned}
M &= C^D \bmod N \\
&= 128^{343} \bmod 527 \\
&= 128^{256} * 128^{64} * 128^{4} * 128^{2} * 128 \bmod 527 \\
&= 35 * 256 * 35 * 101 * 47 * 128 \bmod 527 \\
&= 2 \bmod 527 \quad .
\end{aligned}
$$

Unless surprisingly large improvements are made in factoring, or methods of inverting M^E without calculating D are discovered, the RSA system will remain secure. Because this cryptosystem requires dozens of multiplications of numbers hundreds of digits in length, its operation is quite slow. Rivest has constructed an experimental implementation in TTL hardware at MIT which encrypts data at six kilobits per second as compared with ten megabits for Fairchild's DES implementation.

Example: Trapdoor Knapsacks

Another public key system [7,8] is called the "trapdoor knapsack system," a name imaginatively derived from the notion of attempting to choose just the right set of rods from those in a box so that when packed into a long thin knapsack, the rods would fit tightly and not rattle. Trapdoor knapsacks have their roots in a field called combinatorial mathematics and depend on the fact that given a list of numbers it is easy to add up any specified subset, but given instead a list of numbers and a sum it is extremely difficult to discover a subset which totals to exactly that sum. In order to do encryption in this system, the input block is treated as a specification of which numbers are to be selected from a list and added up; the output is their sum. The trapdoor knapsack system is based on Merkle's discovery that if the list of numbers is constructed correctly, certain details of that construction constitute a secret key which allows the constructor to take the sum and discover which members of the list were added.

Given a vector of integers $\vec{\alpha} = (\alpha_1, \alpha_2, \cdots, \alpha_n)$ and an integer S, the knapsack problem is to find a subset of the α_i such that the sum of the elements of the subset is equal to S. Equivalently, given $\bar{\alpha}$ and S find a binary n-vector x such that $\vec{\alpha} \cdot x = S$.

The knapsack problem is believed to be extremely difficult in general, belonging to a class of problems (the NP complete problems) that are thought not to be solvable in polynomial time on any deterministic computer. Some cases of the knapsack problem are quite simple, however, and Merkle and Hellman's technique is to start with a simple one and convert it into a more complex form.

The vector $\vec{\alpha}$ can be used to encipher a block by forming the dot product $S = \vec{\alpha} \cdot \vec{x}$. Recovery of $\vec{x}$ from S involves solving a knapsack problem and is thus believed to be computationally infeasible if $\vec{\alpha}$ and $\vec{x}$ are chosen randomly.

If the vector α is selected so that each element is larger than the sum of the preceding elements and each of the x_i is either 0 or 1, its knapsack problem is very simple. For example, if $\alpha' = (171,197,459,1191,2410)$ and $S' = 3798$ then x_5 must equal 1. If it were 0 then even if $x_1 = x_2 = x_3 = x_4 = 1$, the dot product $\alpha \cdot \vec{x}$ would be too small. Then, knowing that $x_5 = 1$, $S' - \alpha' = 3797 - 2410 = 1387$ must be a sum of a subset of the first four elements of $\vec{\alpha}$. Because $1387 \geq \alpha_4' = 1191$, x must equal 1. Finally $S' = \alpha_5' - \alpha_4' = 196 = \alpha_2'$ so $x_3 = 0$, $x_2 = 1$, and $x_1 = 0$.

This simple knapsack vector $\vec{\alpha}'$ cannot be used as a public enciphering key because anyone can easily recover $\vec{x}$ from S. The algorithm for generating public keys therefore generates a random simple knapsack vector $\vec{\alpha}'$ (with a hundred or more components) and keeps $\vec{\alpha}'$ secret. It also generates a random number m which is larger than $\sum \vec{\alpha}'$ and a random pair w, w^{-1} such that $ww^{-1} = 1 \bmod m$. It then generates the public knapsack vector or enciphering key a by multiplying each component of α' by w mod m

$$\alpha = w * \alpha' \bmod m \quad .$$

When another user wishes to send the message x to A he computes

$$S = \vec{\alpha} \cdot \vec{x}$$

and sends this to A. A uses his secret information, w^{-1} and m to compute

$$
\begin{aligned}
S' &= wS \bmod m \\
&= w^{-1} \sum \alpha_i x_i \bmod m \\
&= w^{-1} \sum (w\alpha_i' \bmod m) x_i \bmod m \\
&= \sum (w^{-1} w\alpha_i' \bmod m) x_i \bmod m \\
&= \vec{\alpha}' \cdot \vec{x}
\end{aligned}
$$

because $m > \sum \alpha'$. For example, if the secret vector α' is as above, then w = 2550 and M = 8443, results in the public vector, α = (5457,4213,5316,6013,7439), which hides the structure present in α'.

The vector $\vec{\alpha}$ is published by the user as his public key, while the parameters w^{-1} and m are kept secret as his private key. They can be used to decipher any message which has been enciphered with his public key, by computing $S' = w^{-1}S \bmod m$ and then solving the simple knapsack $S' = \vec{\alpha}' \cdot \vec{x}$. This process can be iterated to produce a sequence of vectors with seemingly more difficult knapsack problems by using transformations (w_1,m_1), (w_2,m_2), etc. The overall transformation is not, in general, equivalent to any single (w,m) transformation.

The trapdoor knapsack system requires special adaptation when used to produce signatures [7, 14].

Unlike the RSA system, knapsack systems are quite fast and speeds of one megabit appear easy to obtain. Unfortunately, the public keys are quite large, requiring approximately ten-thousand bits.

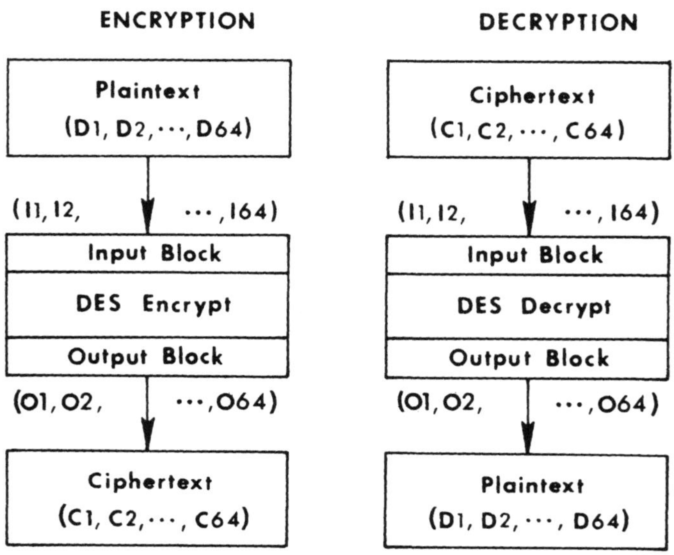

Figure 3. Block mode.

Comparison of Conventional and Public Key Systems

Modes of Operation

Block mode. The basic form of public key systems, and of many conventional systems including DES, is block mode shown schematically in Figure 3: A block of plaintext is transformed under the control of a key into a block of ciphertext in a way which is independent of any other text the system may have processed. This mode of operation is also called electronic code book mode.

Practical requirements for authentication, variable message length, etc., limit actual use of block mode operation to a few special cases such as transmitting a key in encrypted form. Although these do not exhaust the possibilities, most encryption is done in one of three other modes:

Output feedback or key autokey mode. The block cipher is used to produce a long sequence of pseudorandom bits by repeatedly taking the ciphertext output and feeding it back as the plaintext input; Figure 4. The pseudorandom sequence is then XORed with the plaintext.

This mode has the important advantage of not expanding errors which change 0s to 1s or vice versa but the significant disadvantage that loss of even a single bit (bit slip) results in permanent loss of synchronization.

Cipher feedback or ciphertext autokey mode. In cipher feedback mode, each incoming block of plaintext is XORed with the ciphertext output of the previous block; Figure 5. The resulting ciphertext is then fed back as the input to the next round.

In this mode, single errors are expanded into "garbled" blocks. This is sometimes useful for authentication. Loss of synchronization in cipher feedback mode is no worse than

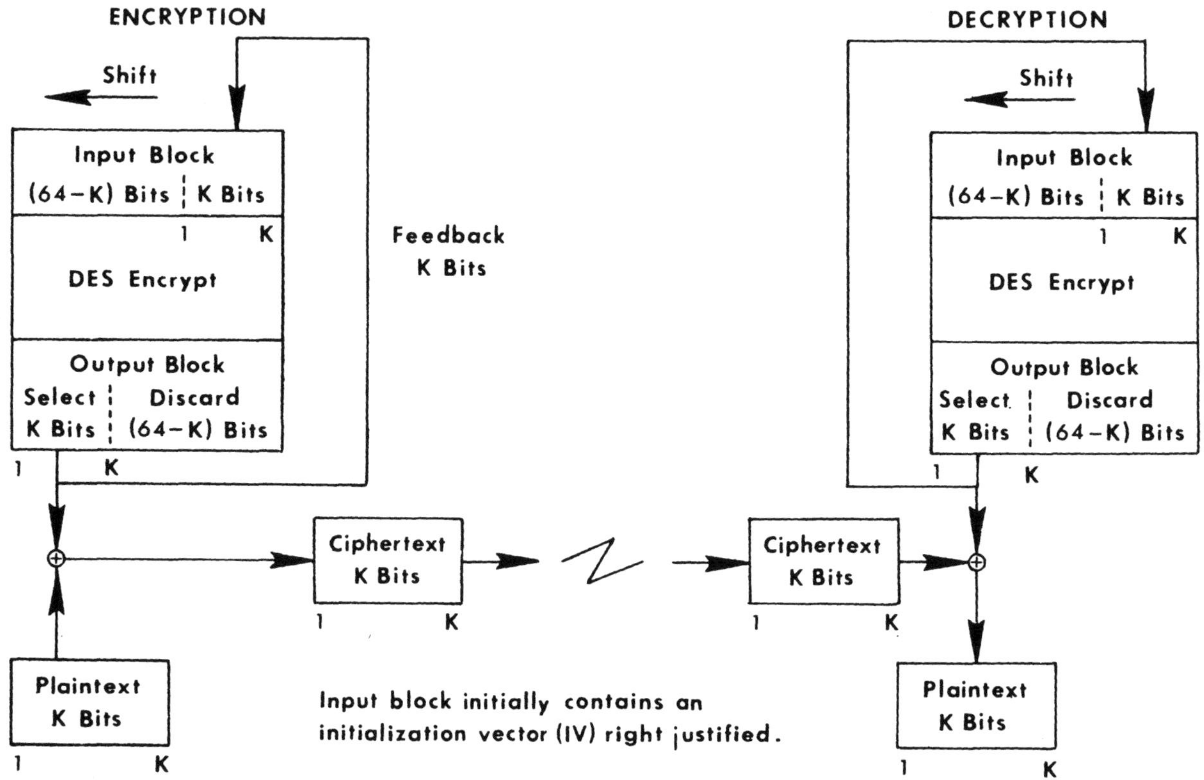

Figure 4. Output feedback (OFB) mode.

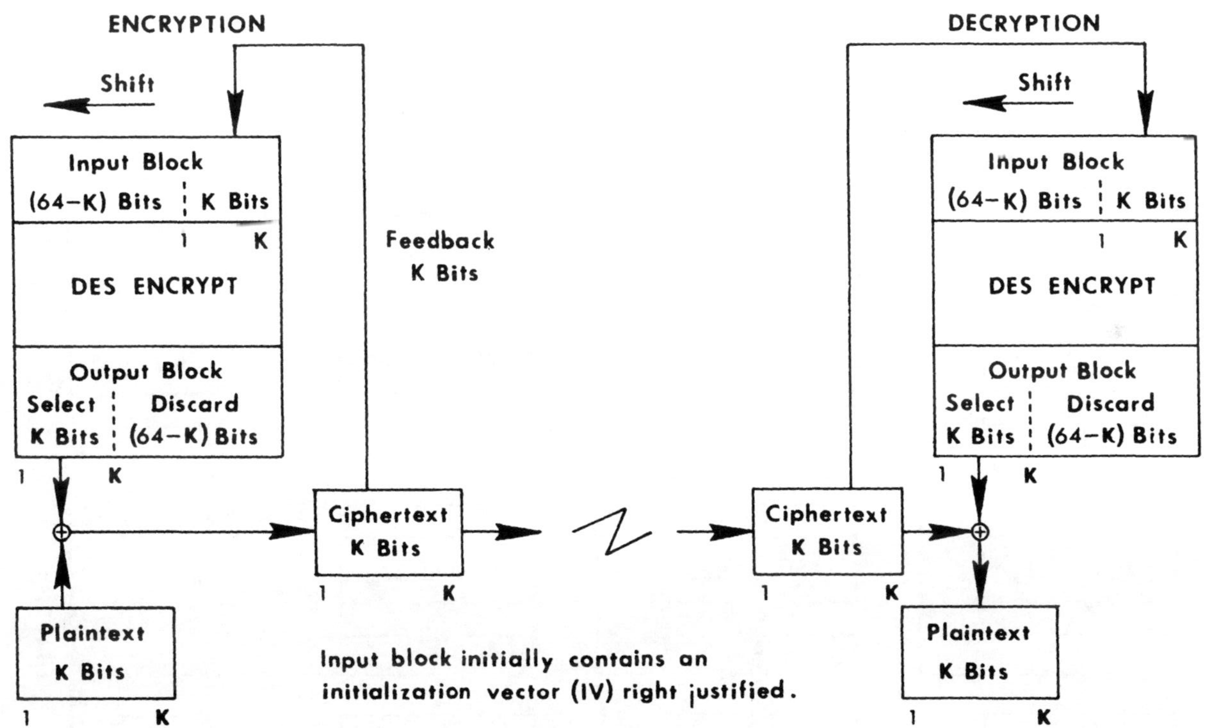

Figure 5. Cipher feedback (CFB) mode.

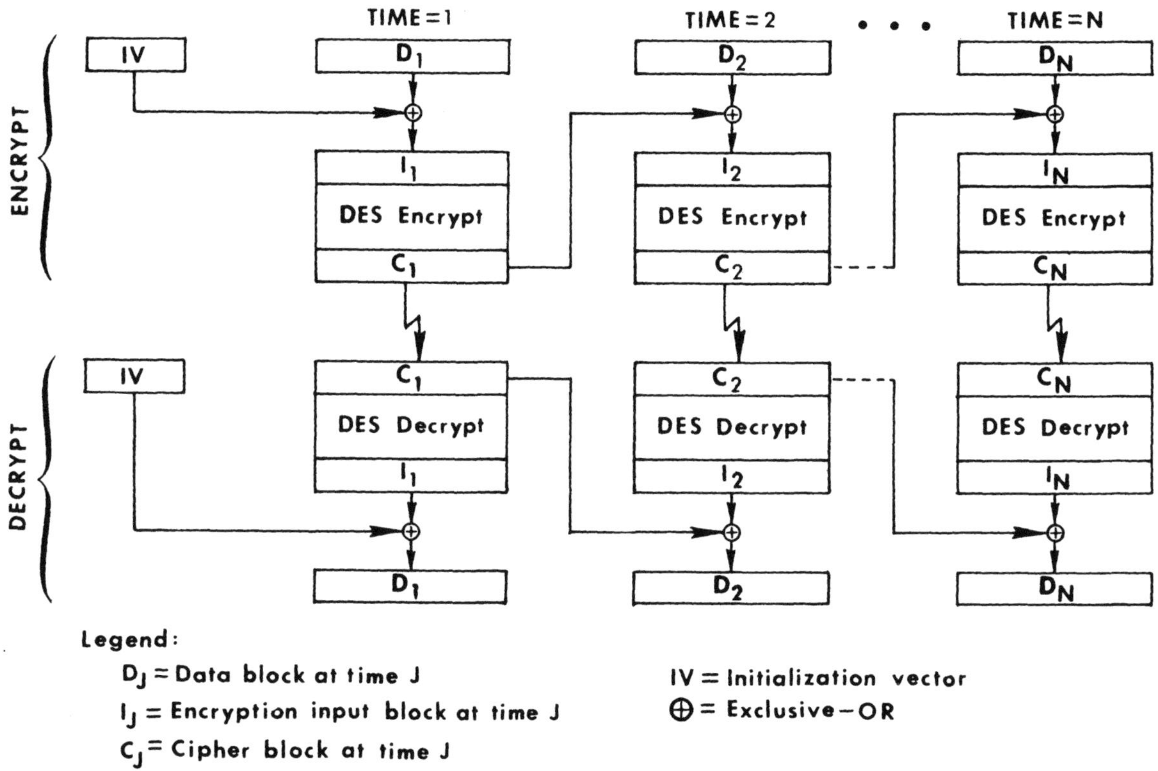

Figure 6. Cipher block chaining (CBC) mode.

any other error, and the system resynchronizes itself after the passage of the next full block.

Cipher block chaining. Cipher block chaining, Figure 6, is similar to cipher feedback in form and consequences. Each plaintext block is XORed with the previous ciphertext block, then encrypted.

The output feedback and cipher feedback modes employ the underlying block system only to encrypt, regardless of whether they are enciphering or deciphering, and therefore cannot be made secure if the enciphering key has been made public.

The block chaining mode uses the underlying block system both to encrypt and decrypt; it can therefore be used in conjunction with the public key property.

Since output feedback mode and cipher feedback mode are often useful, a practical communication system must be able to encipher with secret keys. This enciphering can nonetheless be done with public key systems by not making use of the public key property and keeping both the enciphering and deciphering keys secret. A natural way of doing this is to generate a secret *session key*: a key which is used for the duration of just one session. This key can be transmitted securely from the sender to the receiver encrypted with the receiver's public key.

Privacy and Key Distribution

Public key systems receive their name from the important contribution they make to the problem of distributing keys to cryptographic users.

In a public network with n subscribers, there are n * (n-1)/2 pairs of subscribers, and each pair might want to communicate privately. For this privacy to be guaranteed by conventional cryptography, each pair must use a key which they share with no one else. If the network has a million subscribers, there is a potential demand for just under half a trillion keys, too many for subscribers to want to store and far too many to be distributed in advance.

At first glance, public keys appear to solve this problem completely. Since knowledge of a public key does not convey the ability to decrypt material encrypted with that key, all confidential messages to a given subscriber can be encrypted with the same key, regardless of who sent them. If subscriber A wants to send a private message to subscriber B, he must obtain B's public key. This may come from the same "phonebook" or directory service from which he got B's address, or even directly from B. B's public key requires no protection and can thus be sent in clear.

The problem is one of authentication: The sender of a secret message must authenticate the receiver. Encrypting the message in a public key guarantees that the data will be read only by the holder of the corresponding private key, but the sender must still assure himself that the public key is correct, i.e., that the holder of the private key is the intended recipient. What steps must be taken in order to provide this assurance vary with the communication environment and the degree of security required.

The attitude taken in military communications is that cryptography is the only trustworthy authentication mechanism. It is assumed that the opponents may have altered any aspect of network routing and (aside from cryptographic authentication) can impersonate any user. Under this assumption, A could have no confidence in a key he had received in clear over the network.

Fortunately, in a commercial communications environment, this assumption is rarely justified and faith can usually be placed in the integrity of other communication mechanisms. The stringent military requirement for absolute security (at almost any price) is replaced by an equally stringent requirement for acceptable security at an acceptable price.

The user whose business requires only a moderate grade of security may be satisfied to rely on the integrity of network routing to protect public key distribution. The widespread use of microwave relays makes passive wiretaps easy to place in modern communication networks, but subverting network routing requires an active wiretap that must delete as well as insert messages; such a tap is difficult to construct and more likely to be detected. The commitment and economic resources of an opponent engaged in industrial espionage might be sufficient for placing wiretaps in the subnet, but totally inadequate to undertake the expense or risk of attempting to subvert network routing.

Key distribution becomes much harder to subvert if the public keys are difficult to counterfeit. One approach to this problem is through the use of "certificates" [6]; a certificate is a message of the form: "A's public key is ..." encrypted in the public key of some trusted authority. If the private key of the trusted authority is destroyed after the certificates are generated, no counterfeit public keys can be generated later. Merkle [8] has improved this procedure by applying a process called tree authentication to permit a group of users to generate a tree whose leaves are user names paired with public keys. A member of the group need only remember the root node of the tree to be able to check the authenticity of a leaf. Using this mechanism, Merkle has outlined mechanisms for guaranteeing secure key distribution without resorting to central authority. Security in these schemes, however, is bought at the cost of substantial inflexibility. Once the authentication tree has been built, no more users can be added; new users must wait for the next tree.

A more flexible approach is to employ a *Key Distribution Center (KDC):* a network resource that hands out authenticated keys on demand. The KDC authenticates its transmissions by signing them with its own private key. Each subscriber can assure himself of the authenticity of keys sent by the KDC by knowing just one key (other than his own private key): the KDC's public key.

A little thought shows that a similar arrangement can be made with conventional systems. In this case each subscriber shares a secret key with the KDC. Two subscribers entering into a private conversation contact the KDC and (using the secret keys they share with it) obtain a private session key to use in that conversation. The KDC can ease its own secure storage burden, from thousands or millions of keys down to one, by encrypting all of the subscriber keys in a master key, and decrypting them only as needed.

Analysis of the protocols required shows that the two schemes require about the same number of overhead messages and the same amount of secure storage (one secret key per subscriber plus one for the KDC), and Needham and Schroeder [10] have thus argued that the public keys provide no advantage. This analysis, however, fails to consider the cost to the opponents of penetrating each of these systems.

In order to compromise a network using conventional cryptography, it suffices to corrupt the KDC. This gives the intruder access to sufficient information to recover the session keys used to encrypt past, present, and future messages. These keys, together with information obtained from passive wiretaps, give the corrupt KDC access to the contents of any message ever sent on the system.

A public key network presents a much more difficult problem. In order to compromise the network, the opponents must obtain the KDC's private key, which will allow them to distribute counterfeit public keys. Even with this information, however, a passive wiretap is useless. The KDC's private key is used only to authenticate subscribers' public keys; it does not enable the intruders to decrypt any subscriber's traffic. In order to gain access to this traffic, the intruders must trick subscribers into encrypting messages with phony public keys.

The KDC can spy on messages from subscriber A to subscriber B, by answering A's request for B's public key with a fraudulent key from a pair it generated itself. This will enable the KDC to decrypt any message that A sends to B. If such a message actually reaches B, however, B will be unable to decrypt it and will inform A of the error. The KDC must therefore intercept A's message, decrypt it, and reencrypt it in B's public key in order to maintain the deception. If the KDC wants to understand B's replies to A, it must go through the same procedure with B, translating in both directions.

Since a KDC can function securely without any special privileges, it is connected to the network in the same way as any other subscriber and the corrupt KDC has no special powers on which to call for controlling all traffic between A and B. The intruders will therefore be forced to place one or more active wiretaps in the net to maintain this control, and the number of such wiretaps will grow rapidly with the number of subscribers on which they spy.

Note that in the conventional approach, encryption of keys received from the KDC is indispensible; without this there would be no security whatever. In the public key approach, cryptographic authentication of keys sent by the KDC could be omitted. The system would remain secure unless the opponents could insert active wiretaps.

It is also worth observing that A and B will decrease their security slightly if, after having established contact, they settle on a session key and revert to a conventional mode of operation which does not make use of the public key property. In this case, the intruder does not need to control the channel after the session key has been selected. This threat, however, can be countered, without losing the advantages a session key provides, by periodically (and unpredictably) using the public keys to exchange new session keys.

The above scenario has been described in terms of public key cryptosystems. The situation is very similar for public key distribution systems and also requires the intruder to engage in active wiretapping as well as corrupting the KDC.

Signatures

The object of a digital signature is to provide a pure data equivalent of the written signature -- a datum which the recipient can save as evidence of the sender's authorship of a message. Although no entirely adequate solution to this problem has been found, public key cryptosystems provide an approach which minimizes the amount of additional machinery, such as witnesses, required.

Encrypting a message with a private key fulfills most of the criteria of signing it. Only the holder of the private key could have produced the message, but anyone can check its authorship by decrypting it with the appropriate public key.

Kline and Popek have pointed out that this is not entirely satisfactory because the holder of the secret key can invalidate his signature either accidentally, by losing his private key, or intentionally, by pretending to have lost it in such a way that it becomes public knowledge [4]. This gives rise to a conflict of interest, since the holder of the key used to sign a contract may well stand to benefit if the key is lost. To make matters worse, since there is no intrinsic way of establishing the age of data (as a crime lab can sometimes do with a paper document) all contracts "signed" with a revealed private key will become invalid, not just new ones.

Kline and Popek conclude that any system in which the

user knows his own key will be insecure and recommend a solution in which the user is prevented from revealing his private key by being deprived of all control of it. They propose a "tamper-proof" terminal which authenticates the user through some absolute means such as fingerprints and then signs his transmission with a key for which the system is the custodian. This, they point out, can be done with either public key or conventional systems and neither seems to offer any particular advantage.

Aside from the questionable assumption that a tamper-proof terminal can be made cheap enough for wide availability, this scheme suffers the dangerous vice of forcing the users to place complete faith in the system. If the system were compromised, through either illegal actions or legal manipulation, the users could find their names signed to documents they had never seen.

It is clear that trusted third parties cannot be entirely avoided in any contract system as this is precisely the role played by a court when it adjudicates a contract under dispute. It appears, however, that the makers of a contract must engage a third party at the time they sign the contract rather than waiting for the development of bad faith.

A partial answer is provided by introducing a digital "notary public" which dates the document and signs the date with its own private key. Since the documents can be encrypted, the notary need know nothing about their content, nor need it be aware of the identities of the parties to the transaction. The receiver of a signed message can submit it to one or more notaries without making any statement about its content or purpose and thereby protect himself against later keyloss by the signer.

Notaries public prevent the invalidation of old contracts signed with a key which is reported lost. They are of no help, however, when a key is alleged to have been compromised for some time without the owner's knowledge. To the degree that written signatures can be forged, this threat exists in conventional contract litigation. To counter this threat, contracts for large amounts of money are usually signed in the presence of witnesses and large bank checks require countersignature by a second bank officer. Techniques for carrying such measures over into electronic media are currently under development. Shamir [15], for example, has developed a technique for sharing a key among several people.

Time and Space Efficiency

As a result of the opponent's ability to encipher messages using the public key, an attack is open to him which would not be available to the attacker of a conventional cryptosystem; he can repeatedly encrypt the ciphertext (using the public key) until he gets a result which he recognizes as the plaintext. This inherently excludes small block sizes -- for a 32 bit block, the plaintext could always be recovered in a billion or fewer encryptions. This attack would be quite weak against a system with a 64 bit block, however, and can be completely ignored for blocks of length 128 or greater.

There is no reason to believe that public key systems need to be any worse than this in block size, or to believe that they need be any worse at all in speed, but the systems developed so far are much less efficient than this ideal.

The RSA system requires 500 to 1000 bits of key for real security as compared to 100 for a conventional system. It is also extremely slow. Rivest has constructed a hardware prototype using a 100 digit (320 bit) block size and a 100 digit key, which is estimated to run at six kilobits. This compares sadly with the megabit rate of similar DES implementations.

The trapdoor knapsack system is far better in speed; a typical encryption requires 100 additions of 100 bit words (about 100 microseconds per 100 bits, or one megabit), though decryption is somewhat slower. The size of the public key, however, is a whopping ten thousand bits.

In practice, it seems that use of the current public key systems will have to be restricted to the applications in which they are advantageous (key exchanges and signatures) and conventional systems (using session keys encrypted with public keys) employed for most data transfers [6].

Certification

The ideal way of certifying a cryptographic system would be to give a formal mathematical proof that the value of the work required to break it was greater than the value of the information it was used to protect. At present no mathematical theory capable of giving such proofs is available, and cryptographic certification must rest on less formal kinds of evidence.

Cryptographic systems have traditionally been certified by an adversary procedure: A system which has been designed by one group of cryptographers is subjected to attack by another. The attackers are supplied with all of the information which was known to the designers, and permitted to attack the system under extremely favorable conditions. They may for example submit carefully chosen pieces of plaintext for encryption, or carefully chosen pieces of ciphertext for decryption, and examine the results.

If the system resists attack under these favorable conditions, it is considered to be secure. In addition, the record of this assault is available to potential system customers for their use in evaluating the system.

Adversary attack was the approach used in certifying DES. IBM reported that seventeen manyears of effort were devoted to attacking DES without success. Unfortunately, only the conclusions, and not the results, of this study have been reported.

Another approach is to attempt to make use of mathematical work already done by basing the cryptographic system on a well known mathematical problem in such a way that cryptanalyzing the system is equivalent to solving the problem. This approach is evident in all of the public key systems to date and Rabin has shown that a ciphertext only attack on a variant of the RSA system is equivalent to the well studied integer factoring problem [12]. Rabin's result is a two edged sword, however. His technique is to exhibit a method of factoring the number p × q on the assumption that the factorer can solve cryptograms with modulus p × q (i.e., take square roots). Although the results make the system appear very strong against a known plaintext attack, they show equally clearly that it will collapse immediately against a chosen text attack.

Although equivalence to a well known mathematical problem provides good evidence of the strength of a system, it is not a form of evidence which is widely understood or accepted in the security community. Before any public key system can expect to be accepted, and before its designers can expect to win an implied warranty of fitness suit in the event of its failure, it will have to be subjected to certification by adversary attack.

References

[1] L. Adleman, "A subexponential algorithm for the discrete logarithm problem with applications to cryptography," in Proc. IEEE 20th Annual Symposium of Foundations of Computer Science (Oct. 29-31, 1979), pp. 56-60.

[2] W. Diffie and M. E. Hellman, "New directions in cryp-

tography," IEEE Trans. on Inform. Theory, IT-22 (Nov. 1976), pp. 644-654. (See pp.143-180, this volume.)

[3] W. Diffie and M. E. Hellman, "Multiuser cryptographic techniques," in Proc. Nat. Computer Conf., New York, NY (June 7-10, 1976).

[4] C. S. Kline and G. J. Popek, "Public key vs. conventional key encryption," in Proc. Nat. Computer Conf. (1979).

[5] D. E. Knuth, The Art of Computer Programming, Addison-Wesley, Reading, MA (1969).

[6] L. M. Kornfelder, "Toward a practical public key cryptosystem," MIT Dept. of Electrical Engineering (May 7, 1978).

[7] R. C. Merkle and M. E. Hellman, "Hiding information and signatures in trapdoor knapsacks," IEEE Trans. on Inform. Theory, IT-24, 5 (Sept. 1978), pp. 525-530. (See pp. 197-215, this volume.)

[8] R. C. Merkle, "Secrecy, authentication and public key systems," Ph.D. Thesis, Dept. of Electrical Engineering, Stanford University (June 1979).

[9] "Data encryption standard," National Bureau of Standards, Federal Information Processing Standards Publication No. 46 (January 15, 1977).

[10] R. M. Needham and M. D. Schroeder, "Using encryption for authentication in large networks of computers," CACM, Vol. 21, No. 12 (Dec. 1978), pp. 993-999.

[11] S. C. Pohlig and M. E. Hellman, "An improved algorithm for computing logarithms in GF(p) and its cryptographic significance," IEEE Trans. on Inform. Theory, IT-24 (Jan. 1978), pp. 106-111.

[12] M. O. Rabin, "Digitalized signatures and public key

functions as intractable as factorization," submitted to CACM.

[13] R. L. Rivest, A. Shamir, and L. Adleman, "A method for obtaining digital signatures and public key cryptosystems," CACM, Vol. 21, No. 2 (Feb. 1978), pp. 120-126. (See pp. 217-239, this volume.)

[14] A. Shamir, "A fast signature scheme," MIT Laboratory for Computer Science, Tech. Memo. 107 (July 1978).

[15] A. Shamir, "How to share a secret," MIT Laboratory for Computer Science, Tech. Memo. 134 (May 1979).

[16] B. Shanning, "Data encryption with public key distribution," in Proc. EASCON (1979).

Ralph C. Merkle

4. Protocols for Public Key Cryptosystems

Abstract

New cryptographic protocols which take full advantage of the unique properties of public key cryptosystems are now evolving. Several protocols for public key distribution and for digital signatures are compared with each other and with the conventional alternative.

Introduction

The special strengths of public key systems are illustrated by giving cryptographic protocols for key distribution and digital signatures using both public key and conventional systems. Beyond providing recipes for solving some specific problems, these examples are intended to improve the reader's ability to judge other protocols and, when faced with new problems, to synthesize new protocols.

The reader is assumed to be familiar with the general ideas behind public key cryptosystems, as described in [1,10].

This work was partially supported under NSF Grant ENG 10173.

This paper will also be published in the Communications of the ACM in 1981 and is an expanded version of a preliminary report presented by R. Merkle at the Symposium. Since studies of public key protocols are an important part of current research in this area the author and the editor decided that the purpose of this volume would be best served by including the latest and most complete report available.

For many of the following examples, we shall need the services of two communicants, called A and B, and an opponent E. A and B will attempt to send secret messages and sign contracts, while E will attempt to discover the keys, learn the secrets, and forge contracts. Sometimes, A will attempt to evade a contract he signed with B, or B will attempt to forge A's signature to a new contract.

A and B will need to apply one way functions to various arguments of various sizes, so we define the one way function F with the properties that:

1. F can be applied to any argument of any size. F applied to more than one argument is defined to be the same as F applied to the concatenation of the arguments.
2. F will produce an output of fixed size (perhaps 100 bits).
3. Given F and x it is easy to compute F(x).
4. Given F and F(x) it must be impossible to determine x.
5. Given F, F(x) and x, it must be impossible to determine $x' \neq x$ such that $F(x) = F(x')$.

For a more complete discussion of one way functions, see [2,9,13,19].

Centralized Key Distribution

Centralized key distribution using conventional encryption functions was the only reasonable method of handling key distribution in a multi-user network environment before the discovery of public key distribution methods. Only conventional encryption functions need be used, which presently offers a performance advantage. (Presently known public key systems are less efficient than conventional cryptographic systems. Whether or not this will continue is not now known.

Discovery of new public key systems seems almost inevitable, and discovery of more efficient ones probable.)

In centralized key distribution, A, B, and all other system users somehow deposit a conventional cryptographic key with a central key distribution center. Call X's key k_X, and let C(key, plaintext) be the ciphertext resulting from the conventional encryption function. If A wishes to communicate with B, then A picks a random key k′ and computes $y = C(k_A, \langle k', \text{"send this key to B"}\rangle)$ and sends it to the center along with his name. The center computes $C^{-1}(k_A, y) = \langle k', \text{"send this key to B"}\rangle$ and then computes $z = C(k_B, \langle k' \text{"this key is from A"}\rangle)$ and sends this to B. B computes $C^{-1}(k_B, z) = \langle k', \text{"this key is from A"}\rangle$ and uses k′ in further encrypted communications with A.

This protocol is simple and requires only conventional encryption functions. Its use has been defended in the literature [17, 18, 20].

The major drawback of this protocol is its vulnerability to both centralized loss of security and centralized loss of function. All of the eggs are in a central basket. Theft of the central keys, or bribery of personnel at the central site will compromise all users of the system. Similarly, destruction of the central keys destroys the key distribution mechanism for all users. Users might still be able to communicate, but will no longer be able to establish secure keys. In addition, even though A and B can communicate with each other, if either of them is unable to communicate with the key distribution center they will not be able to establish a secure key. In contrast, public key distribution will continue to function when only two users are left, and only the single communication path between them is functional. Public key systems are much more robust.

The security and reliability of centralized key distribution can be increased by using two or more centers, each with its own keys [1]. Destruction or compromise of a single center will not affect the other centers. If users always use several keys -- one from each center -- both to encrypt and decrypt messages, then compromise of a single key (or a single center) has no effect on user security. Only if all centers are compromised is the user's security compromised. In general, any number of centers can be established; although practical considerations will usually dictate a small number: e.g., two to five.

Security can also be improved if all the user keys are encrypted with a master key by the center. The master key must still be stored securely (and suitable provision made for its backup), but the (encrypted) user keys can be stored anywhere. This approach is used by IBM [23].

Multiple centers forces each user to establish a key with each center. This increases cost, but also increases security. There are two ways of modeling this increase in security. In the first, we argue that the probability of compromising one center is p, so the probability of compromising k centers is p^k. If p is reasonably small, this model predicts a rapid and dramatic increase in security as the number of centers is increased. In the second model we argue that if the cost of compromising one center is d dollars, then the cost of compromising k centers is only $k \times d$ dollars. This model predicts only a small increase in security as new centers are added. The truth probably lies somewhere in between.

This protocol does not fully solve the key distribution problem: some sort of key distribution method must be used between each user X and the center to establish each k_X. This problem is nontrivial because no electronic communications can be used for the transmission of k_X, and inexpensive physical methods, e.g., registered mail, offer only moderate security. The use of couriers is reasonably secure, although more expensive.

Centralized key distribution is more vulnerable to both loss of security and loss of function than well designed public key distribution systems. At the present time, it does provide improved performance because conventional encryption functions are more efficient than public key functions. In addition, certified conventional encryption functions are widely available, while certified public key cryptosystems are not. The latter two situations can be expected to change.

Simple Public Key Distribution

This is the most basic application of public key systems [1, 5, 6, 7, 8]. Its purpose is to allow A and B to agree on a common key k without any prior secret arrangements, even though E overhears all messages. A randomly computes enciphering and deciphering keys E_A and D_A, and sends E_A to B (and E). B picks the random key, k, and transmits $E_A(k)$ to A (and E). A computes $D_A(E_A(k)) = k$. A then discards both E_A and D_A, and B discards E_A. The key in future communications is k. It is used to encrypt all further messages using a conventional encryption function. Once A and B have finished talking, they both discard k. If they later resume the conversation the process is repeated to agree on a new key k'.

This protocol is very simple, and has a great deal to recommend it. First, no keys and no secret materials exist before A and B start communicating, and nothing is retained after they have finished. It is impossible for E to compromise any keys either before the conversation takes place, or after it is over, for the keys exist only during the conversation. Furthermore, if E is passive and does not actively interfere with the messages being sent, then E will understand nothing and the conversation will be secure.

The disadvantage of this protocol is that E might actively interfere with the exchange of keys. Worse yet, E can force a known k on both A and B. All further messages encrypted with k can then be read by E. All E need do is pretend to B that he is A, and pretend to A that he is B. To do this, E blocks transmission of E_A to B, and substitutes E_E. B will compute $E_E(k)$ and transmit it to A. E will block this transmission, learn k by computing $D_E(E_E(k)) = k$ and then send $E_A(k)$ to A. A will compute $D_A(E_A(k)) = k$ as usual. E knows k, and both A and B are none the wiser.

In spite of this disadvantage, the protocol is very useful for two reasons. Passive eavesdropping, by itself, is a major problem. In "The Codebreakers," the authoritative 1164 page history of cryptography by David Kahn [14], the threat was from passive eavesdropping in the vast majority of cases. Use of a simple public key distribution protocol provides protection from this attack, and also provides a positive guarantee against lost or stolen codebooks, bribery or blackmail of code-clerks, and "practical cryptanalysis" by theft of keys. For example, the major vulnerability of the U. S. telephone network today is from technically sophisticated passive eavesdropping. The Russians use their embassy and consulates in the U. S. to house microwave receivers which listen to conversations carried between telephone company microwave towers [11, 12]. They are not jamming or altering phone calls, just listening.

Secondly, if the reader has a preference for any other key distribution protocol which does not provide these blanket guarantees against lost or stolen keys, then it is simple to combine the reader's preferred key distribution protocol with the simple public key distribution protocol to obtain a hybrid which offers the strengths of both. The problem of carelessly lost keys, poor key security, theft of keys, and bribery of clerks or janitors who have access to the key are not minor, as history shows [14]. A blanket guarantee against all passive attacks is extremely comforting.

When guarantees of authenticity are also required, the simple public key distribution protocol can be used together with other methods because of the remarkably strong guarantees it provides against the passive eavesdropper. Even though a "better" method is being used to provide authenticity, its security might have been compromised by theft of keys. In this case it is impossible to guarantee authenticity, but the simple key distribution protocol can at least guarantee secrecy, thus providing "fail-soft" operation.

Authenticated Public-Key Distribution

The now classic protocol [1] for secure and authenticated communications between A and B is: A and B generate E_A and E_B and make them public, while keeping D_A and D_B secret. The public enciphering keys of all users are entered in a public file, allowing easy and authenticated access to E_X for any user, X.

If A and B wish to agree on a common key k, then

1. A looks up E_B in the public file.
2. A generates k_1 randomly and transmits $E_B(k_1)$ to B.
3. B looks up E_A in the public file.
4. B generates k_2 randomly and transmits $E_A(k_2)$ to A.
5. A computes $k = \langle k_1, k_2 \rangle$, where $k_2 = D_A(E_A(k_2))$.
6. B computes $k = \langle k_1, k_2 \rangle$, where $k_1 = D_B(E_B(k_1))$.

At the end of this protocol, A and B have agreed on a common key, k, which is both secret and authenticated. A is assured he is talking to B, for only B can decipher $E_B(k_1)$, while B is assured he is talking to A because only A can decipher $E_A(k_2)$.

This protocol suffers from two weaknesses. First, entries in the public file might be altered. E might create a false entry in A's public file which read:

$$B............E_E \quad .$$

This false entry would let E pretend to A that he was B, to the disadvantage of both A and B.

False entries in the public file can be dealt with both by good physical security, or by using new protocols (see sections 5 and 6) for authenticating the entries in the public file.

Second, secret deciphering keys can be lost. If E should learn D_B, then E could masquerade as B to A without altering the public file. Unless additional precautions are taken, A and B might never find out about the loss. Note that if D_B is compromised but D_A is still secure, then A can no longer be sure he is talking to B, but he can be sure he is talking secretly to some (unauthenticated) person claiming to be B. Again, the public key system has a "fail-soft" ability which is superior to the total compromise that would occur using conventional protocols.

Public-Key Distribution with Certificates

Kohnfelder [3] first suggested that entries in the public file be authenticated by having a Central Authority (CA) sign them with D_{CA}. He called such signed entries *certificates*. The certificate for A, called C_A, is computed by the central authority as:

$$C_A = D_{CA}(\langle\text{"user A"}, E_A\rangle)$$

while similarly C_B is computed as:

$$C_B = D_{CA}(\langle\text{"user B"}, E_B\rangle) \quad .$$

The protocol with certificates is the same as the authenticated protocol, except steps 1 and 3, which involve looking up E_A and E_B are replaced by the steps of obtaining and checking the proper certificates. The modified protocol is:

1. A obtains B's certificate (either from a public file, or requesting it from B) and confirms it by computing
$$E_{CA}(C_B) = \text{"user B"}, E_B \quad .$$
2. A generates k_1 randomly and transmits $E_B(k_1)$ to B.
3. B obtains A's certificate and confirms it by computing
$$E_{CA}(C_A) = \text{"user A"}, E_A \quad .$$
4. B then generates k_2 randomly and transmits $E_A(k_2)$ to A.
5. A computes $k = \langle k_1, k_2 \rangle$, where $k_2 = D_A(E_A(k_2))$.
6. B computes $k = \langle k_1, k_2 \rangle$, where $k_1 = D_B(E_B(k_1))$.

This protocol assures A and B that each has the other's public enciphering key, and not the public enciphering key of some imposter.

The security of this protocol rests on the assumptions that D_A, D_B, and D_{CA} have not been compromised, that A and B have correct copies of E_{CA}, and that the central authority has not issued a bad certificate, either deliberately because it was untrustworthy, or accidentally because it was tricked.

E_{CA} can be published in newspapers and magazines, and sent over all available communication channels: blocking its correct reception would be very difficult.

Security can be improved by having several "Central Authorities," each with its own secret deciphering key. Each user would be given a certificate from each authority (note that although user A might have many certificates, he would still have only one public enciphering key, for all the certificates would be the same message -- "A, E_A" -- signed by different CA's). Compromise of a single "authority" will no longer result in compromise of the system. There is, however, the problem for the users of knowing which of the authorities has been compromised, and hence which issues of certificates are to be viewed as suspect.

If only a single "Central Authority" exists, and D_{CA} is compromised, then it is no longer possible to authenticate the users of the system and their public enciphering keys. The certificates are now worthless because the (unauthorized) person who has learned D_{CA} can produce false certificates at will.

This problem can be greatly reduced by destroying D_{CA} after certificates for all users have been created. If D_{CA} no longer exists, it cannot be compromised. The central authority would create E_{CA} and D_{CA}, sign all the certificates, then immediately destroy D_{CA}. D_{CA} would be vulnerable only during the short time that it was being used to sign certificates.

While it is now impossible for anyone to falsely add new users to the system by creating false certificates, it is also impossible to add legitimate users to the system as well, which is unacceptable. The simplest way of dealing with this problem is for the central authority to issue new certificates with a new (different) secret deciphering key. For example, each month the central authority could create new certificates for that month's new users using a newly created D_{CA}. The new E_{CA} would be published, and the new users would be accepted. The new D_{CA} would be destroyed after use.

Although this method sharply reduces the risk that D_{CA} might be compromised, it still leaves open the possibility that the central authority might issue bad certificates either by intent, or because of some trickery during the short period when new certificates are actually being signed.

These possibilities are eliminated by the next protocol.

Public Key Distribution with Tree Authentication

Key distribution with certificates was vulnerable to the criticism that D_{CA} can be compromised, resulting in system wide loss of authentication. This problem can be solved by using tree authentication [13].

Again, this protocol attempts to authenticate entries in the public file. However, instead of signing each entry in the public file, this protocol applies a one way hash function, H, to the entire public file. Even though H is applied to the entire public file, the output of H is only 100 or 200 bits long. The (small) output of H will be called the root, R, of the public file. If all users of the system know R, then all users can authenticate the correctness of the (whole) public file by computing R = H(public file). Any attempt to introduce changes into the public file will imply R $\neq$ H(altered public file), an easily detected fact.

This method effectively eliminates the possibility of compromising D_{CA} because no secret deciphering key exists. Anyone can compute R = H(public file), and so confirm that the copy of the public file that they have is correct. R, (like E_{CA} in the protocol of section 5) can easily be widely distributed.

Because correct copies of the public file are widely distributed, it is very easy for a user of the system to discover that someone else is attempting to masquerade as him. If E has put the false entry

$$A............E_E$$

into the public file, then A will discover this fact when he looks at his own entry. A cannot be given a specially "printed" public file with his entry correct because then H(public file) would not equal R. If new public files are issued well before they go into use, then all users of the system will have time to assure that they have been correctly entered into the public file. Because the public file will be subjected to the harsh glare of public scrutiny, and because making alterations in the public file is effectively impossible after it has been published, a high degree of assurance that it is correct can be attained.

While this concept is very comforting, forcing each user to keep a complete copy of the public file might not be practical. Fortunately, it is possible to selectively authenticate individual entries in the public file without having to know the whole public file by using Merkle's "tree authentication," [13].

The essence of tree authentication is to authenticate the entire public file by "divide and conquer." If we define $\underline{Y}$ = public file = $Y_1, Y_2, \cdots, Y_n$, (so the i-th entry in the public file is denoted Y_i, and B's entry is Y_B); we can define H(public file) = H($\underline{Y}$) as:

$$H(\underline{Y}) = F(H(\text{first half of } \underline{Y}), H(\text{second half of } \underline{Y})) \quad .$$

Where F is a one way function as defined earlier.

If A wishes to confirm B's public enciphering key, then A need only know the first half of the public file, (which is where Y_B appears) and H(second half of public file) which is only 100 bits long. A can compute H(public file) knowing only this information, and yet A only knew half the entries in the public file.

In a similar fashion, A does not really need to know all of the first half of the public file, for

H(first half of public file) =
F(H(first quarter of public file),
H(second quarter of public file)) .

All A needs to know is the first quarter of the public file (which has Y_B), and H(second quarter of public file).

By applying this concept recursively, A can confirm Y_B in the public file knowing only R, $\log_2$ n intermediate values, and Y_B itself. The information needed to authenticate Y_B, given that R has already been authenticated, lies along the path from R to Y_B and will be called the authentication path.

These definitions are illustrated in Figure 1, which shows the authentication path for Y_5.

This brief sketch of tree authentication should serve to convey the idea. For a more detailed discussion the reader is referred to [13].

Using tree authentication, user A has an authentication path which can be used to authenticate user A's public enciphering key, provided only that R has already been authenticated. An "authentication path" is a new form of certificate, with E_{CA} replaced by R.

The advantage of tree authentication is that no secret deciphering key D_{CA} exists, so D_{CA} cannot be compromised. It is impossible to create false certificates after R is computed.

With tree authentication, it is impossible to have a centralized loss of authentication, but it is also impossible to add new users without issuing a new tree. The tree, once computed, is fixed and unchanging. Therefore, the public file (which is just the leaves of the tree) is also fixed and unchanging. For this reason, it can be carefully and publicly checked for errors. For the same reason, it is impossible to update. A new tree must be issued periodically.

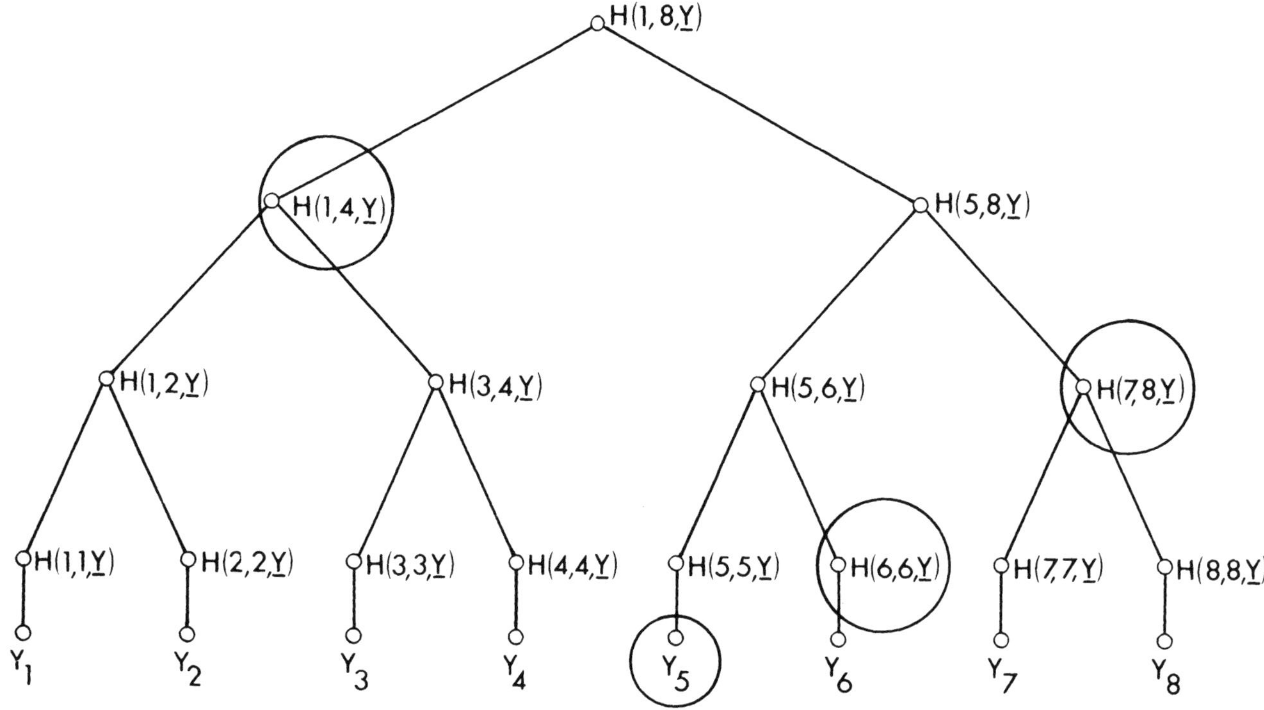
H(1, 8,Y)
H(1,4,Y)
H(5,8,Y)
H(1,2,Y)
H(3,4,Y)
H(5,6,Y)
H(7,8,Y)
H(1,1,Y)
H(2,2,Y)
H(3,3,Y)
H(4,4,Y)
H(5,5,Y)
H(6,6,Y)
H(7,7,Y)
H(8,8,Y)
Y1
Y2
Y3
Y4
Y5
Y6
Y7
Y8

Figure 1.

In summary: If tree authentication is used to authenticate each entry in the public file, the protocol for public key distribution proceeds as follows:

1. A obtains B's entry in the public file and B's authentication path (either from B or from some convenient storage device) and confirms their correctness.
2. A then generates k_1 randomly and transmits $E_B(k_1)$ to B.
3. B obtains A's entry in the public file and A's authentication path and confirms their correctness.
4. B then generates k_2 randomly and transmits $E_A(k_2)$ to A.
5. A computes $k = \langle k_1, k_2 \rangle$, where $k_2 = D_A(E_A(k_2))$.
6. B computes $k = \langle k_1, k_2 \rangle$, where $k_1 = D_B(E_B(k_1))$.

This protocol can only be compromised if: D_A or D_B is compromised, or if R is not correctly known by A or B, or if there is a false and misleading entry in the public file.

The latter two are easily detectable. If either A or B has the wrong R, they will be unable to complete the protocol with any other legitimate user who has the correct R. Complete failure of the protocol is easily detected, and will lead to corrective action. Implicitly, the correct value of R is agreed on by A and B every time each confirms the correctness of the other's authentication path. The correct value of R is therefore being constantly transmitted between pairs of users as they establish keys. This is in addition to other means of confirming R, such as publication.

Because the public file is both open to public scrutiny and unalterable, false or misleading entries can be rapidly detected. In practice, a few users concerned with correctness can verify that the public file satisfies some simple global properties, i.e., each user name appears once and once only in the entire public file; individual users can then verify that their own entry is correct, and need not bother examining the rest of the public file.

The only practical method of compromising this protocol is to compromise D_A or D_B. A user's security is thus dependent on himself and no one else.

It is still possible for A to claim to be the nonexistent C. Because C does not exist, he will never object that A is masquerading as him, allowing A to establish pseudonyms. If it is essential to establish a one-to-one correspondence between named users of the system and real people, some form of physical authentication is necessary. In many applications there is no need to know that user C is really a pseudonym for user A. As long as C pays his bills, his real identity is irrelevant. The identifier "C" is relative, not absolute, and serves simply to tie together a sequence of transactions.

Digital Signatures

The use of public key cryptosystems to provide digital signatures was suggested by Diffie and Hellman [1]. Rivest, Shamir and Adleman [8] have suggested an attractive implementation. Signature techniques based on methods other than public key cryptosystems have been suggested by Lamport and Diffie [1, 24], Rabin [15], and Merkle [13].

Digital signatures, whether based on conventional encryption functions, on public key cryptosystems, on probabilistic computations, or on other techniques share several important properties in common. These common properties are best illustrated by the following now classic example.

A wishes to place a purchase order with his stock broker B. A has just received word that the stock will go up in value, and wishes to purchase it within a few hours. A, on the Riviera, cannot send a written order to B in New York in time. All that A can quickly send to B is information, i.e., a sequence of bits, but B is concerned that A may later disclaim the order. A must somehow generate a sequence of bits (a digital signature) which will convince B (and if need be a judge) that A authorized the order. It must be easy for B to validate the digital signature, but impossible for him (or anyone other than A) to generate it (to prevent charges that B was dabbling in the market illegally with A's money).

The signature must be a function of both the message and the signer, for it must convince B (and a judge) that the particular person, A, has signed a particular message, m. There is basically one situation which the digital signature must resolve: B claims that A signed a message, and A claims he did not. If in fact A signed the message, then he is guilty of disavowal; but if he did not, B is guilty of forgery. To summarize: a digital signature should be message dependent, signer dependent, easy to generate, easy to validate, but impossible to forge or disavow.

There are digital signature schemes which do not involve public-key cryptosystems but it will be convenient notationally to let A sign message m by computing the signature, $D_A(m)$. Checking a signature will then be done by computing $m = E_A(D_A(m))$. If $E_A(D_A(m))$ produces an illegible message (random bits) then the signature is rejected as invalid. This notation is somewhat misleading because the actual method of generating and validating signatures can be very different from this model. This notation is retained because it is widely known and because we will not discuss the differences among different digital signature methods, only their common properties.

Digital signature protocols are naturally divided into three parts: a method of signing messages used by A, a method for authenticating a signature used by B, and a method for resolving disputes, used by the judge. This leads to the important observation that two protocols that differ only in the method of resolving disputes <u>are different</u>. Even though two distinct protocols require that A and B do exactly the same thing in signing and authenticating messages, those protocols are substantively different if the method of resolving disputes used by the judge is different. Failure to understand this point has led to confusion in the literature [17, 20].

We now turn to specific digital signature protocols.

A Conventional Signature Protocol

A conventional "signature" protocol relies on the observation that if A and B trust some central authority CA, and if A and B have a secure method of communicating with CA, then A can "sign" a message simply by sending it to CA and relying on CA to adjudicate disputes. This approach is defended by some [17].

In the following protocol we assume that A and CA know the secret (conventional) key k_A, and that B and CA know k_B. The protocol is given in a somewhat unusual form: we will sometimes *decrypt* plaintext, and *encrypt* the resulting ciphertext. This clarifies the analogies between this protocol and the public key protocol (given later).

1. A signs message m by computing $m_s = C^{-1}(k_A,m)$.
2. B checks signed message m_s by sending it to CA and requesting him to encipher it with k_A, i.e., compute $C(k_A,m_s)$.
3. CA sends the result of step 2 back to B after decrypting it with k_B (for authentication purposes) along with A's name and m_s; that is to say, CA transmits $C^{-1}(k_B, \langle$"Check of A's digital signature", $C(k_A,m_s), m_s\rangle)$.

4. B enciphers the transmission from CA and checks the correctness of the message. If the message is the same as the one B has agreed to, B accepts the signature as valid.

The dispute resolution protocol might be:

1. The judge decides that m_s is a valid signature for m if and only if when CA computes $C(k_A, m_s)$, it is equal to m.

An alternative dispute resolution protocol might be:

1. The judge decides that message m was signed by A if:
   a) no one gives him k_A, and
   b) he is given an m_s such that $C(k_A, m_s)$ computed by CA is equal to m.
2. In all other cases, the judge decides the signed message is not valid.

Both of these protocols are subject to the weaknesses of centralized key distribution (described earlier).

The consequences of destruction of the k_i are more serious for digital signatures than for key distribution. If the central authority loses the k_i, (it might be bombed by someone deeply in debt), then it is impossible to resolve any disputes.

The problems surrounding compromise and possible public display of A's secret key have been emphasized by some authors [16, 17, 20]. Under the first dispute resolution protocol described, if either A's or CA's copy of k_A should be made public, A would have no recourse at all against any claims brought against him, for anyone could use the now public k_A to generate any contract they feel like.

This particular problem is solved by the second protocol. A cannot be held responsible if k_A is compromised and made public, for then it can be presented to the judge, who in accordance with condition 4a will hold the signature invalid. If we assume that A knows k_A, A can disclaim responsibility for any signed message by presenting k_A to the judge. For this reason it has been argued that k_A must not be known by A, and the physical security of k_A must be sufficient to prevent anyone (including A) from finding out what it is. This seems attainable in practice.

Should E steal k_A but not make it public, and if A does not know k_A, then E can forge messages and hold A responsible. It would be desirable to have a protocol that would allow A to report the theft of his secret signing key: this is considered later in the section on the "Time Stamp Protocol."

The Basic Digital Signature Protocol

The first public key based digital signature protocol [1], proceeded as follows:

1. A signs message m by computing $m_s = D_A(m)$ and sending it to B.
2. B looks up E_A in the public file.
3. B authenticates the signed message by computing $E_A(m_s)$. If this value equals m, the signature is valid, otherwise not.

The dispute resolution protocol is:

1. The judge decides that message m was signed by A if and only if given an m_s such that $m = E_A(m_s)$.

This protocol can be criticized [16, 17, 20] on two grounds: First, the public file might have been tampered with. When B looks up E_A in step 2, E might have altered the public file so that E_E appears next to A's name. B will then "check" a signature with the wrong public enciphering key, making B's "check" useless.

Methods of authenticating the public file, discussed previously under key distribution protocols, solve this problem.

A second criticism is that A has no recourse should his secret deciphering key be compromised and made public. Anyone can sign any message they desire with A's compromised D_A, and A will be held responsible.

It seems clear that A will only agree to this digital signature protocol if he can provide very good physical security for D_A. The loss to A if D_A is compromised can be substantial.

Several factors combine to allow extraordinarily good physical security for D_A. First, destruction of D_A is merely inconvenient. A can always generate a new D'_A and E'_A. If theft of D_A is imminent, D_A can be destroyed. Contracts signed with D_A are still valid and E_A still exists to authenticate them, even though D_A no longer exists.

Second, only a single copy of D_A need exist. Because destruction of D_A is only inconvenient, backup copies of D_A need not be kept. D_A could be kept in a small strong box or on a single chip of silicon in a "signet ring" worn by A. Attempts to open the ring would cause destruction of D_A.

A different method of solving this problem is to alter the dispute resolution protocol so that, should A's signing key become public, A can disclaim responsibility.

1. The judge decides that message m was signed by A if:
   a) no one gives his D_A, and
   b) he is given an m_s such that $m = E_A(m_s)$.
2. In all other cases, the judge decides the signed message is not valid.

The fact that altering the dispute resolution procedure creates a different protocol has not been fully appreciated, and the preceding two protocols have been confused with each other for this reason. Some criticism of "the" public key digital signature protocol has actually been of this second protocol, and failed to consider the first protocol at all.

Under this protocol, should A's signing key be made public, A will no longer be held responsible for messages signed with it, for in any dispute A will give D_A to the judge who will then, in accordance with condition 4a, pronounce the signature invalid.

If we assume that A knows D_A, then A can present D_A to the judge in any dispute, effectively disavowing the signed message m_s. For this reason, some critics have argued that this protocol is inadequate.

If we assume that A does not know D_A, then he is unable to disavow his signature under this protocol. It is not clear why critics of public key systems have disregarded this possibility, certainly they have embraced it when dealing with k_A in the conventional signature protocol. Their criticism of public key based digital signature protocols has therefore been directed towards a question of physical security which is largely independent of the protocol being used. Designing a system in which A does not know D_A (or k_A in the conventional case) does not present any great difficulties -- the comments made previously about good physical security still apply. Maintaining a single copy of D_A in a dedicated microcomputer so that A does not know his own signing key can offer extremely good security.

The major difference between this protocol and the preceding one is in the division of risk: B will be left holding the bag if A's signing key is compromised. Clearly, B must be given assurances that this condition is unlikely before he will be willing to use this protocol.

It is interesting to note the parallels between the public key and conventional signature schemes. The following statements hold in both cases:

1. A has a secret key (k_A in the conventional case, D_A in the public key case.)

2. Preservation of the security of A's secret signing key by good physical security is important.
3. A signs messages by deciphering the message with his signing key.
4. Anyone can check a signed message by having it enciphered with A's key. In the conventional case, this must be done by the trusted agent CA, who also knows A's conventional key and is willing to encipher any messages given to him with that key -- but will refuse to decipher messages. In the public key case, the encipherment is done by using E_A, which is publicly available.

The primary difference is the need to trust CA in the conventional case. This

1. forces on-line communications with CA;
2. forces A to trust CA not to disclose or compromise k_A;
3. forces A to trust CA to correctly adjudicate disputes. There is little chance for appeal if A believes CA's resolution of a dispute is wrong, either because of intentional fraud or simple accident. CA, by definition, is trusted.

In addition to trusting CA, A must use (and trust) some sort of key distribution mechanism to establish k_A.

It is interesting to view the conventional signature system as a "hardware" implementation of a public key system. The "public enciphering key" is kept by CA, and it is an "enciphering key" because CA refuses to decipher anything with it. The physical security provided by CA for his copy of k_A and CA's refusal to decipher take the place of the logical security provided by E_A. The secret "deciphering key" is kept by A, and allows him to both encipher and decipher messages at his whim. This analogy carries over to key distribution systems: IBM's key management scheme [23] can be viewed in this way.

The Time Stamp Protocol

A protocol that would allow A to report loss or theft of D_A and disclaim messages signed after the reported loss yet force A to acknowledge the validity of signatures made before the reported loss must involve the concept of time. We introduce time into the following protocol by using timekeepers who can digitally time stamp information given to them. We assume that both A and B have agreed on a set of acceptable timekeepers whose time stamps will be accepted in dispute resolution.

Timekeeper T will time stamp document d by computing $D_T(\langle d, \text{current-time}\rangle)$. T is unconcerned with the nature of d, for T is only attesting that he saw d at a specific time. That d might be a totally false and misleading document is not T's problem.

If A can report that D_A has been lost, then he must report this fact to some agent who will be responsible for answering queries about the current status of D_A, i.e., has it been lost or not. For simplicity, we shall assume this role is played by the central authority, CA. CA will be called on to sign messages stating that A's secret deciphering key has not been compromised as of the current time. These signed messages will be called "validity checks."

The time stamp protocol proceeds as follows:

1. A signs message m by computing $m_s = D_A(m)$ and sending it to B.
2. B authenticates E_A (by using any of the previously described methods, or some other method of his choice).
3. B authenticates the signed message by computing

$E_A(m_s)$. If this value does not equal m, the signature is not valid and is rejected.

4. B requests timekeeper T to time stamp m_s.
5. B requests a validity check from CA. If D_A is still valid, CA computes D_{CA} ("A's secret deciphering key, which corresponds to public enciphering key E_A, is still valid at time ⟨current-time⟩").
6. B compares the time given in the time stamp and the time given in the validity check. If the time stamp preceeded the validity check, B is assured A has not reported a loss, and the signature is valid.

The protocol that A uses to report a loss to CA is:

1. A reports to CA that D_A has been compromised. (CA might optionally demand that A sign this message with D_A to prevent false reports of loss. Note that the signed message D_A ("My secret deciphering key has been compromised") must be valid, even if D_A has been compromised.)
2. CA computes D_{CA} ("A's secret deciphering key, corresponding to public enciphering key E_A, has been compromised as of ⟨current-time⟩.") and sends it to A.
3. A confirms the validity of CA's signed message.

The dispute resolution protocol proceeds as follows:

1. If $E_A(m_s)$ is not equal to m, then the signed message is invalid.
2. If A has not reported the loss of D_A, then m_s is valid if and only if $E_A(m_s) = m$.
3. If A reported the loss of D_A at time t_{loss}, (which must be confirmed by CA's digitally signed statement) then A is responsible for a signed message if and only if it is time stamped prior to t_{loss}.
4. If B has a validly signed message from A, including the time stamp from the timekeeper and the validity

check from CA, and yet A is not responsible for the signed message as in step 3, then the timekeeper and CA have been negligent and are responsible for any loss incurred.

This complex protocol provides very good assurance to all parties that they have been dealt with fairly. The following important points should be noted:

1. If A's security has been adequate and D_A is still secret, then A can never be falsely held responsible for a signed message.
2. If B has obtained both a valid time stamp and validity check, then B will always be able to hold either A responsible, or will be able to hold the timekeeper and CA responsible because of their negligence.
3. If the timekeepers and CA perform their function correctly (which will include careful consideration of timing problems, as discussed by Lamport [22]) and if their security is proof against loss of their secret deciphering keys, then they will never be held negligent.

An important aspect of this protocol is that it holds A responsible for signed messages until he reports the loss. This is not always desirable, for it forces A to bear the risk between the actual time of loss and the time the loss is reported. Present protocols in use in electronic fund transfers (EFT) systems allow the bearer of a credit card to disclaim responsibility for loss if the loss is reported within some fixed time, such as 24 hours, and continue to limit liability thereafter. These protocols take into account more than just the technical possibilities, they are also shaped by social forces; i.e., the feeling that the cardholder should not be responsible for errors or weaknesses in system design.

The major disadvantage of this protocol, as compared with the basic digital signature protocol, is the requirement that B obtain both a time stamp and a validity check, presumably in real time. These requirements force the use of a communications network, which both increases expense and decreases reliability.

If B is willing to obtain the time stamp and the validity check after the transaction has been completed, i.e., within a few days, an off-line system can be used. This modified protocol could be used by B either as a fail-soft protocol during communications outages, or as the standard protocol if communication costs are too high.

Off-line operation is cheaper and more reliable, but it exposes B to some risk: A might have recently reported the loss of D_A and B would not know about it. If physical security for secret deciphering keys is good, this risk should be minimal.

Witnessed Digital Signatures

If the value of a transaction is high enough, it might be desirable to have a witness physically confirm that A signed message m. The witness, W, would compute D_W ("I, W, physically saw A agree to and sign message m."). It would be necessary for A and B to agree in advance on acceptable witnesses.

Such a protocol might be:

1. A signs message m by computing $D_A(m)$.
2. A finds witness W, and W physically confirms that A has agreed to m.
3. W witnesses A's signature by computing D_W ("A has agreed to message m.").
4. Both A's and W's signed statements are given to B.
5. B authenticates E_A and E_W with a method of his choice.

6. B checks the messages signed in steps (1) and (3) above, and accepts the signature as valid only if both are correct.

The dispute resolution procedure is:

1. The judge holds A's signature valid if and only if presented with valid signed statements by A and the witness which both agree that message m was signed.

The primary advantage of this protocol is that it reduces B's risk. The primary disadvantage is that it forces A to find a (physically present) witness to confirm the transaction.

Digital Signature Applications Not Involving Dispute

Not all applications of digital signatures involve contracts between two potentially disputing parties. Digital signatures are also an ideal method of broadcasting authenticated messages from a central source which must be confirmed by many separate recipients, or repeatedly confirmed by the same recipient at different times to insure that the message has not been modified.

The only conventional alternative is to give all the recipients conventional cryptographic keys with which to authenticate transmissions. If these conventional keys are all the same, security is severely degraded: any single recipient can compromise security of the whole system. If these conventional keys are all different, the central source must individually encipher the same message for transmission to each recipient with that recipient's key.

One example of such an application is the distribution of network software to individual nodes of a communications network. It would be clearly undesirable for any node to start executing the wrong software, either through accident or malign intent. On the other hand, it is very desirable to send updates to the nodes over the network itself. The obvious solution is for updates to be digitally signed by an appropriate network administrator, and for the nodes to check the digital signature prior to executing them.

This example leads naturally to another application of digital signatures in operating system security. A major risk to the security of an operating system is the possibility that the system code that it is executing today is not the same that it was executing yesterday: someone might have put a trapdoor into the operating system that lets them do anything they please. To guard against this possibility, the operating system could refuse to execute any code in privileged mode unless that code had been properly signed. Carried to its logical conclusion, the operating system would check the digital signature of privileged programs each time they were loaded into central memory (modifying the program after it had been loaded and its digital signature checked would have to be forbidden). If this check were implemented in hardware, it would be impossible for any software changes to subvert it. The machine would be physically incapable of executing code in privileged mode unless that code was signed.

If privileged programs are digitally signed by the programmer who originally wrote them, as well as by various supervisory levels, and if the computer is physically unable to execute unsigned code in privileged mode, then it is possible to have complete assurance that the privileged programs running on the computer right now have not been modified since they were given there final checkout and signed by the programmer. Of course, this does not necessarily mean that the operating system is secure, but it does eliminate a major class of worries.

If we impose the stronger restriction that the computer will refuse to execute ANY unsigned code, then we can be assured that every program executed must have been digitally signed by some appropriate authority. This can be used to impose very tight control indeed on the programs run on the computer.

Further investigation of these intriguing possibilities is well worthwhile.

Conclusions

The primary purpose of this paper has been to increase the readers insight into the strengths and weaknesses not only of the particular protocols described, but also of cryptographic protocols in general. Certainly, these are not the only ones possible; however, they are valuable tools to the system designer: they illustrate what can be achieved and provide feasible solutions to problems of recurring interest.

Further constructive work in this area is very much needed.

Acknowledgements

It is a great pleasure for the author to acknowledge the pleasant and informative conversations he had with Dov Andelman, Whitfield Diffie, Martin Hellman, Raynold Kahn, Loren Kohnfelder, Frank Olken, and Justin Reyneri.

Bibliography

[1] W. Diffie and M. Hellman, "New directions in cryptography," IEEE Trans. on Inform. Theory, IT-22, 6 (Nov. 1976), 644-654. (See pp. 143-180, this volume.)

[2] A. Evans, W. Kantrowitx and E. Weiss, "A user authentication system not requiring secrecy in the computer," Comm. ACM 17, 8 (Aug. 1974), 437-442.

[3] L. M. Kohnfelder, "Towards a practical public-key cryptosystem," MIT EE Bachelor's thesis.

[4] S. M. Lipton and S. M. Matyas, "Making the digital signature legal -- and safeguarded," Data Communications (Feb. 1978), 41-52.

[5] R. J. McEliece, "A public-key cryptosystem based on algebraic coding theory," DSN Progress Report, JPL (Jan. and Feb. 1978), 42-44.

[6] R. Merkle, "Secure communications over insecure channels," Comm. ACM 21, 4 (Apr. 1978), 294-299. (See pp. 181-196, this volume.)

[7] R. Merkle and M. Hellman, "Hiding information and signatures in trapdoor knapsacks," IEEE Trans. on Inform. Theory, IT-24, 5 (Sept. 1978), 525-530. (See pp. 197-215, this volume.)

[8] R. L. Rivest, A. Shamir and L. Adleman, "A method for obtaining digital signatures and public-key cryptosystems," Comm. ACM 21, 2 (Feb. 1978), 120-126. (See pp. 217-239, this volume.)

[9] M. V. Wilkes, Time-Sharing Computer Systems, Elsevier, New York (1972).

[10] W. Diffie and M. E. Hellman, "Privacy and authentication: an introduction to cryptography," Proceedings of the IEEE Vol. 67, No. 3 (Mar. 1979), 397-427.

[11] J. Squires, "Russ monitor of U.S. phones," Chicago Tribune (June 25, 1975), 123.

[12] R. Davis, "Remedies sought to defeat Soviet eavesdropping on microwave links," Microwave Syst., Vol. 8, No. 6 (June 1978), 17-20.

[13] R. C. Merkle, "A certified digital signature," to appear CACM.

[14] D. Kahn, The Codebreakers, Macmillan, New York (1967).

[15] M. O. Rabin, "Digitalized signatures," in Foundations of Secure Computation, ed. R. A. Demillo, et al., Academic Press, New York (1978), 155-166.

[16] J. Saltzer, "On digital signatures," private communication.

[17] G. J. Popek and C. S. Kline, "Encryption protocols, public key algorithms, and digital signatures in computer networks," in Foundations of Secure Computation, ed. R. A. Demillo, et al., Academic Press, New York (1978), 133-153.

[18] R. M. Needham and M. D. Schroeder, "Using encryption for authentication in large networks of computers," CACM, 21, 12 (Dec. 1978), 993-999.

[19] R. Merkle, "Secrecy, authentication and public-key systems," Stanford Elec. Eng. Ph.D. thesis, ISL SEL 79-017 (1979).

[20] G. J. Popek and C. S. Kline, "Encryption and secure computer networks," Computing Surveys, 11, 4 (Dec. 1979), 331-356.

[21] G. J. Simmons, "Symmetric and asymmetric encryption," Computing Surveys, 11, 4 (Dec. 1979), 305-330. (See pp. 241-298, this volume.)

[22] L. Lamport, "Time, clocks, and the ordering of events in a distributed system," CACM, 21, 7 (July 1978), 558-565.

[23] W. F. Ehrasm, S. M. Matyas, C. H. Meyer and W. L. Tuchman, "A cryptographic key management scheme for implementing the data encryption standard," IBM Sys. Jour., 17, 2 (1978), 106-125.

[24] L. Lamport, "Constructing digital signatures from a one-way function," SRI Intl. CSL-98.

Gustavus J. Simmons

5. Message Authentication Without Secrecy

Introduction

A previously unrecognized class of secure communications problems arose in the late 1960's in the design of systems to verify international compliance with treaties limiting arms production or testing.† Since that time several other problems of the same generic type have arisen, such as the IAEA (International Atomic Energy Agency) RECOVER system that monitors worldwide power reactors to control fissile materials. In all of these applications a collection of sensors‡ is to be emplaced in a physically secure, but unattended, installation to collect data that would with high confidence reveal noncompliance with the terms of a treaty or licensing agreement. This data must then be transmitted to the monitor (receiver) over a public communications channel. In some instances this "channel" may simply consist of the periodic delivery by the host for the sensor emplacement of recordings of data purportedly taken by the monitor's sensors, while in others it may be a conventional communications link such as a

† This article sponsored by the U.S. Department of Energy under Contract DE-AC04-76DP00789.

‡ For example, TV cameras installed in "hot" cells of a power reactor to permit IAEA monitoring of fuel rods, unattended seismic installations emplaced in a host nation to detect underground nuclear testing or activity monitors on a heavy armament production line, etc.

land line, a microwave link, a COMSAT channel, etc. From the viewpoint of the monitor, an opponent, usually assumed to be the host for the sensor emplacement but possibly a third party desiring to undermine the treaty arrangements, may either modify incriminating messages to innocuous ones or else introduce spurious incriminating messages to mislead the monitor into erroneously reporting violations. This latter tactic is especially significant when only a negotiated, but limited, number of on-site verification inspections are permitted the monitor. Obviously (again from the monitor's viewpoint), the probability of having either an altered or counterfeit message be accepted as authentic can be made as small as desired by block encrypting the data from the sensors along with a sufficient number of message identifiers, such as time, date, message number, etc., prior to transmission. This is accomplished, however, at the expense of concealing the content of the message from the host. Such secrecy is generally intolerable to the host (and perhaps to third parties) since the monitor could then cheat on the terms of the agreement by transmitting information concealed in the cipher other than that agreed to. In other words, for such a system to be acceptable, the plaintext message consisting of the output of the sensors as well as the identifying information must be legible to the host at least -- and perhaps to specified third parties. Conversely, for the system to be acceptable to the monitor this exposure of the message content should not increase the probability of an opponent, whether the host or a third party, having either a modified or substitute message be accepted as authentic.

Even if both of these objectives are realized, there is still another subtle aspect to these problems. If the action to be taken by the monitor in the event that a violation of the treaty or agreement is detected involves third parties or arbiters -- such as the United Nations, IAEA, NATO, the World

Bank, etc. -- then it must also be impossible for the monitor to forge messages. Otherwise, the host to the sensors could disavow an incriminating message as having been fabricated by the monitor, an assertion which the monitor could not disprove if it were within his capabilities to create an undetectable forgery. The justification for calling this a subtle problem will become apparent later, when a system is described that, while it prevents the host from forging acceptable messages, leaves open to him a unilateral action that would make it possible for the monitor to forge messages and hence make it impossible for the monitor to prove the authenticity of a message to a third party.

Therefore, a complete solution to this class of problems requires that:

1. No party be able to forge messages that would be accepted as authentic.
2. All parties, i.e., host, monitor and third parties be able to independently verify the authenticity of messages.
3. No unilateral action possible on the part of any party should lessen confidence as to the authenticity of a message.
4. No part of the message be concealed from the host and perhaps from specified third parties.

If these four objectives are met, then the monitor can be confident that should the sensors detect a violation he will receive the incriminating information. He can also be confident that the host can neither substitute innocuous for incriminating information nor spoof him by deliberately substituting false incriminating messages, and that no third party can deceive him with counterfeit messages. The host and any agreed upon third parties have real time access to the messages, and hence can be reassured that no information other than that agreed to is being transmitted. Finally, authorized third parties can be confident that an incriminating message could only have been generated by the sensors, since no party has the ability to forge messages that would deceive them as authentic.

Authentication

Before discussing authentication without secrecy, it is necessary to discuss the principles of authentication; principles that hold for communications either with or without secrecy. In the simplest terms possible, authentication is merely the determination that a received message is or is not in a subset of acceptable messages M out of the set of all possible messages $\mathfrak{M}$. To illustrate this point assume that the receiver knows that the transmitter will send only four letter words as messages. However for various reasons, perhaps due to a noisy communications channel that may alter symbols in transmission or, as we shall discuss later, an opponent that deliberately modifies messages, the receiver may receive a four letter group different than what was transmitted. There are $26^4 = 456{,}976$ four English letter groups: aaaa to zzzz. Let this set be $\mathfrak{M}$. Based on the number of four letter entries in the Webster's Third International Unabridged Dictionary including meaningful English words, selected common occurrence foreign language words, place and chemical names, widely known proper names and established abbreviations and acronyms, there are 64,800 four letter "words" in the language. Let this set be M. In this simple example, shown schematically in Figure 1 (p. 110), the receiver would accept any four letter word† as an "authentic" message and reject all other four letter groups as unauthentic. The ratio of acceptable messages to the total number of four letter groups, $|M|/|\mathfrak{M}|$, is very nearly 1/7. Therefore the probability that a four letter

† Scrabble rules: "If it's in the dictionary, it's a word."

group generated randomly -- with equiprobable selection of each of the letters from the alphabet -- will be acceptable as an authentic message is $\approx 1/7$, and conversely that it will be rejected as unauthentic is $\approx 6/7$. The important point to this example is that the number of bits transmitted is greater than the number of bits of information communicated -- and that the difference, i.e., the redundant information in the message, exactly accounts for the authentication capability. $\text{Log}_2|M| \approx 16$ bits of information are needed to specify an $m \in M$. Actually $2^{16} = 65{,}536$, so that 16 bits could distinguish among a few more (736) words than there are in the language, but $\log_2|\mathfrak{M}| = 18.8$ bits are needed to identify an element of $\mathfrak{M}$. The redundant 2.8 bits is used to discriminate between authentic and unauthentic messages. As one would expect, $2^{-2.8} \approx 1/7$.

In the example, because of structural constraints in the English language, vowel and consonant usage for example, or of prohibited structure, i.e., qx where $x \neq u$, and of the wide variation in the frequency of occurrence of letters, digraphs, trigraphs, etc., M is a strongly structured subset of $\mathfrak{M}$. In other words it is possible to delimit much of the membership in M in a more concise way than by exhibiting the unabridged Webster's. This observation merely says that the partitioning of the message space $\mathfrak{M}$ into words and nonwords is intermediate in complexity of description to a random selection of the subset M that can only be described through enumeration (which we shall attempt to approximate through encryption) and the usual military usage of an authenticator as a fixed (one time use) suffix known only to the transmitter and receiver and appended to whatever message is sent by the transmitter to confirm his identity to the receiver. In the latter case M is described by the suffix.

Thus far in the discussion, authentication appears to be more a question of error detection than message authentica-

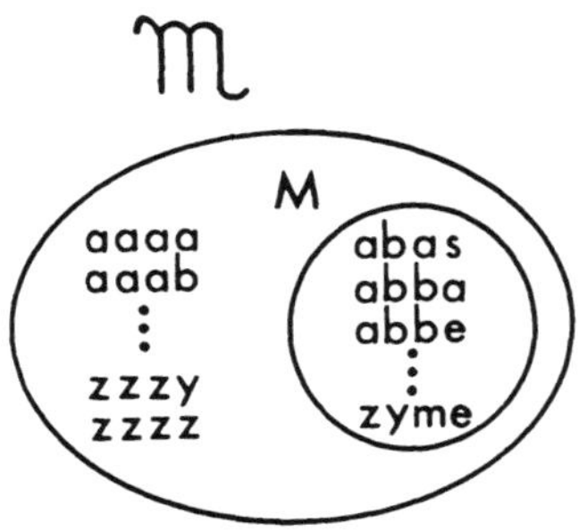

Figure 1.

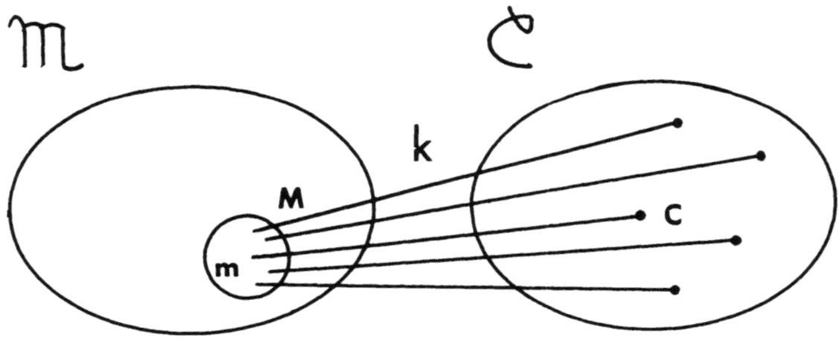

Figure 2.

tion. To appreciate the difference consider the following very simple problem. A commander has a number of subordinates whose function it is to execute a serious and irreversible act, such as firing missiles, on receipt of his order to do so. If both parties trust each other, then the system at its simplest need only provide authentication to the subordinate that a fire order came from his commander. This could be accomplished by including a preagreed upon, but secret from all other parties, message (authenticator as described above) in the fire order. If the concern is only with accidental misunderstanding or with an outsider attempting to impersonate the superior commander, such a naive safeguard might suffice. It could not protect against a third party who intercepted the commander's order to learn the authenticator and then included it in an altered order to the subordinate in a "postal chess" ploy.

In order to avoid this threat, the message m with the appended authenticator (redundant information) must be altered in such a way that an opponent cannot separate the authenticator from the message and affix it to some other message of his choosing. There are two, superficially distinct, ways this may be accomplished. The appended authenticator can be constructed to be a noninvertible (to the opponent) function of the message or the entire transmission can be constructed to be a noninvertible (again to the opponent) function of the message and the redundant authenticating information. For the moment, we consider the latter -- block encryption of the message and authenticator by the transmitter prior to transmission. When this is done, the opponent will observe the cipher c, Figure 2, but wishes to substitute some other cipher c' that would decrypt to an $m' \in M$. If the cryptosystem is secure, c' will map into $\mathfrak{M}/M$ with probability $1 - |M|/|\mathfrak{M}|$, and hence his probability of a

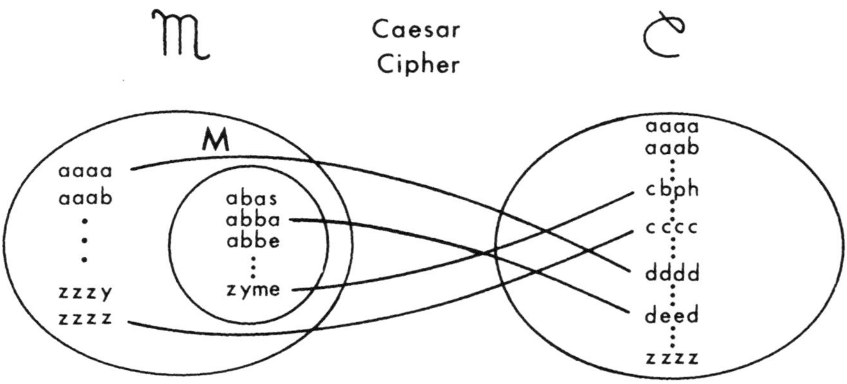

Figure 3.

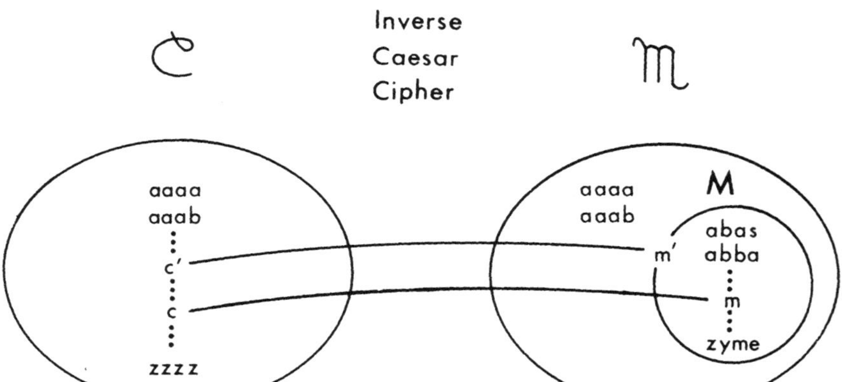

Figure 4.

successful substitution or alteration will be $|M|/|\mathfrak{M}|$, i.e., the random guessing chance of success. In this case the authentication system is said to be perfect in the sense that the best possible use is made of the redundant information to introduce equivocation or uncertainty to the opponent.

Using the four letter example discussed earlier, and the Caesar cipher† -- which is of negligible security to even a schoolboy -- we observe the permutation of letter groups shown in Figure 3. If the opponent were unable to break the Caesar cipher his chance of having some other cipher c' be accepted as authentic would be $\approx 1/7$, etc., as discussed above and shown in Figure 4. In fact the user views the authentication problem in the large scale as communication through a "game theoretic" channel, as depicted in Figure 5, under the control of an opponent whose objective is to find and use his optimal strategy to introduce messages, or message modifications, and have them be accepted by the receiver as authentic. This is a zero sum game, so that the transmitter/receiver's objective is to devise an optimal (read perfect in the sense defined before) authentication strategy to thwart the opponent.

We shall discuss several authentication problems [8], of generally increasing complexity, and their solution, as a means of explaining the principles of authentication.

In the example of the military commander communicating orders to a subordinate, if the superior commander requires verification of receipt of the order, another prearranged message (countersign to his sign -- or a matched authenticator to his authenticator) from the subordinate would have to be returned. In fact, many military command and control situations are as simple as this. Mutual trust is assumed,

† Each letter is replaced by its successor three positions ahead in the alphabet considered cyclically; a → c, etc.

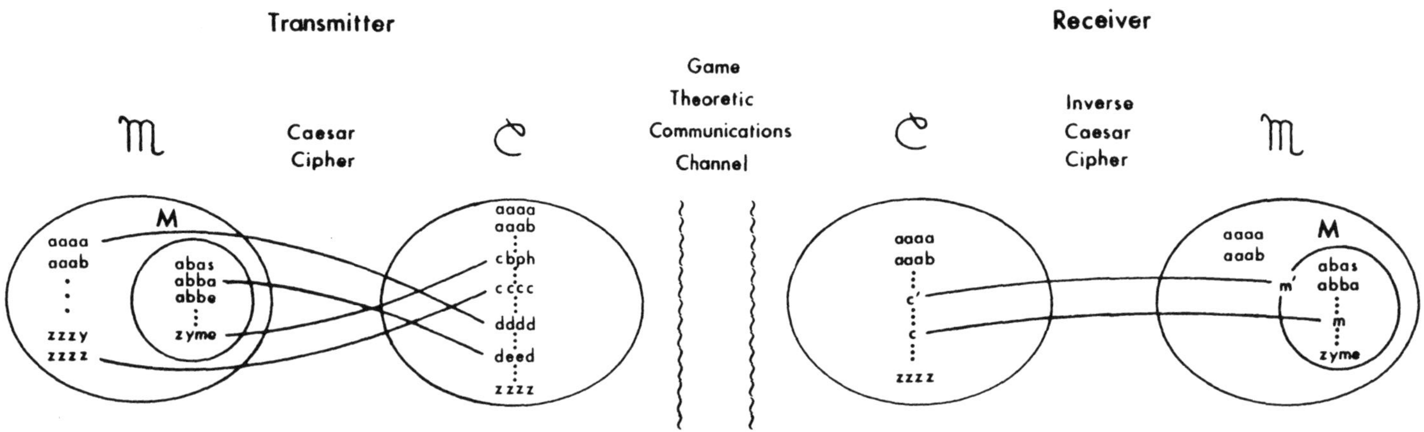

Probability that $m' \in M$ is $\frac{|M|}{|\mathfrak{M}|}$ if the encryption algorithm is an equiprobable random mapping of symbols -- which the Caesar cipher is not.

Figure 5.

since either party can claim to have received the prearranged identifiers when in fact they didn't (which in this case is equivalent to their being able to generate undetectable forgeries, i.e., to select any other $m \in M$), so that this system can only detect unauthentic messages introduced by third parties, but cannot protect against deceit by either communicant. Because authentication, i.e., the determination that a message is in M, is invariably dependent on recognizing the presence of an already known or derivable (to the authorized users) redundancy in the message, the receiver can only be prevented from making forgeries by denying him the ability to introduce the requisite redundant information into a fraudulent message. We shall explore in detail how this can be accomplished using either one key (symmetric) or two key (asymmetric) encryption techniques, both when the information in the message is known to -- or secret from -- the opponent.

Authentication against deceit by insiders can be achieved using a symmetric encryption system such as the DES in a simple variation of the common way such systems are used to provide password file security in computer log-in systems. The problem with an unprotected, i.e., raw, user password file is that anyone having or gaining access to the file could impersonate any user by submitting the user's identifying password. The solution, devised by Needham [2,4] was to file not the user's password but a function of the user's password where the function -- which must be exposed in the computer, of course -- is noninvertible or "one way." Almost from the beginning it was recognized that any secure cryptosystem could be used as a one way function to provide the desired password file protection. In a symmetric system, the cipher (message) can be found given the key and message (cipher) while the key cannot be recovered from a knowledge of the cipher and message (known plaintext attack), hence a one way function exists between the key and the message-cipher pair. In password file protection the user's password is therefore the key and the message is some fixed test phrase that is encrypted with each user's key into the cipher stored in the file. Anyone having access to the encryption algorithm, the test phrase and the cipher file would still be unable to impersonate a user, while a user can reliably authenticate himself by presenting the key that encrypts the test phrase to a cipher that matches his stored cipher. Lamport [3] was apparently the first to note that this same technique could be used to provide a one time authentication of a transmitter to a receiver. The reason that it can only be used once for this purpose but repeatedly for access to the computer is that while the computer is assumed to not record the key nor to have deceitful objectives, it is deceit by the receiver that the authentication system is attempting to prevent. The receiver doesn't know the key until the transmitter reveals it -- and thereafter he does. One way to use this idea in the present example would be for the commander to select a message and a key with which he computes a test cipher. He then gives the test cipher and message to his subordinate and to a higher level of command that will arbitrate any disputes that may arise as to whether the subordinate commander carried out an authentic order from his superior or not but keeps the key secret to himself. When the superior wishes to order the missiles fired he sends his key as an authenticator. The subordinate decrypts the test cipher and matches the messages to verify the authenticity of the order. He can later prove that he received the order from his superior since he can exhibit the key that he could only have obtained by either receiving it from his superior commander as arranged or by breaking the cryptosystem to recover the key from the known plaintext and the test cipher. The return acknowledgment could be handled in a similar fashion.

What has been described is a mapping of $\mathcal{C}$ into $\mathfrak{M}$ by a fixed point $k \in \mathcal{K}$; Figure 6. But by hypothesis, k cannot be recovered from a knowledge of the message/cipher pair m and c so that such a scheme is cryptosecure. In this example only the decryption of c by the specific key $k \in \mathcal{K}$ selected by the superior commander would be accepted as authentic and the subspace of acceptable messages consists of only the single element m. One could equally well say in this case that the mapping is of $\mathcal{K}$ into $\mathfrak{M}$ by the fixed point $c \in \mathcal{C}$. When only a single message-cipher-key triple is involved, these are indeed functionally equivalent. As we shall see later there is a significant difference when $|M| > 1$.

The reason for giving c and m to the arbiter in advance is that otherwise the subordinate could encrypt a message of his choice, m, with an arbitrary key k' to generate a cipher c' that he could attribute to his superior. Consequently, a necessary, but not sufficient, condition for a message/cipher pair to be judged authentic is that it have been filed with the arbiter in advance of a dispute.

Much more serious though in the scheme just described is the limitation that only a single transmission (authenticated) of a prechosen message can be made since the secret key must be revealed to authenticate the message. If there were two or more messages that could be authenticated by exhibiting the same key k, the receiver could choose any one of these and substitute it for the message actually received in the same way that he could claim (and not be refuted) to have received any $m \in M$ in the open system first described.

By prearranging a large number of battle plans and ciphers (i.e., by enlarging the codebook), an execute signal could be authenticated for any particular plan by revealing the appropriate key. It is in this more general setting that some of the subleties of authentication are revealed. As has

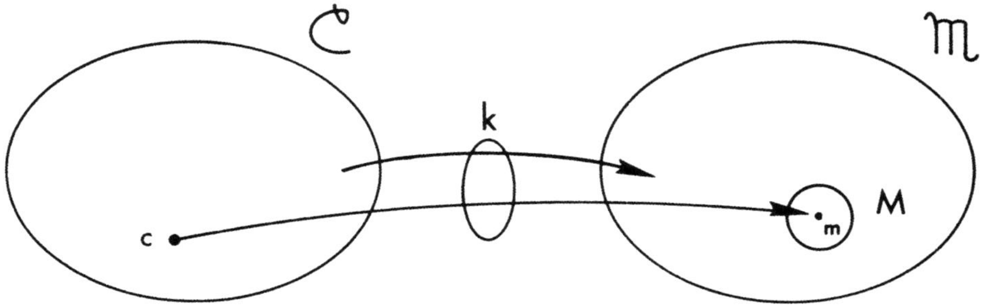

Figure 6.

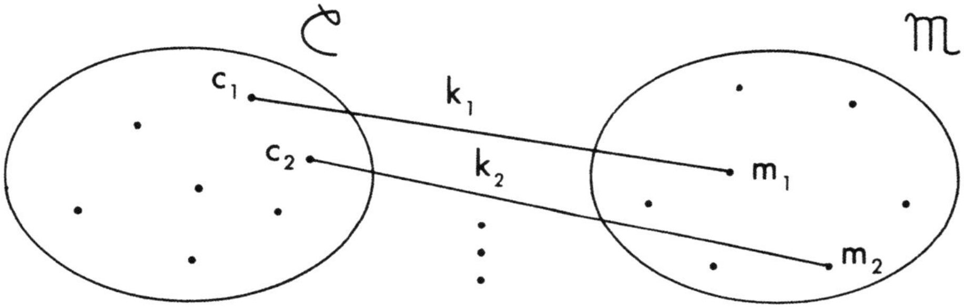

Figure 7.

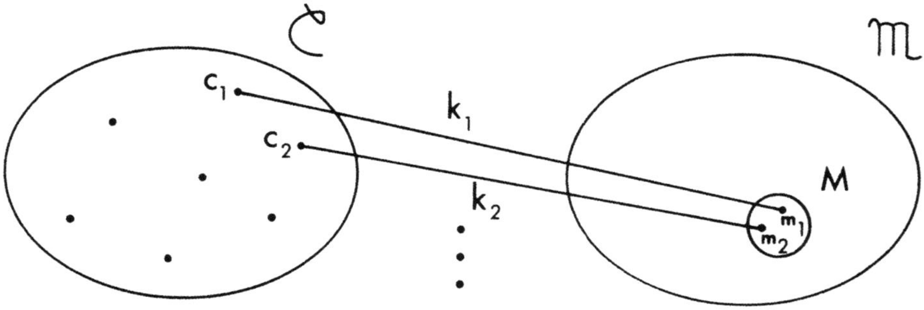

Figure 8.

already been remarked, one cannot use the same k to authenticate all of the messages. Schematically, the analog to the single message-cipher case for multiple messages is shown in Figure 7, where the keys k_i could either be chosen to be all different or randomly chosen from $\mathcal{K}$ with negligible effect on the authentication security. The scatter of the points of M in $\mathfrak{M}$ and of their ciphers in $\mathcal{C}$ in Figure 7 is intended to suggest that neither is capable of a succinct (functional) description but that a tabular description of both subsets would be needed. Obviously, one or the other of these two subsets could be chosen to have a simple description and the other (computed using the k_i) would be devoid of structure, i.e., would have to be tabulated if the k_i are to be concealed. As a consequence of $\mathcal{K}$ being the key space for a secure cryptosystem it doesn't matter whether the points in the one set are drawn randomly or chosen to be near each other (using some metric) or in fact irrespective of any relationship that they may have in the containing set, the images are randomly scattered in the other set. What is more, since the cryptosystem is immune to a known plaintext attack, there is no computationally feasible way for a user who is given the cryptosystem to impose order or structure on the images since this would be tantamount to solving for keys given plaintext information and cipher -- which by hypothesis cannot be done. This is shown schematically in Figure 8 for the decrypt function ($\mathcal{C} \rightarrow \mathfrak{M}$). A converse mapping would apply for the encrypt function.

As described above, either the tabulation of the pairs $\{m_i, c_i\}$, or the description of M (indexed by i) and a tabulation of $\{c_i\}$ or conversely the description of the ciphers C (indexed by i) and a tabulation of $\{m_i\}$ would be given to both the intended receiver and to the arbiter in advance of communication. The transmitter would authenticate a message m_i by revealing key k_i.

Clearly only the tabular listing or the functional description of C has to be revealed in advance in order to permit authentication. The transmitter would then reveal the missing pair of elements, m_i and k_i, to authenticate a transmission. Let $\{c_i\} = C$ be the published list, then the receiver has only to find some key-message pair whose cipher is in the table in order to be able to utter an undetectable forgery. But for any key k^*, there is some cipher c_i which is the encryption of m_i. Therefore the chance that c_i when decrypted by k^* will be in M is $|M|/|\mathfrak{M}|$ -- so that we have a variant of the "birthday problem" in searching for arbitrary key-cipher pairs whose message is in M with perhaps unacceptable authentication security as $|M|$ becomes large [10]. If M alone were given to the receiver, irrespective of whether it was an unordered tabular listing or a functional description, he could choose any $m \in M$ and encrypt it with an arbitrary key k to obtain a cipher c_i. He could then claim that this pair had been sent to him by the transmitter as authentication for m.

The conclusion is that the receiver (and the arbiter) must be given C and may also be given M in order that they may authenticate messages as having come from the transmitter. The probability of the receiver being able to falsely attribute a message to the transmitter in the two cases is different, but potentially acceptable in either case. For this reason, in all variants of this scheme, the receiver and the arbiter must be content with a codebook to permit them to decide if a message is to be accepted as authentic or not.

The crucial difference between symmetric and asymmetric systems in simple message authentication is that it is possible to avoid the need to distribute the random entry codebook in advance! In the direct analog to the authentication system just described using symmetric cryptosystems in asymmetric cryptosystems the existence of the two keys d and e that act as functional inverses to each other makes it possible for the transmitter to compute a cipher c, using e, that will decrypt into $m \in M$ using d. Therefore, the receiver and arbiter could be given d and a succinct (functional) description of M; for example, all acceptable messages will end in a time, date and message number. Since e is concealed from a knowledge of d by a computationally infeasible task, the receiver even though he knows M has no better chance of constructing a cipher c' which will decrypt into an $m' \in M$ than does a third party who must guess at ciphers. The transmitter on the other hand authenticates messages simply by being in possession of a cipher that he can reveal that decrypts into an acceptable message.

It is also possible in an asymmetric system to give the receiver (and the arbiter if there is a need for arbitration) the decryption key in advance and then to authenticate a message by presenting a message-cipher pair in which the cipher will decrypt using the receiver's key to the message. This technique is the basis of being able to authenticate without requiring secrecy for the message. We first discuss an application of this technique in which secrecy was unimportant.

The first application [11] of the principles described here and indeed the first application of a two key cryptographic system in the open literature is in an access control system designed by the Sandia National Laboratories and successfully installed by the Sandia Safeguards Development Department and operated at the Idaho National Engineering Laboratory, Idaho. This system, designated as a Positive Personnel Identity Verification (PPIV) device is an optional supplementary subsystem to the International Nuclear Material Containment Portal used by the International Atomic Energy

Agency (IAEA) to prevent the unauthorized removal of nuclear materials from a facility.

The way the technique is implemented is that a central facility is entrusted by all of the sites that will need to verify individual identities with the task of first verifying the identity of individuals to whatever degree of certainty that is deemed necessary and of then generating ID records that are given to the individuals they identify. The record consists of some collection of personal attributes (photograph, fingerprints, hand geometry, voiceprint, retinal prints, signature, etc.) encrypted along with descriptive identifiers such as name, social security number, etc., using the encrypt key of an asymmetric cryptosystem. Needless to say, the authentication function is totally dependent on the central site keeping the encrypt key secret. The decrypt key would be delivered as an authenticated, but not necessarily secret, message to the sites that would have to protect the integrity but not the privacy of the key. When, at some later time, an individual appears at a site with a claimed identity, he would present the cipher record in his possession and permit his individual attributes to be reread by equipment located at the site. Using the decrypt key, the site would decrypt the ID cipher and check for a suitable agreement with the individual attributes just measured. If a match is achieved, the identity of the individual would be confirmed since the cipher could only have been generated using the (assumed) secret encrypt key held by the enrollment station that was responsible for establishing the identity of the individual before issuing the ID cipher. The only advance communication between the site and the central facility is the authenticated (but not necessarily secret) exchange of the decrypt key. The other channel of communication is the public one of the user bringing his own ID cipher to the site. The contents of his ID cipher, and indeed the decrypt key with which it was generated, may be known to the bearer, hence the remark that secrecy is unimportant in this application. Since in a two key cryptosystem in which the sender's key is known to be secure, authentication is possible, the site can be certain (to the same level as the two key cryptosystem is cryptosecure) that the ID records it has received are authentic, i.e., issued by the central authority. Then, to the degree that the information in the ID records can identify an individual, they can be confident of the identification. No communication with the central facility is required at the time that individual identification is made. The crucial point is that the separation of the encryption and the decryption capabilities in two key cryptosystems has been exploited to devolve the authentication capability from the sender to the receiver -- and hence has transferred the ability to determine the veracity of the ID records supplied by the applicant to the receiver (site). The fact about two key cryptosystems on which this concept depends is that it is possible to transfer the ability to authenticate (messages) over an authentication channel.

Authentication Without Secrecy

As explained above, authentication depends on partitioning the message space $\mathcal{M}$ (or equivalently the cipher space $\mathcal{C}$) into two sets; the set of acceptable, i.e., authentic, messages M and the set of remaining unacceptable (inauthentic) messages $\mathcal{M}/M$. In the case of authentication with secrecy, i.e., where the message content is concealed from the opponent, we were able to assume with no loss of generality that the redundant information was all contained in an authenticator appended to the message. The resulting extended message then had to be block encrypted, both to conceal the content of the message, and to "spread" the redundant information through all bit positions in the resulting cipher in a manner

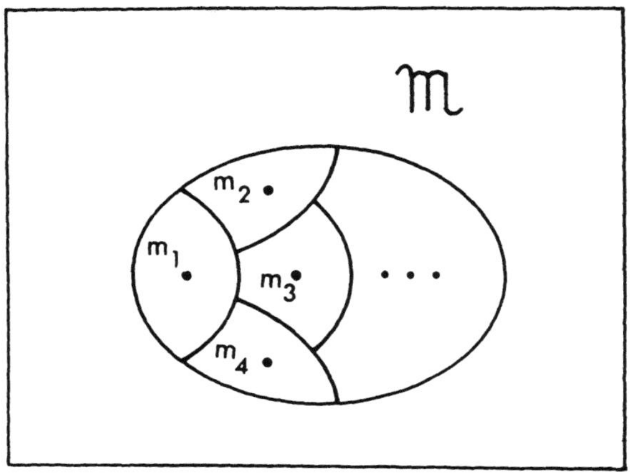

Figure 9.

inscrutable to the opponent. Pictorially $\mathfrak{M}$ is partitioned into $|M|$ parts, each containing (labeled by) a single acceptable message with the anticipated authenticator appended: Figure 9. The opponent in the case of authentication with secrecy, may or may not know the partitioning function φ on $\mathfrak{M}$, but by definition he does not know the partitioning function ϕ of C induced by encrypting the parts of $\mathfrak{M}$. In the case of authentication without secrecy, however, the opponent(s) are given the function φ on the message space $\mathfrak{M}$ onto the message space M in <u>advance</u> of the communication, i.e., they know the induced labeled partition π_φ of $\mathfrak{M}$, where each part P_i is labeled by an element m_i of M. At the time of the transmission of an extended message q_{ji} the opponent is also assumed to know by independent means (to his satisfaction) the message $m_i \in M$ that is to be communicated so that he can verify that q_{ji} comes from, i.e., is the jth element in, the part labeled by m_i. This is the "without secrecy" part of the system -- what the opponent does not know, of course, is which message(s) would be accepted in the other parts. Since the opponent's objective is to substitute an element from some other part and have the receiver accept it as an authentic transmission from the transmitter, there are some obvious constraints on π_φ. If any part, other than the one labeled by the transmitted message, contains only a single message, then the opponent is certain of a successful substitution. Although we shall not attempt to make these ideas precise here, an easy consequence of this observation is that if messages (the labels for parts) are equiprobable, then the parts should be of the same cardinality (contain equal numbers of extended messages). In this event -- if the transmitter/receiver have preselected a single message in each part to be "authentic" -- the opponents probability of success, given that he has seen q_{ji} in the part labeled by i, will be

$$\frac{|M| - 1}{|\mathcal{M}| - |\mathcal{M}|/|M|} = \frac{|M|}{|\mathcal{M}|}$$

or just his guessing probability of success in advance of observing q_{ji} being transmitted to communicate m_i. Clearly the transmitter/receiver's strategy cannot do better. On the other hand the transmitter/receiver can "cheat" in this scheme to communicate in secret some information that would be concealed from the opponent even though he knows π_φ, m_i and the extended message q_{ji}. If the part p_i labeled by m_i contains $|\mathcal{M}|/|M|$ extended messages, the opponent would reject as a violation the transmission of a q from any other part -- but would have to accept as legitimate the transmission of any element in P_i. This makes it possible for the transmitter/receiver to communicate up to $\log_2|\mathcal{M}| - \log_2|M|$ bits of secret (from the opponent) information, by selecting preagreed upon elements in P_i, at the expense of giving up an ability to authenticate these messages. In the extreme, they would accept any element as authentic -- but could communicate $\log_2|M| - \log_2|M|$ bits in secret. Since, as was explained in the introductory remarks, authentication without secrecy problems are characteristically ones in which both parties must be assumed to cheat if at all possible, it is essential that the transmitter/receiver not be able to misuse the redundancy introduced into the message for the purpose of authentication to accomplish secret (from the opponent or arbiter) communication.

The best known example of an authentication without secrecy application is in the systems designed by the Sandia National Laboratories to monitor compliance with an underground nuclear test ban treaty [8]. Although the problem has been described before, we repeat the essential points here.

Assume that the United States and the Soviet Union sign a comprehensive test ban treaty in which each party agrees to stop all underground testing of nuclear weapons. Each side wishes to verify that the other is complying, that is, is not surreptitiously carrying out underground tests. One of the most reliable techniques for detecting underground tests is to measure the ground motions resulting from an underground detonation using seismic sensors. Just how small a test can be detected is a function of -- among other things -- how close the detectors can be emplaced to the point of the detonation. Since the purpose of a comprehensive test ban treaty is to stop the development (proof testing) of new nuclear weapons technology, the sensors would have to be emplaced close enough to possible test sites to detect all meaningful weapons tests, which includes testing of low yield devices. In the case of the Soviet Union and the U. S. this would require that the seismic sensors be emplaced within the host nations national boundaries. These techniques are highly reliable, though, so that either nation could have confidence that the data (message) from their seismic instruments suitably located in the host (other) nation's territory would indicate violations by the other party. It is not difficult to secure the instruments physically in subsurface emplacements; only the data stream sent through an open communications channel would be subject to, perhaps undetected, attack. If the host nation could successfully substitute innocuous seismic records for the incriminating records of underground tests, it could cheat undetected, or if the host (or third parties) could substitute what appeared to be seismic records of underground tests for innocuous seismic data, this could cause the monitor to expend his limited (negotiated) number of on-site inspections as well as undermining his faith in the system itself.

This problem first arose in the 1960's before the open literature publication of descriptions of asymmetric (two key) cryptosystems. Consequently, it was first "solved" using symmetric (one key) systems. Authentication, to the monitor's satisfaction is easy to achieve. He need only encrypt the seismic data along with as many identifiers -- station ID number, date, clocks, etc. -- as are needed to provide the redundant information required for authentication. The monitor would be as confident of authentication as he is of the security of the encryption system used to produce the cipher. However this solution would almost certainly be unacceptable to the host nation (in whose territory the seismic observatory is placed), which would be ignorant of the contents of the enciphered messages and would hence fear that the cipher contained information other than the agreed-upon seismic data; for example, weather data or R. F. signal surveys, etc. If the host nation were given the key to a symmetric encryption system (so that it could decrypt the cipher and verify message content at the time of its transmission), it would also, by definition be able to generate counterfeit ciphers.

One option would be for the monitor to give the host the key used to encrypt the message immediately after he had satisfied himself as to its authenticity. Unfortunately (and unacceptably) this requires that the host trust the monitor for the full content of a transmission ($\approx 10^8$ bits/day for each seismic station) during which time the monitor could transmit illicit information in the entire block of data. Of course the host would refuse to cooperate for future transmissions if he detected deception by the monitor -- but depending on the time and nature of the transmission the damage could already have been done. A compromise solution is to form an authenticator much shorter than the entire message where the authenticator depends on all the symbols in the message through some hashing function. The authenticator must be encrypted, but the message need not be.

For example, one could use the Data Encryption Standard (DES) in a simple modification of the Cipher Block Chaining (CBC) Mode [12] to generate the authenticator; Figure 10. Assume, for ease of discussion, that a block of data consisting of 64K bits is to be authenticated. A 64 bit initialization vector known only to the monitor (consisting of 56 bits of key and 8-parity check bits would be used to encrypt the first 64 bit block of data. The resulting 64 bit cipher would not be transmitted, but instead a preselected subset of 56 bits would be used as key to encrypt the second block of 64 bits of data, etc. The raw data could have been transmitted as it was generated -- with the final 64 bit cipher appended as an authentication. The monitor (knowing the secret key) would duplicate the block chain encryption of the data as it is received -- and would accept the transmission as authentic only if the appended authenticator received with the message matches the one calculated locally. From the standpoint of the host this is a great improvement over the concealment from him (by encryption) of the entire message consisting of 64K bits, since only 64 bits are inscrutable to him and hence are potentially available to the monitor for illicit message concealment. After the monitor has satisfied himself of the authenticity of the message, the initialization vector (key) would be given to the host who would (presumably) duplicate the generation of the observed authenticator.

Ironically, the host and monitor each trust this system to the same level of confidence for the same reason. The monitor trusts the authentication since in order to create a forgery the host would have to invert from a known plaintext/cipher pair to find the key used by the monitor. On the other hand, the host is satisfied that the monitor didn't conceal information in the preceding transmission if the key he is given generates the authenticator that was transmitted

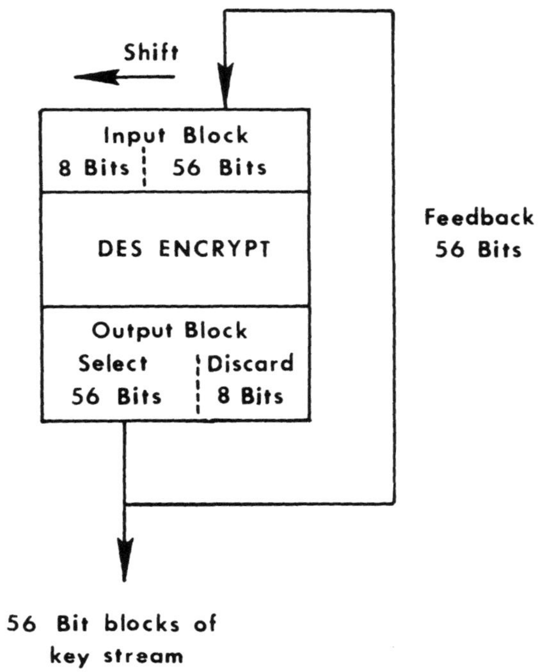

Figure 10. Output feedback (OFB) mode key stream generator. Input block initially contains an initialization vector (IV) right justified.

since the monitor would have had to solve for the (unique?) key relating the plaintext and the desired bogus authenticator; i.e., precisely the same problem on which the host bases his confidence in the authenticator.

The system as described is "one-shot" in the sense that after the first block of 64K bits of message are authenticated and the key is revealed to the host -- no further authentication is possible with that key. What is needed, of course, is (effectively) as many keys as there are blocks of data to be authenticated. Since it is impractical to store so many keys -- a separate DES encryption system is used as a key generator, with a single key that remains concealed from the host. The key must be kept secret at least throughout the period of unattended operation of the system, i.e., until the next manned (by the monitor) initialization, and perhaps even for the life of the system because of the difficulty of <u>securely</u> entering a new key into a down-hole system after the seismic sensor package has been emplaced. Using DES in 56 bit Output Feedback (OFB) Mode, Figure 11, as many "keys" as are needed can be generated from a single initial key set in secret by the monitor at the time the system is put into operation.

If unilateral response by the monitor, such as abrogation of a treaty or resumption of atmospheric testing of nuclear weapons as the U. S. did in 1962 in response to the Soviets 1961 violation of the joint understanding of a moratorium on such tests, is the only action to result from a detection by the monitor of a violation of the agreement, the compromise system just described suffices. If, however, the action to be taken by the monitor in the event of a violation being detected involves third parties or arbiters, such as the United Nations, NATO, etc., then it must be impossible for the monitor to forge messages. Otherwise, the host could

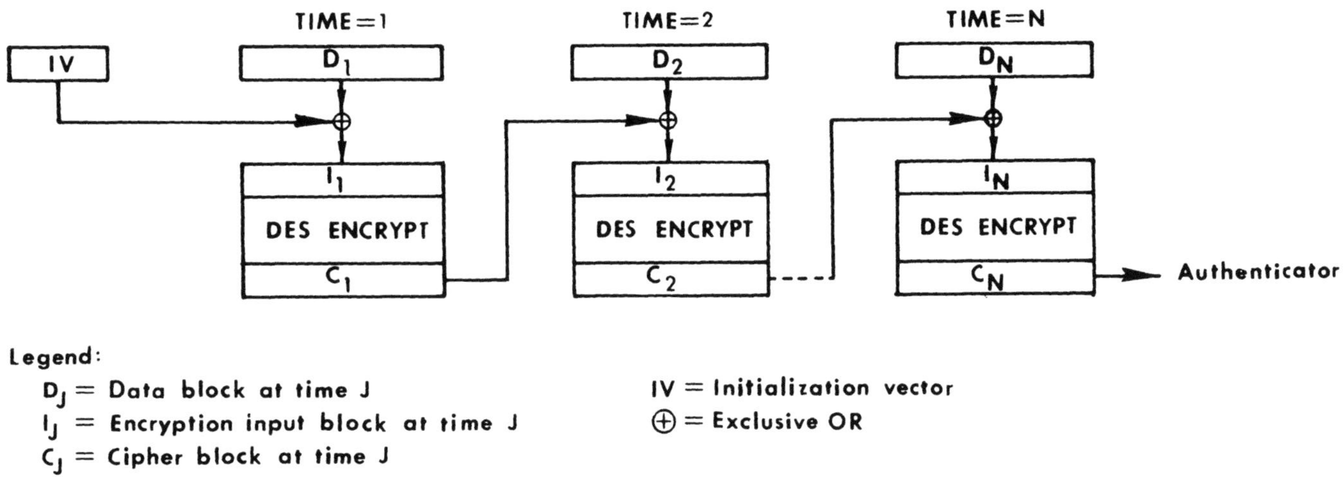

Figure 11. Cipher block chaining (CBC) authentication.

disavow an incriminating message as having been fabricated by the monitor -- an assertion which the monitor could not disprove if he has the known ability to create an undetectable forgery. Using symmetric cryptosystems this latter problem appears to be insolvable. Before discussing how the problem can be completely solved using asymmetric encryption techniques, we first remind the reader of what has (and has not) been achieved using symmetric techniques.

The monitor can be confident of the authenticity of a received message to the same degree that he is confident of the cryptosecurity of the system. The host is at risk that unauthorized information may have been concealed in the purported authenticator until he is given the key used for its generation, after which he is equally (to the monitor) confident that this did not occur for the same reasons that the monitor was confident. The monitor has compromised (over what he could and probably would have otherwise done) by introducing only a small fraction of redundant information per message block -- thus forcing him to use sophisticated error-correcting super encoding, etc., if he is to hold the rejection rate due to errors to very low levels. The host on the other hand, has to "trust" that the monitor has not misused this small amount of information at the time each block of data is communicated -- although he can refuse to allow future transmissions if he detects cheating. Finally, a third party cannot be persuaded of the hosts duplicity by the monitor's proving the authenticity of an incriminating message -- although he and the host both know it to be genuine.

We describe two systems using asymmetric techniques that address these points of compromise. Although the systems could conceptually be implemented using an as yet undiscovered asymmetric cryptosystem, we shall base our discussion on the scheme chosen by the Sandia National Laboratories: the RSA

(Rivest, Shamir, Adleman) algorithm. It is not appropriate to this paper to do more than sketch how this algorithm works. The reader is referred to any of several good references for further details [1,6,8]. In the RSA system, the user chooses a pair of primes p and q so large that factoring $n = pq$ is beyond all projected computational capabilities. He also chooses a pair of numbers e and d, where $(e,\varphi(n)) = 1$, and $ed \equiv 1 \bmod \varphi(n)$; $\varphi(n) = (p-1)(q-1)$.† In other words, e and d are multiplicative inverses in the group of residue classes modulo $\varphi(n)$.

A message m is encrypted in this system to the cipher c by the transmitter using key $k = (e,n)$ by the rule

$$m^e \equiv \pmod{n} \quad ,$$

and c is decrypted by the authorized receiver using $k = (d,n)$ by the rule

$$c^d \equiv \pmod{n} \quad .$$

For example, if $p = 421$ and $q = 577$ so that $n = pq = 242{,}917$ and $\varphi(n) = 241{,}920$, then for $e = 101$, $d = 9581$. Using these values $k = (101{:}242{,}917)$ and $k' = (9581{:}242{,}917)$ so that the message $m = 153{,}190$ encrypts by

$$c = 153{,}190^{101} \equiv 203{,}272 \pmod{242{,}917} \quad ,$$

and c decrypts by

$$m = 203{,}272^{9581} \equiv 153{,}190 \pmod{242{,}917} \quad .$$

The cryptosecurity of the RSA system is based on the difficulty (infeasibility?) of factoring n [1,5]. Obviously, if an opponent can factor n to recover p and q, he can then calculate the multiplicative inverse of e using the Euclidean algorithm just as the user did to set up the system and hence

† $\varphi(x)$ is the Euler phi function or totient of x (x, a positive integer) and is simply the number of positive integers less than x that have no factor other than 1 in common with x.

be able to decrypt ciphers. Since computing the multiplicative inverse d of e from a knowledge of e and n is essentially the same as factoring n or determining $\varphi(n)$, d is secure from an opponent knowing only n and e. Conversely, computing e from a knowledge of d and n is of the same difficulty. Therefore, so long as p and q, and one of the pair of exponents d and e are kept secret, the RSA system is as secure as factoring is difficult -- which with reasonable conditions imposed on the choices for p and q is now generally accepted to be a computationally infeasible problem.

The simplest possible implementation of an authentication without secrecy system using an asymmetric encryption algorithm solves some of the problems left unsolved in systems based on symmetric encryption algorithms. In this scheme the monitor would choose the primes p and q and one of the exponents e or d, then calculate the inverse exponent (d or e respectively). As part of the initialization procedure by the monitor, n = pq and e would be securely entered into the downhole seismic package. The decryption key d and n would be given to the host -- and of course retained by the monitor. In operation, the seismic data as well as the redundant identifying information would be block encrypted using the key e and n. The host could decrypt in real time, even delaying transmission in a buffer until decryption was completed, to reassure himself that no information was concealed in the message. Recall that he is assumed to know the actual seismic data (message) either from his own sensors or from data links to the monitors sensors ahead of the authentication operation. The monitor, on the other hand, can be certain of the authenticity of a message (containing message numbers, clock readout, etc.) since by hypothesis neither the host nor any third party can compute e from the exposed n and d. Thus the host need not trust the monitor at all, while the monitor is free to introduce as much redundant (but pre-known to the host) information as he wishes to provide authentication confidence. This system fails in exactly the same way that the one based on symmetric techniques did when a third party must be convinced that a violation has been detected, since the monitor could still generate undetectable forgeries.

In our final design, even this problem can be solved. Clearly, no party can be in possession of e, since they could then (by definition) generate undetectable forgeries. Since there are no scenarios in which the objectives of the monitor and of the host are furthered by their collaborating to create undetectable forgeries, it might at first seem that a solution would be to split the knowledge of e between the host and the monitor in such a way that neither alone could recover e. For example, the monitor and host might each enter a random binary number, R_m and R_h, respectively, and their exclusive OR (mod 2) sum taken as e. Neither the host nor the monitor could infer anything about e from their knowledge of the random component they had selected, hence neither is capable of uttering an undetectable forgery. The host, however, can still cheat in the following way. He could test with impunity, and when incriminating records are exhibited by the monitor claim that his copy of R_h has been compromised; i.e., one of his people has defected, his files have been rifled, etc. The point is that he can either deliberately or inadvertantly make it possible for the monitor to generate undetectable forgeries, and hence unilaterally make it impossible for the monitor to prove to an unbiased third party that he did not do so.

The solution therefore, is for the equipment to generate p and q in secret from all parties and then to select e (also in secret from all parties) revealing only n and d which it calculates using p, q and e. We have mentioned the need for selecting "good" primes, the most obvious condition being the magnitude of the numbers, but also such that p - 1 and q - 1 have large prime factors, etc. All of these criteria can be programmed in, along with a nondeterminate random number generator that provides an unknown seed to start the prime generation process. For example, if a 100 bit start is needed, a random process, radioactive decay, say could be observed for 100 intervals of sufficient length that many decays would occur in each interval. At the end of each interval a 0 or 1 is entered in the corresponding bit position according as to whether an even or odd numbered particles had been counted. Using the resulting random start, the next larger "good" prime would be found and used as p or q. e would be generated in a similar manner and d calculated using the Euclidean algorithm. The decryption key n and d would be output at the end of the initialization process to the monitor, the host and to any arbiters needed. In such a system only the downhole equipment could generate authentic messages -- and unlike the various compromise systems described above, all of the objectives of each of the parties are completely realized:

1. No party is able to forge messages that would be accepted as authentic.
2. All parties, i.e., host, monitor and third parties are able to independently verify the authenticity of messages.
3. No unilateral action possible on the part of any party can lessen the confidence of any party as to the authenticity of messages.
4. No part of the message is concealed from the host or from specified third parties.

Conclusion

The applications of authentication without secrecy discussed here (to arms control, nuclear materials control and to the verification of international compliance with nuclear weapons testing moratoria) may appear exotic and of little commercial or personal interest. It is the author's opinion, however, that almost the opposite is true and that these systems may be more properly viewed as a paradigm for public access systems to valuable resources or facilities. For example, the treaty verification problem is one-to-one equivalent to a problem in international banking in which the correspondents each have branch national banks in foreign host countries [7]. The bottom line is that by using asymmetric cryptosystems, all of the functions desired of an authentication without secrecy system can be achieved, even though all parties are assumed to cheat whenever possible.

References

[1] W. Diffie and M. E. Hellman, "New directions in cryptography," IEEE Trans. Inform. Theory, IT-22, 6 (Nov. 1976), 644-654. (See pp. 143-180, this volume.)

[2] A. Evans, Jr. and W. Kantrowitz, "A user authentication scheme not requiring secrecy in the computer," Comm. ACM, 17, 8 (Aug. 1974), 437-442.

[3] L. Lamport, "Constructing digital signatures from a one way function," SRI International Computer Science Laboratory Report No. CSL-98 (Oct. 18, 1979).

[4] R. M. Needham and M. D. Schroeder, "Using encryption for authentication in large networks of computers," Comm. ACM, 21, 12 (Dec. 1978), 993-999.

[5] M. O. Rabin, "Digitalized signatures and public key functions as intractable as factorization," Tech. Rep. MIT/LCS/TR-212, MIT Lab. Comput. Sci., Cambridge, Mass. (Jan. 1979).

[6] R. Rivest, A. Shamir and L. Adleman, "A method for obtaining digital signatures and public-key cryptosystems," Comm. ACM, 21, 2 (Feb. 1978), 120-126. (See pp. 217-239, this volume.)

[7] G. J. Simmons, "Cryptology: the mathematics of secure communication," Math. Intelligencer, 1, 4 (Jan. 1979), 233-246.

[8] G. J. Simmons, "Symmetric and asymmetric encryption," Computing Surveys, 11, 4 (Dec. 1979), 305-330. (See pp. 241-298, this volume.)

[9] G. J. Simmons, "Secure communications in the presence of pervasive deceit," Proceedings of the 1980 Symposium on Security and Privacy (April 1980), 84-93.

[10] G. Yuval, 'How to swindle Rabin," Cryptologia, 3, 3 (July 1979), 187-189.

[11] P. D. Merillat, "Secure stand alone positive personnel identity verification system (SSA-PPIV)," Technical Rpt. SAND79-0070, Sandia National Laboratories, Albuquerque, NM (March 1979).

[12] "DES modes of operation," Federal Information Processing Standards Publication 81, National Bureau of Standards, Washington, D.C. (Sept. 25, 1980).

Part 2

The Origins of the Subject

Whitfield Diffie, Martin E. Hellman

6. New Directions in Cryptography

Abstract

Two kinds of contemporary developments in cryptography are examined. Widening applications of teleprocessing have given rise to a need for new types of cryptographic systems, which minimize the need for secure key distribution channels and supply the equivalent of a written signature. This paper suggests ways to solve these currently open problems. It also discusses how the theories of communication and computation are beginning to provide the tools to solve cryptographic problems of long standing.

I. Introduction

We stand today on the brink of a revolution in cryptography. The development of cheap digital hardware has freed it from the design limitations of mechanical computing and brought the cost of high grade cryptographic devices down to

---

This work was partially supported by the National Science Foundation under NSF Grant ENG 10173. Portions of this work were presented at the IEEE Information Theory Workshop, Lenox, MA, June 23-25, 1975, and the IEEE International Symposium on Information Theory in Ronneby, Sweden, June 21-24, 1976.

where they can be used in such commercial applications as remote cash dispensers and computer terminals. In turn, such applications create a need for new types of cryptographic systems which minimize the necessity of secure key distribution channels and supply the equivalent of a written signature. At the same time, theoretical developments in information theory and computer science show promise of providing provably secure cryptosystems, changing this ancient art into a science.

The development of computer controller communication networks promises effortless and inexpensive contact between people or computers on opposite sides of the world, replacing most mail and many excursions with telecommunications. For many applications these contacts must be made secure against both eavesdropping and the injection of illegitimate messages. At present, however, the solution of security problems lags well behind other areas of communications technology. Contemporary cryptography is unable to meet the requirements, in that its use would impose such severe inconveniences on the system users, as to eliminate many of the benefits of teleprocessing.

The best known cryptographic problem is that of privacy: preventing the unauthorized extraction of information from communications over an insecure channel. In order to use cryptography to insure privacy, however, it is currently necessary for the communicating parties to share a key which is known to no one else. This is done by sending the key in advance over some secure channel such as private courier or registered mail. A private conversation between two people with no prior acquaintance is a common occurrence in business, however, and it is unrealistic to expect initial business contacts to be postponed long enough for keys to be transmitted by some physical means. The cost and delay imposed by this key distribution problem is a major barrier to the transfer of business communications to large teleprocessing networks.

Section III proposes two approaches to transmitting keying information over public (i.e., insecure) channels without compromising the security of the system. In a *public key cryptosystem* enciphering and deciphering are governed by distinct keys, E and D, such that computing D from E is computationally infeasible (e.g., requiring 10^{100} instructions). The enciphering key E can thus be publicly disclosed without compromising the deciphering key D. Each user of the network can, therefore, place his enciphering key in a public directory. This enables any user of the system to send a message to any other user enciphered in such a way that only the intended receiver is able to decipher it. As such, a public key cryptosystem is a multiple access cipher. A private conversation can therefore be held between any two individuals regardless of whether they have ever communicated before. Each one sends messages to the other enciphered in the receiver's public enciphering key and deciphers the messages he receives using his own secret deciphering key.

We propose some techniques for developing public key cryptosystems, but the problem is still largely open.

Public key distribution systems offer a different approach to eliminating the need for a secure key distribution channel. In such a system, two users who wish to exchange a key communicate back and forth until they arrive at a key in common. A third party eavesdropping on this exchange must find it computationally infeasible to compute the key from the information overheard. A possible solution to the public key distribution problem is given in Section III, and Merkle [1] has a partial solution of a different form.

A second problem, amenable to cryptographic solution, which stands in the way of replacing contemporary business communications by teleprocessing systems is authentication. In current business, the validity of contracts is guaranteed by signatures. A signed contract serves as legal evidence of an agreement which the holder can present in court if necessary. The use of signatures, however, requires the transmission and storage of written contracts. In order to have a purely digital replacement for this paper instrument, each user must be able to produce a message whose authenticity can be checked by anyone, but which could not have been produced by anyone else, even the recipient. Since only one person can originate messages but many people can receive messages, this can be viewed as a broadcast cipher. Current electronic authentication techniques cannot meet this need.

Section IV discusses the problem of providing a true, digital, message dependent signature. For reasons brought out there, we refer to this as the one-way authentication problem. Some partial solutions are given, and it is shown how any public key cryptosystem can be transformed into a one-way authentication system.

Section V will consider the interrelation of various cryptographic problems and introduce the even more difficult problem of trap doors.

At the same time that communications and computation have given rise to new cryptographic problems, their off-spring, information theory, and the theory of computation have begun to supply tools for the solution of important problems in classical cryptography.

The search for unbreakable codes is one of the oldest themes of cryptographic research, but until this century all proposed systems have ultimately been broken. In the nineteen twenties, however, the "one time pad" was invented, and shown to be unbreakable [2, pp. 398-400]. The theoretical basis underlying this and related systems was put on a firm foundation a quarter century later by information theory [3]. One time pads require extremely long keys and are therefore prohibitively expensive in most applications.

In contrast, the security of most cryptographic systems resides in the computational difficulty to the cryptanalyst of discovering the plaintext without knowledge of the key. This problem falls within the domains of computational complexity and analysis of algorithms, two recent disciplines which study the difficulty of solving computational problems. Using the results of these theories, it may be possible to extend proofs of security to more useful classes of systems in the foreseeable future. Section VI explores this possibility.

Before proceeding to newer developments, we introduce terminology and define threat environments in the next section.

II. Conventional Cryptography

Cryptography is the study of "mathematical" systems for solving two kinds of security problems: privacy and authentication. A privacy system prevents the extraction of information by unauthorized parties from messages transmitted over a public channel, thus assuring the sender of a message that it is being read only by the intended recipient. An authentication system prevents the unauthorized injection of messages into a public channel, assuring the receiver of a message of the legitimacy of its sender.

A channel is considered public if its security is inadequate for the needs of its users. A channel such as a telephone line may therefore be considered private by some users and public by others. Any channel may be threatened with eavesdropping or injection or both, depending on its use. In telephone communication, the threat of injection is paramount, since the called party cannot determine which phone is calling. Eavesdropping, which requires the use of a wiretap, is technically more difficult and legally hazardous. In radio, by comparison, the situation is reversed. Eavesdropping is passive and involves no legal hazard, while injection exposes the illegitimate transmitter to discovery and prosecution.

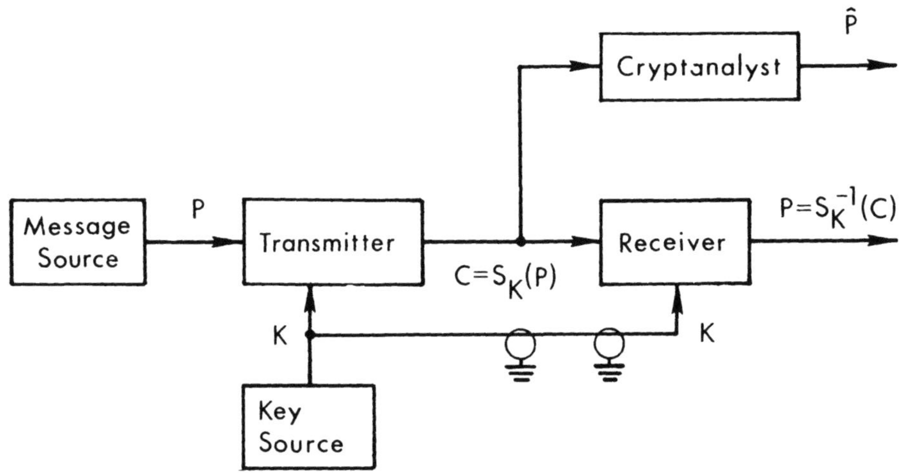

Figure 1. Flow of information in conventional cryptographic system.

Having divided our problems into those of privacy and authentication we will sometimes further subdivide authentication into message authentication, which is the problem defined above, and user authentication, in which the only task of the system is to verify that an individual is who he claims to be. For example, the identity of an individual who presents a credit card must be verified, but there is no message which he wishes to transmit. In spite of this apparent absence of a message in user authentication, the two problems are largely equivalent. In user authentication, there is an implicit message "I AM USER X," while message authentication is just verification of the identity of the party sending the message. Differences in the threat environments and other aspects of these two subproblems, however, sometimes make it convenient to distinguish between them.

Figure 1 illustrates the flow of information in a conventional cryptographic system used for privacy of communications. There are three parties: a transmitter, a receiver, and an eavesdropper. The transmitter generates a plaintext or unenciphered message P to be communicated over an insecure channel to the legitimate receiver. In order to prevent the eavesdropper from learning P, the transmitter operates on P with n invertible transformation S_K to produce the ciphertext or cryptogram $C = S_K(P)$. The key K is transmitted only to the legitimate receiver via a secure channel, indicated by a shielded path in Fig. 1. Since the legitimate receiver knows K, he can decipher C by operating with S_K^{-1} to obtain $S_K^{-1}(C) = S_K^{-1}(S_K(P)) = P$, the original plaintext message. The secure channel cannot be used to transmit P itself for reasons of capacity or delay. For example, the secure channel might be a weekly courier and the insecure channel a telephone line.

A *cryptographic system* is a single parameter family $\{S_K\}_{K \in \{K\}}$ of invertible transformations

$$S_K:\{P\} \rightarrow \{C\} \tag{1}$$

from a space $\{P\}$ of plaintext messages to a space $\{C\}$ of ciphertext messages. The parameter K is called the key and is selected from a finite set $\{K\}$ called the keyspace. If the message spaces $\{P\}$ and $\{C\}$ are equal, we will denote them both by $\{M\}$. When discussing individual cryptographic transformations S_K, we will sometimes omit mention of the system and merely refer to the transformation K.

The goal in designing the cryptosystem $\{S_K\}$ is to make the enciphering and deciphering operations inexpensive, but to ensure that any successful cryptanalytic operation is too complex to be economical. There are two approaches to this problem. A system which is secure due to the computational cost of cryptanalysis, but which would succumb to an attack with unlimited computation, is called *computationally secure*; while a system which can resist any cryptanalytic attack, no matter how much computation is allowed, is called *unconditionally secure*. Unconditionally secure systems are discussed in [3] and [4] and belong to that portion of information theory, called the Shannon theory, which is concerned with optimal performance obtainable with unlimited computation.

Unconditional security results from the existence of multiple meaningful solutions to a cryptogram. For example, the simple substitution cryptogram XMD resulting from English text can represent the plaintext messages: now, and, the, etc. A computationally secure cryptogram, in contrast, contains sufficient information to uniquely determine the plaintext and the key. Its security resides solely in the cost of computing them.

The only unconditionally secure system in common use is the *one time pad* in which the plaintext is combined with a randomly chosen key of the same length. While such a system is provably secure, the large amount of key required makes it impractical for most applications. Except as otherwise noted, this paper deals with computationally secure systems since these are more generally applicable. When we talk about the need to develop provably secure cryptosystems we exclude those, such as the one time pad, which are unwieldly to use. Rather, we have in mind systems using only a few hundred bits of key and implementable in either a small amount of digital hardware or a few hundred lines of software.

We will call a task *computationally infeasible* if its cost as measured by either the amount of memory used or the run-time is finite but impossibly large.

Much as error correcting codes are divided into convolutional and block codes, cryptographic systems can be divided into two broad classes: *stream ciphers* and *block ciphers*. Stream ciphers process the plaintext in small chunks (bits or characters), usually producing a pseudorandom sequence of bits which is added modulo 2 to the bits of the plaintext. Block ciphers act in a purely combinatorial fashion on large blocks of text, in such a way that a small change in the input block produces a major change in the resulting output. This paper deals primarily with block ciphers, because this *error propagation* property is valuable in many authentication applications.

In an authentication system, cryptography is used to guarantee the authenticity of the message to the receiver. Not only must a meddler be prevented from injecting totally new, authentic looking messages into a channel, but he must be prevented from creating apparently authentic messages by combining, or merely repeating, old messages which he has copied in the past. A cryptographic system intended to guarantee privacy will not, in general, prevent this latter form of mischief.

To guarantee the authenticity of a message, information is added which is a function not only of the message and a secret key, but of the date and time as well; for example, by attaching the date and time to each message and encrypting the entire sequence. This assures that only someone who possesses the key can generate a message which, when decrypted, will contain the proper date and time. Care must be taken, however, to use a system in which small changes in the ciphertext result in large changes in the deciphered plaintext. This intentional error propagation ensures that if the deliberate injection of noise on the channel changes a message such as "erase file 7" into a different message such as "erase file 8," it will also corrupt the authentication information. The message will then be rejected as inauthentic.

The first step in assessing the adequacy of cryptographic systems is to classify the threats to which they are to be subjected. The following threats may occur to cryptographic systems employed for either privacy or authentication.

A *ciphertext only attack* is a cryptanalytic attack in which the cryptanalyst possesses only ciphertext.

A *known plaintext attack* is a cryptanalytic attack in which the cryptanalyst possesses a substantial quantity of corresponding plaintext and ciphertext.

A *chosen plaintext attack* is a cryptanalytic attack in which the cryptanalyst can submit an unlimited number of plaintext messages of his own choosing and examine the resulting cryptograms.

In all cases it is assumed that the opponent knows the general system $\{S_K\}$ in use since this information can be obtained by studying a cryptographic device. While many users of cryptography attempt to keep their equipment secret, many commercial applications require not only that the general system be public but that it be standard.

A ciphertext only attack occurs frequently in practice. The cryptanalyst uses only knowledge of the statistical properties of the language in use (e.g., in English, the letter e occurs 13 percent of the time) and knowledge of certain "probable" words (e.g., a letter probably begins "Dear Sir:"). It is the weakest threat to which a system can be subjected, and any system which succumbs to it is considered totally insecure.

A system which is secure against a known plaintext attack frees its users from the need to keep their past messages secret, or to paraphrase them prior to declassification. This is an unreasonable burden to place on the system's users, particularly in commercial situations where product announcements or press releases may be sent in encrypted form for later public disclosure. Similar situations in diplomatic correspondence have led to the cracking of many supposedly secure systems. While a known plaintext attack is not always possible, its occurrence is frequent enough that a system which cannot resist it is not considered secure.

A chosen plaintext attack is difficult to achieve in practice, but can be approximated. For example, submitting a proposal to a competitor may result in his enciphering it for transmission to his headquarters. A cipher which is secure against a chosen plaintext attack thus frees its users from concern over whether their opponents can plant messages in their system.

For the purpose of certifying systems as secure, it is appropriate to consider the more formidable cryptanalytic threats as these not only give more realistic models of the working environment of a cryptographic system, but make the assessment of the system's strength easier. Many systems which are difficult to analyze using a ciphertext only attack can be ruled out immediately under known plaintext or chosen plaintext attacks.

As is clear from these definitions, cryptanalysis is a system identification problem. The known plaintext and chosen plaintext attacks correspond to passive and active system identification problems, respectively. Unlike many subjects in which system identification is considered, such as automatic fault diagnosis, the goal in cryptography is to build systems which are difficult, rather than easy, to identify.

The chosen plaintext attack is often called an IFF attack, terminology which descends from its origin in the development of cryptographic "identification friend or foe" systems after World War II. An IFF system enables military radars to distinguish between friendly and enemy planes automatically. The radar sends a time-varying challenge to the airplane which receives the challenge, encrypts it under the appropriate key, and sends it back to the radar. By comparing this response with a correctly encrypted version of the challenge, the radar can recognize a friendly aircraft. While the aircraft are over enemy territory, enemy cryptanalysts can send challenges and examine the encrypted responses in an attempt to determine the authentication key in use, thus mounting a chosen plaintext attack on the system. In practice, this threat is countered by restricting the form of the challenges, which need not be unpredictable, but only nonrepeating.

There are other threats to authentication systems which cannot be treated by conventional cryptography, and which require recourse to the new ideas and techniques introduced in this paper. The *threat of compromise of the receiver's authentication data* is motivated by the situation in multiuser networks where the receiver is often the system itself. The receiver's password tables and other authentication data are then more vulnerable to theft than those of the transmitter (an individual user). As shown later, some techniques for protecting against this threat also protect against the *threat of dispute*. That is, a message may be sent but later repudiated by either the transmitter or the receiver. Or, it may be alleged by either party that a message was sent when in fact none was. Unforgeable digital signatures and receipts are needed. For example, a dishonest stockbroker might try to cover up unauthorized buying and selling for personal gain by forging orders from clients, or a client might disclaim an order actually authorized by him but which he later sees will cause a loss. We will introduce concepts which allow the receiver to verify the authenticity of a message, but prevent him from generating apparently authentic messages, thereby protecting against both the threat of compromise of the receiver's authentication data and the threat dispute.

III. Public Key Cryptography

As shown in Fig. 1, cryptography has been a derivative security measure. Once a secure channel exists along which keys can be transmitted, the security can be extended to other channels of higher bandwidth or smaller delay by encrypting the messages sent on them. The effect has been to limit the use of cryptography to communications among people who have made prior preparation for cryptographic security.

In order to develop large, secure, telecommunications systems, this must be changed. A large number of users n results in an even larger number, $(n^2 - n)/2$ potential pairs who may wish to communicate privately from all others. It is unrealistic to assume either that a pair of users with no prior acquaintance will be able to wait for a key to be sent by some secure physical means, or that keys for all $(n^2 - n)/2$ pairs can be arranged in advance. In another paper [5], the authors have considered a conservative approach requiring no new development in cryptography itself, but this involves diminished security, inconvenience, and restriction of the network to a starlike configuration with respect to initial connection protocol.

We propose that it is possible to develop systems of the type shown in Fig. 2, in which two parties communicating

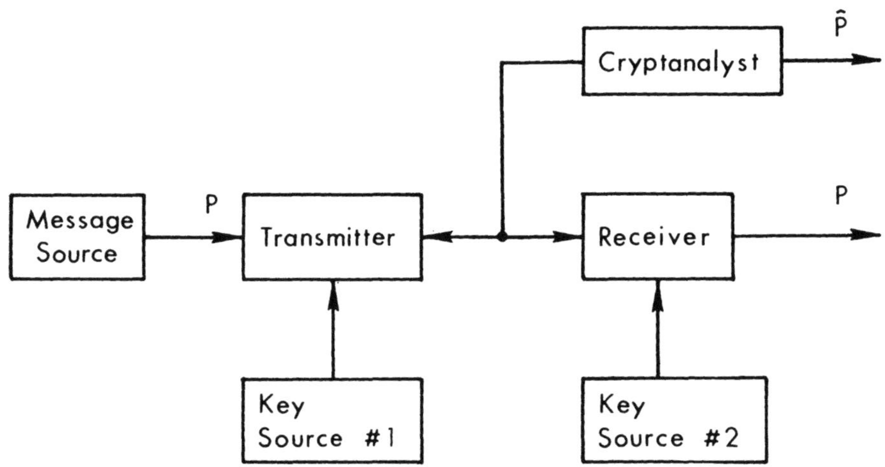

Figure 2. Flow of information in public key system.

solely over a public channel and using only publicly known techniques can create a secure connection. We examine two approaches to this problem, called public key cryptosystems and public key distribution systems, respectively. The first are more powerful, lending themselves to the solution of the authentication problems treated in the next section, while the second are much closer to realization.

A *public key cryptosystem* is a pair of families $\{E_K\}_{K \in \{K\}}$ and $\{D_K\}_{K \in \{K\}}$ of algorithms representing invertible transformations,

$$E_K: \{M\} \rightarrow \{M\} \tag{2}$$

$$D_K: \{M\} \rightarrow \{M\} \tag{3}$$

on a finite message space $\{M\}$, such that

1) for every $K \in \{K\}$, E_K is the inverse of D_K,
2) for every $K \in \{K\}$ and $M \in \{M\}$, the algorithms E_K and D_K are easy to compute,
3) for almost every $K \in \{K\}$, each easily computed algorithm equivalent to D_K is computationally infeasible to derive from E_K,
4) for every $K \in \{K\}$, it is feasible to compute inverse pairs E_K and D_K from K.

Because of the third property, a user's enciphering key E_K can be made public without compromising the security of his secret deciphering key D_K. The cryptographic system is therefore split into two parts, a family of enciphering transformations and a family of deciphering transformations in such a way that, given a member of one family, it is infeasible to find the corresponding member of the other.

The fourth property guarantees that there is a feasible way of computing corresponding pairs of inverse transformations when no constraint is placed on what either the enciphering or deciphering transformation is to be. In practice, the cryptoequipment must contain a true random number generator (e.g., a noisy diode) for generating K, together with an algorithm for generating the E_K - D_K pair from its outputs.

Given a system of this kind, the problem of key distribution is vastly simplified. Each user generates a pair of inverse transformations, E and D, at his terminal. The deciphering transformation D must be kept secret, but need never be communicated on any channel. The enciphering key E can be made public by placing it in a public directory along with the user's name and address. Anyone can then encrypt messages and send them to the user, but no one else can decipher messages intended for him. Public key cryptosystems can thus be regarded as *multiple access ciphers*.

It is crucial that the public file of enciphering keys be protected from unauthorized modification. This task is made easier by the public nature of the file. Read protection is unnecessary and, since the file is modified infrequently, elaborate write protection mechanisms can be economically employed.

A suggestive, although unfortunately useless, example of a public key cryptosystem is to encipher the plaintext, represented as a binary n-vector $\mathbf{m}$, by multiplying it by an invertible binary n × n matrix E. The cryptogram thus equals $E\mathbf{m}$. Letting $D = E^{-1}$ we have $\mathbf{m} = D\mathbf{c}$. Thus, both enciphering and deciphering require about n^2 operations. Calculation of D from E, however, involves a matrix inversion which is a harder problem. And it is at least conceptually simpler to obtain an arbitrary pair of inverse matrices than it is to invert a given matrix. Start with the identity matrix I and do elementary row and column operations to obtain an arbitrary invertible matrix E. Then starting with I do the inverses of these same elementary operations in reverse order to obtain $D = E^{-1}$. The sequence of elementary operations could be easily determined from a random bit string.

Unfortunately, matrix inversion takes only about n^3 operations. The ratio of "cryptanalytic" time (i.e., computing D from E) to enciphering or deciphering time is thus at most n, and enormous block sizes would be required to obtain ratios of 10^6 or greater. Also, it does not appear that knowledge of the elementary operations used to obtain E from I greatly reduces the time for computing D. And, since there is no round-off error in binary arithmetic, numerical stability is unimportant in the matrix inversion. In spite of its lack of practical utility, this matrix example is still useful for clarifying the relationships necessary in a public key cryptosystem.

A more practical approach to finding a pair of easily computed inverse algorithms E and D; such that D is hard to infer from E, makes use of the difficulty of analyzing programs in low level languages. Anyone who has tried to determine what operation is accomplished by someone else's machine language program knows that E itself (i.e., what E does) can be hard to infer from an algorithm for E. If the program were to be made purposefully confusing through addition of unneeded variables and statements, then determining an inverse algorithm could be made very difficult. Of course, E must be complicated enough to prevent its identification from input-output pairs.

Essentially what is required is a one-way compiler: one which takes an easily understood program written in a high level language and translates it into an incomprehensible program in some machine language. The compiler is one-way because it must be feasible to do the compilation, but infeasible to reverse the process. Since efficiency in size of program and run time are not crucial in this application, such compilers may be possible if the structure of the machine language can be optimized to assist in the confusion.

Merkle [1] has independently studied the problem of distributing keys over an insecure channel. His approach is different from that of the public key cryptosystems suggested above, and will be termed a *public key distribution system.* The goal is for two users, A and B, to securely exchange a key over an insecure channel. This key is then used by both users in a normal cryptosystem for both enciphering and deciphering. Merkle has a solution whose cryptanalytic cost grows as n^2 where n is the cost to the legitimate users. Unfortunately the cost to the legitimate users of the system is as much in transmission time as in computation, because Merkle's protocol requires n potential keys to be transmitted before one key can be decided on. Merkle notes that this high transmission overhead prevents the system from being very useful in practice. If a one megabit limit is placed on the setup protocol's overhead, his technique can achieve cost ratios of approximately 10,000 to 1, which are too small for most applications. If inexpensive, high bandwidth data links become available, ratios of a million to one or greater could be achieved and the system would be of substantial practical value.

We now suggest a new public key distribution system which has several advantages. First, it requires only one "key" to be exchanged. Second, the cryptanalytic effort appears to grow exponentially in the effort of the legitimate users. And, third, its use can be tied to a public file of user information which serves to authenticate user A to user B and vice versa. By making the public file essentially a read only memory, one personal appearance allows a user to authenticate his identity many times to many users. Merkle's technique requires A and B to verify each other's identities through other means.

The new technique makes use of the apparent difficulty of computing logarithms over a finite field GF(q) with a prime number q of elements. Let

$$Y = \alpha^X \bmod q \quad , \qquad \text{for} \qquad 1 \leq X \leq q - 1 \quad , \tag{4}$$

where α is a fixed primitive element of GF(q), then X is referred to as the logarithm of Y to the base α, mod q:

$$X = \log_\alpha Y \bmod q \quad , \qquad \text{for} \qquad 1 \leq Y \leq q - 1 \quad . \tag{5}$$

Calculation of Y from X is easy, taking at most $2 \times \log_2 q$ multiplications [6, pp. 398-422]. For example, for X = 18,

$$Y = \alpha^{18} = \left(\left((\alpha^2)^2\right)^2\right)^2 \times \alpha^2 \quad . \tag{6}$$

Computing X from Y, on the other hand can be much more difficult and, for certain carefully chosen values of q, requires on the order of $q^{1/2}$ operations, using the best known algorithem [7, pp. 9, 575-576], [8].

The security of our technique depends crucially on the difficulty of computing logarithms mod q, and if an algorithm whose complexity grew as $\log_2 q$ were to be found, our system would be broken. While the simplicity of the problem statement might allow such simple algorithms, it might instead allow a proof of the problem's difficulty. For now we assume that the best known algorithm for computing logs mod q is in fact close to optimal and hence that $q^{1/2}$ is a good measure of the problem's complexity, for a properly chosen q.

Each user generates an independent random number X_i chosen uniformly from the set of integers $\{1,2,\cdots,q-1\}$. Each keeps X_i secret, but places

$$Y_i = \alpha^{X_i} \bmod q \tag{7}$$

in a public file with his name and address. When users i and j wish to communicate privately, they use

$$K_{ij} = \alpha^{X_i X_j} \bmod q \tag{8}$$

as their key. User i obtains K_{ij} by obtaining Y_j from the public file and letting

$$K_{ij} = Y_j^{X_i} \bmod q \tag{9}$$

$$= (\alpha^{X_j})^{X_i} \bmod q \tag{10}$$

$$= \alpha^{X_j X_i} = \alpha^{X_i X_j} \bmod q \quad . \tag{11}$$

User j obtains K_{ij} in the similar fashion

$$K_{ij} = Y_i^{X_j} \bmod q \quad . \tag{12}$$

Another user must compute K_{ij} from Y_i and Y_j, for example, by computing

$$K_{ij} = Y_i^{(\log_\alpha Y_j)} \bmod q \quad . \tag{13}$$

We thus see that if logs mod q are easily computed the system can be broken. While we do not currently have a proof of the converse (i.e., that the system is secure if logs mod q are difficult to compute), neither do we see any way to compute K_{ij} from Y_i and Y_j without first obtaining either X_i or X_j.

If q is a prime slightly less than 2^b, then all quantities are representable as b bit numbers. Exponentiation then takes at most 2b multiplications mod q, while by hypothesis taking logs requires $q^{1/2} = 2^{b/2}$ operations. The cryptanalytic effort therefore grows exponentially relative to legitimate efforts. If b = 200, then at most 400 multiplications are required to compute Y_i from X_i, or K_{ij} from Y_i and X_j, yet taking logs mod q requires 2^{100} or approximately 10^{30} operations.

IV. One-Way Authentication

The problem of authentication is perhaps an even more serious barrier to the universal adoption of telecommunications for business transactions than the problem of key distribution. Authentication is at the heart of any system involving contracts and billing. Without it, business cannot function. Current electronic authentication systems cannot meet the need for a purely digital, unforgeable, message dependent signature. They provide protection against third party forgeries, but do not protect against disputes between transmitter and receiver.

In order to develop a system capable of replacing the current written contract with some purely electronic form of communication, we must discover a digital phenomenon with the same properties as a written signature. It must be easy for anyone to recognize the signature as authentic, but impossible for anyone other than the legitimate signer to produce it. We will call any such technique *one-way authentication.* Since any digital signal can be copied precisely, a true digital signature must be recognizable without being known.

Consider the "login" problem in a multiuser computer system. When setting up his account, the user chooses a password which is entered into the system's password directory. Each time he logs in, the user is again asked to provide his password. By keeping this password secret from all other users, forged logins are prevented. This, however, makes it vital to preserve the security of the password directory since the information it contains would allow perfect impersonation of any user. The problem is further compounded if system operators have legitimate reasons for accessing the directory. Allowing such legitimate accesses, but preventing all others, is next to impossible.

This leads to the apparently impossible requirement for a new login procedure capable of judging the authenticity of passwords without actually knowing them. While appearing to be a logical impossibility, this proposal is easily satisfied. When the user first enters his password PW, the computer automatically and transparently computes a function f(PW) and stores this, not PW, in the password directory. At each successive login, the computer calculates f(X), where X is the proffered password, and compares f(X) with the stored value f(PW). If and only if they are equal, the user is accepted as being authentic. Since the function f must be calculated once per login, its computation time must be small. A million instructions (costing approximately $0.10 at bicentennial prices) seems to be a reasonable limit on this computation. If we could ensure, however, that calculation of f^{-1} required 10^{30} or more instructions, someone who had subverted the system to obtain the password directory could not in practice obtain PW from f(PW), and could thus not perform an unauthorized login. Note that f(PW) is not accepted as a password by the login program since it will automatically compute f(f(PW)) which will not match the entry f(PW) in the password directory.

We assume that the function f is public information, so that it is not ignorance of f which makes calculation of f^{-1} difficult. Such functions are called one-way functions and were first employed for use in login procedures by R. M. Needham [9, p. 91]. They are also discussed in two recent papers [10], [11] which suggest interesting approaches to the design of one-way functions.

More precisely, a function f is a *one-way function* if, for any argument x in the domain of f, it is easy to compute the corresponding value f(x), yet, for almost all y in the range of f, it is computationally infeasible to solve the equation y = f(x) for any suitable argument x.

It is important to note that we are defining a function which is not invertible from a computational point of view, but whose noninvertibility is entirely different from that normally encountered in mathematics. A function f is normally called "noninvertible" when the inverse of a point y is not unique, (i.e., there exist distinct points x_1 and x_2 such that $f(x_1) = y = f(x_2)$). We emphasize that this is not the sort of inversion difficulty that is required. Rather, it must be overwhelmingly difficult, given a value y and knowledge of f, to calculate any x whatsoever with the property that $f(x) = y$. Indeed, if f is noninvertible in the usual sense, it may make the task of finding an inverse image easier. In the extreme, if $f(x) \equiv y_0$ for all x in the domain, then the range of f is $\{y_0\}$, and we can take any x as $f^{-1}(y_0)$. It is therefore necessary that f not be too degenerate. A small degree of degeneracy is tolerable and, as discussed later, is probably present in the most promising class of one-way functions.

Polynomials offer an elementary example of one-way functions. It is much harder to find a root x_0 of the polynomial equation $p(x) = y$ than it is to evaluate the polynomial $p(x)$ at $x = x_0$. Purdy [11] has suggested the use of sparse polynomials of very high degree over finite fields, which appear to have very high ratios of solution to evaluation time. The theoretical basis for one-way functions is discussed at greater length in Section VI. And, as shown in Section V, one-way functions are easy to devise in practice.

The one-way function login protocol solves only some of the problems arising in a multiuser system. It protects against compromise of the system's authentication data when it is not in use, but still requires the user to send the true password to the system. Protection against eavesdropping must be provided by additional encryption, and protection against the threat of dispute is absent altogether.

A public key cryptosystem can be used to produce a true one-way authentication system as follows. If user A wishes to send a message M to user B, he "deciphers" it in his secret deciphering key and sends $D_A(M)$. When user B receives it, he can read it, and be assured of its authenticity by "enciphering" it with user A's public enciphering key E_A. B also saves $D_A(M)$ as proof that the message came from A. Anyone can check this claim by operating on $D_A(M)$ with the publicly known operation E_A to recover M. Since only A could have generated a message with this property, the solution to the one-way authentication problem would follow immediately from the development of public key cryptosystems.

One-way message authentication has a partial solution suggested to the authors by Leslie Lamport of Massachusetts Computer Associates. This technique employs a one-way function f mapping k-dimensional binary space into itself for k on the order of 100. If the transmitter wishes to send an N bit message he generates 2N, randomly chosen, k-dimensional binary vectors $x_1, X_1, x_2, X_2, \cdots, x_N, X_N$ which he keeps secret. The receiver is given the corresponding images under f, namely $y_1, Y_1, y_2, Y_2, \cdots, y_N, Y_N$. Later, when the message $\mathbf{m} = (m_1, m_2, \cdots, m_N)$ is to be sent, the transmitter sends x_1 or X_1 depending on whether $m_1 = 0$ or 1. He sends x_2 or X_2 depending on whether $m_2 = 0$ or 1, etc. The receiver operates with f on the first received block and sees whether it yields y_1 or Y_1 as its image and thus learns whether it was x_1 or X_1, and whether $m_1 = 0$ or 1. In a similar manner the receiver is able to determine $m_2, m_3, \cdots, m_N$. But the receiver is incapable of forging a change in even one bit of $\mathbf{m}$.

This is only a partial solution because of the approximately 100-fold data expansion required. There is, however, a modification which eliminates the expansion problem when N is roughly a megabit or more. Let g be a one-way mapping from binary N-space to binary n-space where n is approximately 50. Take the N bit message $\mathbf{m}$ and operate on it with g to obtain the n bit vector $\mathbf{m}'$. Then use the previous scheme to send $\mathbf{m}'$. If $N = 10^6$, $n = 50$, and $k = 100$, this adds $kn = 5000$ authentication bits to the message. It thus entails only a 5 percent data expansion during transmission (or 15 percent if the initial exchange of $y_1, Y_1, \cdots, y_N$ is included). Even though there are a large number of other messages (2^{N-n} on the average) with the same authentication sequence, the one-wayness of g makes them computationally infeasible to find and thus to forge. Actually g must be somewhat stronger than a normal one-way function, since an opponent has not only **m′** but also one of its inverse images **m**. It must be hard even given **m** to find a different inverse image of **m′**. Finding such functions appears to offer little trouble (see Section V).

There is another partial solution to the one-way user authentication problem. The user generates a password X which he keeps secret. He gives the system $f^T(X)$, where f is a one-way function. At time t the appropriate authenticator is $f^{T-t}(X)$, which can be checked by the system by applying $f^t(X)$. Because of the one-wayness of f, past responses are of no value in forging a new response. The problem with this solution is that it can require a fair amount of computation for legitimate login (although many orders of magnitude less than for forgery). If for example t is incremented every second and the system must work for one month on each password then T = 2.6 million. Both the user and the system must then iterate f an average of 1.3 million times per login. While not insurmountable, this problem obviously limits use of the technique. The problem could be overcome if a simple method for calculating $f^{(2\uparrow n)}$, for n = 1,2,··· could be found, much as $X^8 = ((X^2)^2)^2$. For then binary decompositions of T - t and t would allow rapid computation of f^{T-t} and f^t. It may be, however, that rapid computation of f^n precludes f from being one-way.

V. Problem Interrelations and Trap Doors

In this section, we will show that some of the cryptographic problems presented thus far can be reduced to others, thereby defining a loose ordering according to difficulty. We also introduce the more difficult problem of trap doors.

In Section II we showed that a cryptographic system intended for privacy can also be used to provide authentication

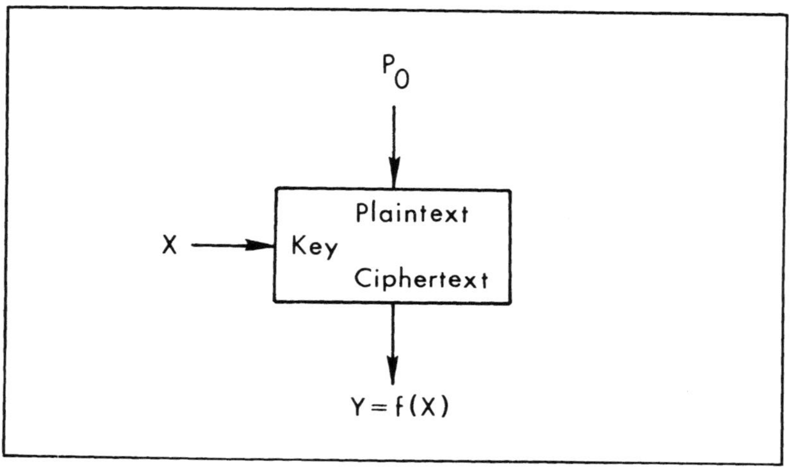

Figure 3. Secure cryptosystem used as one-way function.

against third party forgeries. Such a system can be used to create other cryptographic objects, as well.

A cryptosystem which is secure against a known plaintext attack can be used to produce a one-way function.

As indicated in Fig. 3, take the cryptosystem $\{S_K:\{P\} \rightarrow \{C\}\}_{K \in \{K\}}$ which is secure against a known plaintext attack, fix $P = P_0$ and consider the map

$$f:\{K\} \rightarrow \{C\} \tag{14}$$

defined by

$$f(X) = S_X(P_0) \quad . \tag{15}$$

This function is one-way because solving for X given f(X) is equivalent to the cryptanalytic problem of finding the key from a single known plaintext-cryptogram pair. Public knowledge of f is now equivalent to public knowledge of $\{S_K\}$ and P_0.

While the converse of this result is not necessarily true, it is possible for a function originally found in the search for one-way functions to yield a good cryptosystem. This actually happened with the discrete exponential function discussed in Section III [8].

One-way functions are basic to both block ciphers and key generators. A key generator is a pseudorandom bit generator whose output, the keystream, is added modulo 2 to a message represented in binary form, in imitation of a one-time pad. The key is used as a "seed" which determines the pseudorandom keystream sequence. A known plaintext attack thus reduces to the problem of determining the key from the keystream. For the system to be secure, computation of the key from the keystream must be computationally infeasible. While for the system to be usable, calculation of the keystream from the key must be computationally simple. Thus a good key generator is, almost by definition, a one-way function.

Use of either type of cryptosystem as a one-way function suffers from a minor problem. As noted earlier, if the function f is not uniquely invertible, it is not necessary (or possible) to find the actual value of X used. Rather any X with the same image will suffice. And, while each mapping S_K in a cryptosystem must be bijective, there is no such restriction on the function f from key to cryptogram defined above. Indeed, guaranteeing that a cryptosystem has this property appears quite difficult. In a good cryptosystem the mapping f can be expected to have the characteristics of a randomly chosen mapping (i.e., $f(X_i)$ is chosen uniformly from all possible Y, and successive choices are independent). In this case, if X is chosen uniformly and there are an equal number of keys and messages (X and Y), then the probability that the resultant Y has k + 1 inverses is approximately $e^{-1}/k!$ for $k = 0,1,2,3,\cdots$. This is a Poisson distribution with mean $\lambda = 1$, shifted by 1 unit. The expected number of inverses is thus only 2. While it is possible for f to be more degenerate, a good cryptosystem will not be too degenerate since then the key is not being well used. In the worst case, if $f(X) \equiv Y_0$ for some Y_0, we have $S_K(P_0) \equiv C_0$, and encipherment of P_0 would not depend on the key at all!

While we are usually interested in functions whose domain and range are of comparable size, there are exceptions. In the previous section we required a one-way function mapping long strings onto much shorter ones. By using a block cipher whose key length is larger than the blocksize, such functions can be obtained using the above technique.

Evans et al. [10] have a different approach to the problem of constructing a one-way function from a block cipher. Rather than selecting a fixed P_0 as the input, they use the function

$$f(X) = S_X(X) \quad . \tag{16}$$

This is an attractive approach because equations of this form are generally difficult to solve, even when the family S is comparatively simple. This added complexity, however, destroys the equivalence between the security of the system S under a known plaintext attack and the one-wayness of f.

Another relationship has already been shown in Section IV.

A public key cryptosystem can be used to generate a one-way authentication system.

The converse does not appear to hold, making the construction of a public key cryptosystem a strictly more difficult problem than one-way authentication. Similarly, a public key cryptosystem can be used as a public key distribution system, but not conversely.

Since in a public key cryptosystem the general system in which E and D are used must be public, specifying E specifies a complete algorithm for transforming input messages into output cryptograms. As such a public key system is really a set of *trap-door one-way functions*. These are functions which are not really one-way in that simply computed inverses exist. But given an algorithm for the forward function it is computationally infeasible to find a simply computed inverse. Only through knowledge of certain *trap-door information* (e.g., the random bit string which produced the E-D pair) can one easily find the easily computed inverse.

Trap-doors have already been seen in the previous paragraph in the form of *trap-door, one-way functions* but other variations exist. A *trap-door cipher* is one which strongly resists cryptanalysis by anyone not in possession of *trap-door information* used in the design of the cipher. This allows the designer to break the system after he has sold it to a client and yet falsely to maintain his reputation as a builder of secure systems. It is important to note that it is not greater cleverness or knowledge of cryptography which allows the designer to do what others cannot. If he were to lose the trap-door information he would be no better off than anyone else. The situation is precisely analogous to a combination lock. Anyone who knows the combination can do in seconds what even a skilled locksmith would require hours to accomplish. And yet, if he forgets the combination, he has no advantage.

A trap-door cryptosystem can be used to produce a public key distribution system.

For A and B to establish a common private key, A chooses a key at random and sends an arbitrary plaintext cryptogram pair to B. B, who made the trap-door cipher public, but kept the trap-door information secret, uses the plaintext-cryptogram pair to solve for the key. A and B now have a key in common.

There is currently little evidence for the existence of trap-door ciphers. However they are a distinct possibility and should be remembered when accepting a cryptosystem from a possible opponent [12].

By definition, we will require that a trap-door problem be one in which it is computationally feasible to devise the trap-door. This leaves room for yet a third type of entity for which we shall use the prefix "quasi." For example a *quasi one-way function* is not one-way in that an easily computed inverse exists. However, it is computationally infeasible even for the designer, to find the easily computed inverse. Therefore a quasi one-way function can be used in place of a one-way function with essentially no loss in security.

Losing the trap-door information to a trap-door one-way function makes it into a quasi one-way function, but there may also be one-way functions not obtainable in this manner.

It is entirely a matter of definition that quasi one-way functions are excluded from the class of one-way functions. One could instead talk of one-way functions in the wide sense or in the strict sense.

Similarly, a quasi secure cipher is a cipher which will successfully resist cryptanalysis, even by its designer, and yet for which there exists a computationally efficient cryptanalytic algorithm (which is of course computationally infeasible to find). Again, from a practical point of view, there is essentially no difference between a secure cipher and a quasi secure one.

We have already seen that public key cryptosystems imply the existence of trap-door one-way functions. However the converse is not true. For a trap-door one-way function to be usable as a public key cryptosystem, it must be invertible (i.e., have a unique inverse).

VI. Computational Complexity

Cryptography differs from all other fields of endeavor in the ease with which its requirements may appear to be satisfied. Simple transformations will convert a legible text into an apparently meaningless jumble. The critic, who wishes to claim that meaning might yet be recovered by cryptanalysis, is then faced with an arduous demonstration if he is to prove his point of view correct. Experience has shown, however, that few systems can resist the concerted attack of skillful cryptanalysts, and many supposedly secure systems have subsequently been broken.

In consequence of this, judging the worth of new systems has always been a central concern of cryptographers. During the sixteenth and seventeenth centuries, mathematical arguments were often invoked to argue the strength of cryptographic methods, usually relying on counting methods which showed the astronomical number of possible keys. Though the problem is far too difficult to be laid to rest by such simple methods, even the noted algebraist Cardano fell into this trap [2, p. 145]. As systems whose strength had been so argued were repeatedly broken, the notion of giving mathematical proofs for the security of systems fell into disrepute and was replaced by certification via cryptanalytic assault.

During this century, however, the pendulum has begun to swing back in the other direction. In a paper intimately connected with the birth of information theory, Shannon [3] showed that the one time pad system, which had been in use since the late twenties offered "perfect secrecy" (a form of unconditional security). The provably secure systems investigated by Shannon rely on the use of either a key whose length grows linearly with the length of the message or on perfect source coding and are therefore too unwieldy for most purposes. We note that neither public key cryptosystems nor one-way authentication systems can be unconditionally secure because the public information always determines the secret information uniquely among the members of a finite set. With unlimited computation, the problem could therefore be solved by a straightforward search.

The past decade has seen the rise of two closely related disciplines devoted to the study of the costs of computation: computational complexity theory and the analysis of algorithms. The former has classified known problems in computing into broad classes by difficulty, while the latter has concentrated on finding better algorithms and studying the resources they consume. After a brief digression into complexity theory, we will examine its application to cryptography, particularly the analysis of one-way functions.

A function is said to belong to the complexity class **P** (for polynomial) if it can be computed by a deterministic Turing Machine in a time which is bounded above by some polynomial function of the length of its input. One might think of this as the class of easily computed functions, but it is more accurate to say that a function not in this class must be hard to compute for at least some inputs. There are problems which are known not to be in the class **P** [13, pp. 405-425].

There are many problems which arise in engineering which cannot be solved in polynomial time by any known techniques, unless they are run on a computer with an unlimited degree of parallelism. These problems may or may not belong to the class **P**, but belong to the class **NP** (for nondeterministic, polynomial) of problems solvable in polynomial time on a "nondeterministic" computer (i.e., one with an unlimited degree of parallelism). Clearly the class **NP** includes the class **P**, and one of the great open questions in complexity theory is whether the class **NP** is strictly larger.

Among the problems known to be solvable in **NP** time, but not known to be solvable in **P** time, are versions of the traveling salesman problem, the satisfiability problem for propositional calculus, the knapsack problem, the graph coloring problem, and many scheduling and minimization problems [13, pp. 363-404], [14]. We see that it is not lack of interest or effort which has prevented people from finding solutions in **P** time for these problems. It is thus strongly believed that at least one of these problems must not be in the class **P**, and that therefore the class **NP** is strictly larger.

Karp has identified a subclass of the **NP** problems, called **NP** complete, with the property that if any one of them is in **P**, then all **NP** problems are in **P**. Karp lists 21 problems which are **NP** complete, including all of the problems mentioned above [14].

While the **NP** complete problems show promise for cryptographic use, current understanding of their difficulty includes only worst case analysis. For cryptographic purposes, typical computational costs must be considered. If, however, we replace worst case computation time with average or typical computation time as our complexity measure, the current proofs of the equivalences among the **NP** complete problems are no longer valid. This suggests several interesting topics for research. The ensemble and typicality concepts familiar to information theorists have an obvious role to play.

We can now identify the position of the general cryptanalytic problem among all computational problems.

The cryptanalytic difficulty of a system whose encryption and decryption operations can be done in **P** *time cannot be greater than* **NP.**

To see this, observe that any cryptanalytic problem can be solved by finding a key, inverse image, etc., chosen from a finite set. Choose the key nondeterministically and verify in **P** time that it is the correct one. If there are M possible keys to choose from, an M-fold parallelism must be employed. For example in a known plaintext attack, the plaintext is encrypted simultaneously under each of the keys and compared with the cryptogram. Since, by assumption, encryption takes only **P** time, the cryptanalysis takes only **NP** time.

We also observe that the general cryptanalytic problem is **NP** complete. This follows from the breadth of our definition of cryptographic problems. A one-way function with an **NP** complete inverse will be discussed next.

Cryptography can draw directly from the theory of **NP** complexity by examining the way in which **NP** complete problems can be adapted to cryptographic use. In particular, there is an **NP** complete problem known as the knapsack problem which lends itself readily to the construction of a one-way function.

Let $y = f(x) = \mathbf{a} \cdot \mathbf{x}$ where $\mathbf{a}$ is a known vector of n integers $(a_1, a_2, \cdots, a_n)$ and $\mathbf{x}$ is a binary n-vector. Calculation of y is simple, involving a sum of at most n integers. The problem of inverting f is known as the knapsack problem and requires finding a subset of the $\{a_i\}$ which sum to y.

Exhaustive search of all 2^n subsets grows exponentially and is computationally infeasible for n greater than 100 or so. Care must be exercised, however, in selecting the parameters of the problem to ensure that shortcuts are not possible. For example if n = 100 and each a_i is 32 bits long, y is at most 39 bits long, and f is highly degenerate; requiring on the average only 2^{38} tries to find a solution. Somewhat more trivially, if $a_i = 2^{i-1}$ then inverting f is equivalent to finding the binary decomposition of y.

This example demonstrates both the great promise and the considerable shortcomings of contemporary complexity theory. The theory only tells us that the knapsack problem is probably difficult in the worst case. There is no indication of its difficulty for any particular array. It appears, however, that choosing the $\{a_i\}$ uniformly from $\{0,1,2,\cdots,2^{n-1}\}$ results in a hard problem with probability one as $n \to \infty$.

Another potential one-way function, of interest in the analysis of algorithms, is exponentiation mod q, which was suggested to the authors by Prof. John Gill of Stanford University. The one-wayness of this function has already been discussed in Section III.

VII. Historical Perspective

While at first the public key systems and one-way authentication systems suggested in this paper appear to be unportended by past cryptographic developments, it is possible to view them as the natural outgrowth of trends in cryptography stretching back hundreds of years.

Secrecy is at the heart of cryptography. In early cryptography, however, there was a confusion about what was to be kept secret. Cryptosystems such as the Caesar cipher (in which each letter is replaced by the one three places further on, so A is carried to D, B to E, etc.) depended for their security on keeping the entire encryption process secret.

After the invention of the telegraph [2, p. 191], the distinction between a general system and a specific key allowed the general system to be compromised, for example by theft of a cryptographic device, without compromising future messages enciphered in new keys. This principle was codified by Kerchoffs [2, p. 235] who wrote in 1881 that the compromise of a cryptographic system should cause no inconvenience to the correspondents. About 1960, cryptosystems were put into service which were deemed strong enough to resist a known plaintext cryptanalytic attack, thereby eliminating the burden of keeping old messages secret. Each of these developments decreased the portion of the system which had to be protected from public knowledge, eliminating such tedious expedients as paraphrasing diplomatic dispatches before they were presented. Public key systems are a natural continuation of this trend toward decreasing secrecy.

Prior to this century, cryptographic systems were limited to calculations which could be carried out by hand or with simple slide-rule-like devices. The period immediately after World War I saw the beginning of a revolutionary trend which is now coming to fruition. Special purpose machines were developed for enciphering. Until the development of general purpose digital hardware, however, cryptography was limited to operations which could be performed with simple electromechanical systems. The development of digital computers has freed it from the limitations of computing with gears and has allowed the search for better encryption methods according to purely cryptographic criteria.

The failure of numerous attempts to demonstrate the soundness of cryptographic systems by mathematical proof led to the paradigm of certification by cryptanalytic attack set down by Kerchoffs [2, p. 234] in the last century. Although some general rules have been developed, which aid the designer in avoiding obvious weaknesses, the ultimate test is an assault on the system by skilled cryptanalysts under the most favorable conditions (e.g., a chosen plaintext attack). The development of computers has led for the first time to a mathematical theory of algorithms which can begin to approach the difficult problem of estimating the computational difficulty of breaking a cryptographic system. The position of mathematical proof may thus come full circle and be reestablished as the best method of certification.

The last characteristic which we note in the history of cryptography is the division between amateur and professional cryptographers. Skill in production cryptanalysis has always been heavily on the side of the professionals, but innovation, particularly in the design of new types of cryptographic systems, has come primarily from the amateurs. Thomas Jefferson, a cryptographic amateur, invented a system which was still in use in World War II [2, pp. 192-195], while the most noted cryptographic system of the twentieth century, the rotor machine, was invented simultaneously by four separate people, all amateurs [2, pp. 415, 420, 422-424]. We hope this will inspire others to work in this fascinating area in which participation has been discouraged in the recent past by a nearly total government monopoly.

References

[1] R. Merkle, "Secure communication over an insecure channel," submitted to Communications of the ACM.

[2] D. Kahn, The Codebreakers, The Story of Secret Writing. New York: Macmillan, 1967.

[3] C. E. Shannon, "Communication theory of secrecy systems," Bell Syst. Tech. J., Vol. 28, pp. 656-715, Oct. 1949.

[4] M. E. Hellman, "An extension of the Shannon theory approach to cryptography," submitted to IEEE Trans. Inform. Theory, Sept. 1975.

[5] W. Diffie and M. E. Hellman, "Multiuser cryptographic techniques," presented at National Computer Conference, New York, June 7-10, 1976.

[6] D. Knuth, The Art of Computer Programming, Vol. 2, Semi-Numerical Algorithms. Reading, MA: Addison-Wesley, 1969.

[7] _____, The Art of Computer Programming, Vol. 3, Sorting and Searching. Reading, MA.: Addison-Wesley, 1973.

[8] S. Pohlig and M. E. Hellman, "An improved algorithm for computing algorithms in GF(p) and its cryptographic significance," submitted to IEEE Trans. Inform. Theory.

[9] M. V. Wilkes, Time-Sharing Computer Systems. New York: Elsevier, 1972.

[10] A. Evans, Jr., W. Kantrowitz, and E. Weiss, "A user authentication system not requiring secrecy in the computer," Communications of the ACM, Vol. 17, pp. 437-442, Aug. 1974.

[11] G. B. Purdy, "A high security log-in procedure," Communications of the ACM, Vol. 17, pp. 442-445, Aug. 1974.

[12] W. Diffie and M. E. Hellman, "Cryptanalysis of the NBS data encryption standard" submitted to Computer, May 1976.

[13] A. V. Aho, J. E. Hopcroft, and J. D. Ullman, The Design and Analysis of Computer Algorithms. Reading, MA: Addison-Wesley, 1974.

[14] R. M. Karp, "Reducibility among combinatorial problems," in Complexity of Computer Computations. R. E. Miller and J. W. Thatcher, Eds. New York: Plenum, 1972, pp. 85-104.

Ralph C. Merkle

7. Secure Communications over Insecure Channels

Abstract

According to traditional conceptions of cryptographic security, it is necessary to transmit a key, by secret means, before encrypted messages can be sent securely. This paper shows that it is possible to select a key over open communications channels in such a fashion that communications security can be maintained. A method is described which forces any enemy to expend an amount of work which increases as the square of the work required of the two communicants to select the key. The method provides a logically new kind of protection against the passive eavesdropper. It suggests that further research on this topic will be highly rewarding, both in a theoretical and a practical sense.

Introduction

People have been communicating with each other for many millennia. They often wish to communicate secretly. Since the first use of Caesar's cipher, some two thousand years ago, people have employed a number of ciphers and codes in attempts to keep their correspondence secret. These have met with varying degrees of success until the modern age. The modern digital computer has made it possible to create ciphers which are, in practical terms, unbreakable.[1] (At least, if anyone has broken them, they are maintaining a discreet silence.) Underlying this success has been a very definite paradigm, which makes very definite assumptions about the nature of the encryption process, and the conditions under which secret communications can take place. It is the purpose of this paper to consider this paradigm, and to question the assumptions which underlie it. One assumption (that we must transmit a key, by secret means, prior to an attempt to communicate securely) which has traditionally been regarded as a necessary precondition for cryptographically secure communications is not, in fact, necessary. This is demonstrated by exhibiting a solution which allows two communicants to select a key publicly, but in such a fashion that no one else can easily determine it.

The body of the paper begins with an explanation of the traditional paradigm and then develops a new paradigm, which differs significantly from the traditional one. We then argue that the new paradigm is consistent with secret and secure communications. Finally, the implications of the new paradigm are explored in more detail, with the aid of some examples.

Review

Secure communication takes place between two individuals when they communicate privately in spite of efforts by a third person to learn what is being communicated. We shall, therefore, introduce three protagonists into our paradigm, X and Y, the two communicants, and Z, the third person, who wishes to find out what X and Y are communicating. X and Y have avail-

---

[1] As mentioned by Kahn, in [3], p. 711, "In one case, I.D.A. (Institute for Defense Analyses) cryptanalysts were given 1,000,000 letters of error-free text in a top military cryptosystem. They put in the equivalent of six man years on it -- and finally gave up in defeat."

able some method of encrypting and decrypting messages that they send to each other. X, Y, and Z all know the general method of encryption. X and Y also have available a normal communications channel, over which they send the bulk of their messages. To allow X and Y to be secure, we also assume that they know a key, which is unknown to Z. The general method uses this key as a parameter, and will perform a particular transformation on messages for a particular key. Because Z does not know this key, he cannot perform the particular transformation, and thus cannot encrypt or decrypt messages.

X and Y must both know what the key is, and must insure that Z does not know what it is. In the traditional paradigm for cryptography, this situation comes about by the transmission of the key from X to Y over some special and secure communications channel, which we shall refer to as the key channel. Z cannot intercept messages sent on this channel, and the key is therefore safe.

The reason that the key channel is not used for normal communications is because of its expense and inconvenience. Radio and telephone cannot be used, as both are vulnerable to passive eavesdropping. Registered mail might be acceptable for moderate security. Word of mouth is better, but listening devices might compromise it. Perhaps the only safe method is to send a trusted courier, with an attache case chained to his wrist. This requires that you trust the courier. Whatever the method used, if Z should manage to discover the key by "practical cryptanalysis," then X and Y might very well continue in blissful ignorance of the fact.

In view of the central position that the key channel will occupy in this paper, it would be wise to state, somewhat more clearly, the conditions which it must satisfy. 1) All attempts by Z to modify or alter messages on the key channel, or to inject false or spurious messages, can be detected. 2) Z is unable to determine the content of any message sent over the key channel, i.e., Z cannot intercept the messages.

The paradigm, as stated so far, is not new, and has appeared previously in the literature (see, for example, Shannon [6]). We will now make a modification to the traditional paradigm, as given, which has not previously been considered.

The New Approach

We modify the traditional paradigm by dropping the second restriction on the key channel: that is to say, we no longer demand that Z be unable to determine what is sent on the key channel. Even stronger, we assume that Z has perfect knowledge of everything that is sent over this channel.[2]

It is the thesis of this paper that secure communications between X and Y can still take place, even under the highly restictive conditions we have described.

The reader should clearly understand that no key lurks in the background. There is no method by which X and Y can communicate other than the normal channel and the key channel. They have made no secret preparations prior to the time that they wish to communicate securely.

We must carefully consider what constitutes a solution. If X and Y eventually agree upon a key, and if the work required of Z to determine the key is much higher than the work put in by either X or Y to select the key, then we have a solution. Note that, in theory at least, Z can determine the key used in most methods simply by trying all possible keys and seeing which one produces a legible message. However,

---

[2] A somewhat different approach is taken in [7]. In this paper, the author considers the problem of security in the face of a wiretap, and where no previous preparations have been made. However, he makes the critical assumption that the enemy has inferior reception of the messages being transmitted. By taking advantage of this inferior reception, the enemy can be completely confused.

this means that Z must put in an amount of work that is exponentially larger than the amount of work put in by X or Y. The current solution is not exponential. The amount of work required of Z to determine the key will increase as the square of the amount of work put in by X and Y to select the key. Clearly, it would be desirable to find a solution in which the amount of work put in by Z increases exponentially as a function of the amount of work put in by X and Y. We see no reason why such exponential methods should not exist.

The Method

The method used is based on a single concept: that of a "puzzle." We define a puzzle as a cryptogram which is meant to be broken. To solve the puzzle, we must cryptanalyze the cryptogram. Having done this, we learn the information that was "enpuzzled," the plaintext of the cryptogram. Just as we can encrypt plaintext to produce a cryptogram, so we can enpuzzle information to produce a puzzle. A puzzle, though, is meant to be solved, while ideally, a cryptogram cannot be cryptanalyzed. To solve a puzzle, all one need do is put in the required amount of effort.

To sharpen our definition, we will consider the following method of creating puzzles. First, select a strong encryption function. We are not interested in the details of how this encryption function works: our only interest is that it does work. The reader can select any encryption function that he feels is particularly strong and effective. A concrete example might be the Lucifer encryption function [2], which is currently felt to be quite strong.

After selecting an encryption function, we create our puzzle by encrypting some piece of information with that function. Of course, if our encryption function is really good, our puzzle is unsolvable, which is not what we want. To avoid this problem, we artificially restrict the size of the key space used with the encryption function. If the key is normally 128 bits, we might use only 30 bits. While searching through 2 ↑ 128 possible keys[3] seems completely infeasible, searching through 2 ↑ 30 is tedious, but quite possible. We can control the difficulty of solving a puzzle, simply by changing the restriction on the size of the key space used. To make the puzzle harder to solve, we might select a 40 bit key, while to make it easier, we might select a 20 bit key.

The puzzles we create by this method are precisely as difficult to break as we desire. We rely on the strength of the underlying encryption function to insure that our puzzle can only be solved by exhaustive search through the key space, and we adjust the size of the key space to control the difficulty of solving the puzzle.

There is still one more point that must be brought out. In cryptanalyzing an encrypted message, the cryptanalyst relies on the redundancy in the message. If the information we enpuzzle is random, there will be no redundancy, and thus no way of solving the puzzle. We must deliberately introduce redundancy into our puzzle, so that it can be solved. This can be done easily enough by encrypting, along with the information, a constant that is known to X, Y, and Z. When we try to decrypt the puzzle with a particular key, then the recovery of this constant part can be taken as evidence that we have selected the right key, and thus have solved the puzzle. Contrariwise, the absence of the constant part in the decrypted puzzle indicates that we have used the wrong key, and should try again.

With the concept of "puzzle" in hand, we can proceed. We let X and Y agree upon the value of N which they wish to use. X then generates N puzzles, and transmits these N puzzles to Y over the key channel. X chooses the size of the key space so that each puzzle requires O(N) efforts to break.

---

[3] 2 ↑ 128 denotes 2^{128} (note added in reprinting).

(That is, X selects a key space of size C * N, for a constant, C). Each puzzle contains, within itself, two pieces of information. Neither piece of information is readily available to anyone examining the puzzle. By devoting O(N) effort to solving the puzzle, it is possible to determine both these pieces of information. One piece of information is a puzzle ID, which uniquely identifies each of the N puzzles. The ID's were assigned by X at random. The other piece of information in the puzzle is a puzzle key, i.e., one of the possible keys to be used in subsequent encrypted communications. To distinguish the puzzle keys, one for each puzzle, from the keys randomly selected from the restricted key space to create the puzzles, we will call the former "puzzle keys," and the latter, "random keys," Thus, N puzzle keys are enpuzzled, and in the process of enpuzzling each puzzle key, a random key is used. (The puzzle key is also selected by X at random.)

When Y is presented with this menu of N puzzles, he selects a puzzle at random, and then spends the amount of effort required to solve the puzzle. Y then transmits the ID back to X over the key channel, and uses the puzzle key found in the puzzle as the key for further encrypted communications over the normal channel.

At this point, we summarize who knows what. X, Y, and Z all know the N puzzles. They also know the ID, because Y transmitted the ID over the key channel. Y knows the corresponding puzzle key, because Y solved the correct puzzle. X knows the corresponding puzzle key, because X knows which puzzle key is associated with the ID that Y sent. Z knows only the ID, but does not know the puzzle key. Z cannot know which puzzle contains the puzzle key that Y selected, and which X and Y are using, even though he knows the ID. To determine which puzzle is the correct one, he must break puzzles at random until he encounters the correct one.

If Z desires to determine the key which X and Y are using, then, on an average, Z will have to solve $(\frac{1}{2})$ N puzzles before reaching the puzzle that Y solved. Each puzzle has been constructed so that it requires O(N) effort to break, so Z must spend, on an average, O(N ↑ 2) effort to determine the key. Y, on the other hand, need only spend O(N) effort to break the one puzzle he selected, while X need only spend O(N) effort to manufacture the N puzzles. Thus, both X and Y will only put in O(N) effort.

Having given an outline of the method, we shall now turn to a detailed look at its implementation. Before proceeding, a few points of notation must be cleared up. F will be used to designate an encryption function. Note that F can be any encryption function the reader feels is particularly powerful and effective. F will accept an arbitrary number of arguments. The first argument is the key, and remaining arguments are the message to be encrypted. All of the data objects will be bit strings of arbitrary length. We imagine that the bit strings that make up the message are first concatenated into one long bit string, which is then encrypted using F. To illustrate, we might have the following call on F:

F(1001010110,011110100001,0100000010110101 1,0010111) .

The first bit string is to be used as the key, and the remaining three bit strings form the message.

We shall also use the function, RAND. RAND(P) generates a random number between 1 and P, inclusive. Note that the normal random number generator on a computer is not suited for this. We require either truly random numbers, or pseudorandom numbers generated by a very powerful pseudorandom number generator. Of course, such a pseudorandom number generator will have to be initialized with a truly random seed.

When we have finished making the puzzle, we will transmit it using the function, TRANSMIT(ARG).

To summarize:

- N Total number of puzzles.
- C Arbitrary constant. The random key is selected from a key space of size C * N.
- F A strong encryption function. Its inverse is called "FINVERSE".

In the algorithm presented, we generate neither the ID's nor the puzzle keys at random. The ID's are generated by encrypting the numbers 1 through N. With a good encryption function, this can be viewed as a method of generating pseudorandom numbers. The puzzle keys are generated by encrypting the ID's. Again, this can be viewed as a good pseudorandom number generator. It has the additional property that the puzzle key can be quickly and easily generated from the ID. Two auxiliary keys, K1 and K2, are used in these two encryption processes, and provide the truly random "seed" for these somewhat unorthodox pseudorandom number generators.

Using these conventions, we can write the algorithm for X, who is generating the puzzles, in the following fashion:

```
var ID, KEY, CONSTANT, RANDOMKEY, PUZZLE,
    K1, K2: bit string;

begin
  K1: = RAND(LARGE);
  K2: = RAND(LARGE);
  CONSTANT: = RAND(LARGE);
  TRANSMIT(CONSTANT);
  for I: = 1 to N do

    begin
      ID: = F(K1,I);
      KEY: = F(K2,ID);
      RANDOMKEY: = RAND(C * N);
      PUZZLE: = F(RANDOMKEY,ID,KEY,CONSTANT);
         TRANSMIT(PUZZLE);
    end;

end;
```

We can now write Y's code. We will need a new primitive for Y: RECEIVE(ARG) is a procedure which returns the value of the next puzzle in ARG. We also need to clarify some notation. If we encrypt some arguments with F, we wish to be able to decrypt those arguments. If we say:

CIPHERTEXT: = F(SOMEKEY,A,B,C);

we want to be able to invert this by saying:

A,B,C: = FINVERSE(SOMEKEY,CIPHERTEXT); .

The meaning of this should be obvious, in spite of the fact that we have three variables, A, B, and C on the left-hand side of the assignment statement. With these additional conventions, the code for Y would then appear as follows:

```
var ID, KEY, CONSTANT, SELECTEDPUZZLEID, THEPUZZLE,
      CURRENTPUZZLE, TEMPCONSTANT: bit string;

begin
  SELECTEDPUZZLEID: = RAND(N);
  RECEIVE(CONSTANT);
  for I: = 1 to N do

    begin
      RECEIVE(CURRENTPUZZLE);
      if I = SELECTEDPUZZLEID then THE PUZZLE: =
        CURRENTPUZZLE;
    end;

    comment: The computation to find the randomkey
used by A follows;

  for I: = 1 to C * N do

    begin
      ID,KEY,TEMPCONSTANT: = FINVERSE(I,THEPUZZLE);
      if TEMPCONSTANT = CONSTANT then go to DONE;
    end;

  print ("should not reach this point.");
  panic;
DONE: TRANSMIT(ID);
end;
```

At the very end, X must receive the ID that Y transmitted, and deduce the key. The last actions that X must perform are as follows:

```
begin
   RECEIVE(ID);
   KEY: = F(K2,ID);
   comment: KEY now has the same value in both X and Y.
      All they have to do is use KEY as the key with
      which to encrypt further transmissions.
end;
```

The only information available to Z is the code executed by X and Y, and the values actually transmitted over the key channel. Thus, Z is in possession of N, the CONSTANT, the ID that Y transmitted to X, and also the puzzles that X transmitted to Y. All other variables are known either exclusively by X, or exclusively by Y.

In summary: the method allows the use of channels satisfying assumption 1, and not satisfying assumption 2, for the transmission of key information. We need only guarantee that messages are unmodified, and we no longer require that they be unread. If the two communicants, X and Y, put in O(N) effort, then the third person, Z, must put in O(N ↑ 2) effort to determine the key. We now turn to the consideration of various implications of this work.

Some Implications

There is no reason to assume an exponential method is impossible. We will discuss the implications of the new paradigm, but will not limit ourselves to the O(N ↑ 2) method presented. To attain realistic levels of security using the O(N ↑ 2) method would require a large value for N, which would be costly. An exponential method would eliminate this cost, and so be more attractive. The existence of such an exponential method will be implicit in the following discussion.

We will assume that whatever method we are using can, like the O(N ↑ 2) method, be cast into the following form: first X transmits some information, then Y makes a return transmission, after which the key is known to X and Y. We will refer to the information that X transmits to Y as the first transmission, and the information that Y transmits to X as the return transmission. In the O(N ↑ 2) method presented, the constant and the N puzzles would be the first transmission, while the ID would be the return transmission.

First, we do not care if Z knows the first transmission. Therefore, we can maintain multiple copies of it without a loss of security. We can maintain a permanent log of it, and we can transmit it by any means that is available to us. We can publish it, and propagate so many copies of it that Z will be hard pressed to find them all, let alone alter them.

Second, we can detect a violation of assumption 1. If Z does, in fact, falsify or alter a message, then what X transmitted, and what Y received, will be different. There is no way that Z can get around this fact. In effect, if Z wishes to break the method by tampering with the messages actually sent, he must post a large sign, saying "I know and understand your current cryptographic setup, I have broken your current keys, and even now, I am listening to what you say." Needless to say, Z might be reluctant to do this.

What, in practical terms, are the implications we can foresee from these relaxations of the security required on a key channel? We can see these better by means of some examples. We first consider the key distribution problem. Using the traditional method, codebooks are generated and distributed under tight security. Strong controls are needed to account for all copies and to prevent duplication of the codebook. Loss of a codebook is a disasterous breach of security. What effect would the current ideas have on this picture? In essence, they imply that codebooks can be lost without compromising security. We can give codebooks to the enemy, and still leave him in no better position than he was in before. The general simplification of security procedures that this would allow would be a significant advantage. Even more important would be the increase in actual security.

A key distribution system based on the current ideas might proceed as follows. First, each unit or command that wished to be in the codebook would generate its own first transmission. These would all be sent to a central site, where the names and first transmissions of all involved communicants would be entered into the codebook. The codebook would then be distributed. In essence, we are simply specifying the nature of the communication channel between X and Y. It is not a direct communication channel, but is somewhat round-about. X publishes his first transmission in the codebook, along with his name. The return transmission from Y to X can now take place over normal communication channels. Y is assured that he is talking to X, because Y looked up X's first transmission in the codebook. At this point X and Y have established a common key, but X does not know that he is talking to Y. Anyone could have sent the return transmission, claiming they were Y. To avoid this, X and Y repeat the process of selecting a key, but X now looks up Y in the codebook, and sends a return transmission to Y, based on Y's first transmission. The return transmission will be meaningful only to Y, because the return transmission is based on Y's first transmission. X knows Y's first transmission came from Y, because it is entered in the codebook. If X and Y now use both keys, then they are assured they are talking to each other, and no one else. To summarize: using only a codebook, which is assumed to be correct, but which is not assumed to be secret, X and Y have established an authenticated, secure communications channel. They have done so quickly and easily. The key need be used for only a short period of time (a single conversation), and can then be changed with equal ease.

The new paradigm also has implications for network security. In a computer network, with many users with diverse needs, security is difficult to maintain. If the codebook in the previous example were compiled at the same time and by the same people who normally compile the directory of network users, the additional effort required would be minimal. Those network users interested in security would submit a first transmission to be included next to their entry in the network directory. They would also make sure that their copy of the network directory was correct. Those users not interested in security would ignore the security procedures. Diverse needs, ranging from no security, to very tight security, could then be met on the same network.

As a final example, consider the following situation. Assume two forces, Us and Them, are fighting. They are winning, because they have broken our codes and ciphers. We only find out about this when we discover that they attack exactly where we are weakest, retreat just before our attacks, and generally seem to know too much too quickly. Our forces are in the field, fully deployed, with no chance for distributing new keys in accordance with the traditional paradigm. Under the traditional paradigm, we are lost. Using the new paradigm, we can easily change all our keys, and re-establish security. The difference is dramatic.

We summarize the discussion to the current point. The traditional paradigm for cryptographically secure communications was examined. A new paradigm was proposed, and a method of key distribution was described which is consistent with the new paradigm. The only weakness in the method is that it is O(N ↑ 2), and not exponential. The weaker restrictions on the key channel demanded by the new paradigm open up the possibility of using more normal, i.e., cheaper, channels of communication with which to update keys. In addition, violation of the weaker restriction on the key channel can be detected, and corrective action taken. Violation of the stronger restriction that the key channel must be unreadable might go unnoticed, and result in catastrophic loss of security. This possibility is eliminated with the new paradigm. In the event that there is no channel available which satisfies the stronger restriction, but there is a channel which satisfies the weaker restriction, then the current method provides an option which is otherwise unavailable.

Conclusion

This paper has thus far dealt with a method which is O(N ↑ 2). If an exponential method were possible, it would offer such significant advantages over traditional techniques that it would almost surely supplant them in short order. The problem appears to offer enough leverage that it can be attacked, as witness the current solution, and an exponential solution would offer significant practical advantages over traditional techniques. The problem merits serious consideration. The author will make the following conjecture: An exponential method is possible. The reader is invited to consider the problem.

Addenda

Further progress has been made since the original submittal of this paper. Diffie and Hellman have published a paper [1] which gives a broad overview of the new class of cryptographic problems. It should be mentioned that the "puzzle" approach used in this paper can easily be recast as a public key cryptosystem, in the terminology of [1]. The author and Martin Hellman [4] have devised an exponential method (public key cryptosystem). Rivest, Shamir, and Adleman [5] have also proposed a public key cryptosystem. Further research is in progress, and the results have been extremely encouraging.

Acknowledgments

The author wishes to thank the following people for their kind contributions of time, thought, facilities, references, and encouragement: (in alphabetical order) B. Englar, R. S. Fabry, S. L. Graham, and F. Olken.

References

1. Diffie, W., and Hellman, M. New directions in cryptography. IEEE Trans. on Inform. IT-22, 6 (Nov. 1976), 644-654.
2. Feistel, H. Cryptography and computer privacy. Sci. Amer. 228, 5 (May 1973), 15-23.
3. Kahn, D. The Codebreakers. MacMillan, New York, 1976.
4. Merkle, R., and Hellman, M. Hiding information and receipts in trap door knapsacks. To appear, IEEE Trans. on Inform.
5. Rivest, R. L., Shamir, A., and Adleman, L. A method for obtaining digital signatures and public-key cryptosystems. Comm. ACM 21, 2 (Feb. 1978), 120-126.
6. Shannon, C. E. Communication theory of secrecy systems. Bell Syst. Tech. J. 28 (1949), 654-715.
7. Wyner, A. D. The wire tap channel. Bell Syst. Tech. J. 54, 8 (Oct. 1975), 1355-1387.

Ralph C. Merkle, Martin E. Hellman

8. Hiding Information and Signatures in Trapdoor Knapsacks

Abstract

The knapsack problem is an NP-complete combinatorial problem that is strongly believed to be computationally difficult to solve in general. Specific instances of this problem that appear very difficult to solve unless one possesses "trapdoor information" used in the design of the problem are demonstrated. Because only the designer can easily solve problems, others can send him information hidden in the solution to the problems without fear that an eavesdropper will be able to extract the information. This approach differs from usual cryptographic systems in that a secret key is not needed. Conversely, only the designer can generate signatures for messages, but anyone can easily check their authenticity.

I. Introduction

Given a one-dimensional knapsack of length S and n rods of lengths $a_1, a_2, \cdots, a_n$, the knapsack problem is to find a subset of the rods that exactly fill the knapsack, if such a

This work was supported by the National Science Foundation under Grant ENG 10173.

subset exists. Equivalently, find a binary n-vector **x** such that S = **a** * **x**, if such an **x** exists (* applied to vectors denotes dot product, otherwise normal multiplication).

A supposed solution **x** is easily checked in at most n additions, but finding a solution is believed to require a number of operations that grows exponentially in n. Exhaustive trial and error search over all 2^n possible **x** is computationally infeasible if n is larger than 100 or 200. The best published method for solving knapsacks of the form considered here requires $2^{n/2}$ complexity both in time and memory [1]. In addition, Schroeppel [2] has devised an algorithm that takes $O(2^{n/2})$ time and $O(2^{n/4})$ space. Theory supports these beliefs because the knapsack problem is known to be an NP-complete problem,[1] and is therefore one of the most difficult computational problems of a cryptographic nature [3, pp. 363-404], [4]. Its degree of difficulty, however, is crucially dependent on the choice of **a**. If **a** = $(1,2,4,\cdots,2^{n-1})$, then solving for **x** is equivalent to finding the binary representation of S. Somewhat less trivially, if for all i

$$a_i > \sum_{j=1}^{i-1} a_j \quad , \tag{1}$$

---

[1]Other definitions of the knapsack problem exist in the literature [1], [5]. The definition used here is adapted from Karp [14]. To be precise, Karp's knapsack problem is to determine whether or not a solution **x** exists, while the corresponding cryptographic problem is to determine **x**, given that it exists. The cryptographic problem is not NP-complete, but it is just as hard as the corresponding NP-complete problem. If there is an algorithm for solving the cryptographic problem in time T(n), i.e., for determining **x** given that it exists, then we can determine whether or not an **x** exists in time T(n), i.e., solve the corresponding NP-complete problem. If the algorithm determines **x** in time T(n), then some **x** exists. If the algorithm does not determine **x** in time T(n) or determines an incorrect **x** -- which is easily checked -- then no such **x** exists.

then **x** is also easily found. $x_n = 1$ if and only if $S \geq a_n$, and for $i = n - 1, n - 2, \cdots, 1$, $x_i = 1$ if and only if

$$S - \sum_{j=i+1}^{n} x_j * a_j \geq a_j \quad . \tag{2}$$

While the theory of NP-complete problems and these examples demonstrate that the knapsack problem is only difficult from a worst case point of view, it is probably true that choosing the a_i independently and uniformly from the integers between 1 and 2^n generates a difficult problem with probability tending to one as n tends to infinity. While several efficient algorithms exist for solving the knapsack problem under special conditions [1], [5], [6], none of these special conditions is applicable to trapdoor knapsacks generated as suggested in this paper.

A trapdoor knapsack [4] is one in which careful choice of $\mathbf{a}$ allows the designer to easily solve for any **x** but prevents anyone else from finding the solution. We will describe two methods for constructing trapdoor knapsacks and indicate how they can be used to hide information. Each user I in a system generates a trapdoor knapsack vector $\mathbf{a}(I)$ and places it in a public file with his name and address. When someone wishes to send the information **x** to the Ith user, he sends $S = \mathbf{x} * \mathbf{a}(I)$. The intended recipient can recover **x** from S, but no one else can. Section VI shows how trapdoor knapsacks can be used to generate electronic signatures and receipts [4].

Before proceeding, a word of caution is in order. First, as is usually the case in cryptography, we cannot yet prove that the systems described in this paper are secure. For brevity, however, we will not continue to repeat this. Second, the trapdoor knapsacks described in this paper form a proper subset of all possible knapsacks, and their solutions are therefore not necessarily as difficult as for the hardest knapsacks. It is the hardest knapsacks with which NP theory is concerned.

II. A Method for Constructing Knapsacks

The designer chooses two large numbers m and w such that w is invertible modulo m (equivalently gcd(w,m) = 1). He selects a knapsack vector $\mathbf{a}'$ which satisfies (1) and therefore allows easy solution of $S' = \mathbf{a}' * \mathbf{x}$. He then transforms the easily solved knapsack vector $\mathbf{a}'$ into a trapdoor knapsack vector $\mathbf{a}$ via the relation

$$a_i = w * a_i' \bmod m \quad . \tag{3}$$

The a_i are pseudo-randomly distributed, and it therefore appears that anyone who knows $\mathbf{a}$, but not w and m, would have great difficulty in solving a knapsack problem involving $\mathbf{a}$. The designer then can easily compute

$$S' = w^{-1} * S \bmod m \tag{4}$$

$$= w^{-1} * \sum x_i * a_i \bmod m \tag{5}$$

$$= w^{-1} * \sum x_i * w * a_i' \bmod m \tag{6}$$

$$= \sum x_i * a_i' \bmod m \quad . \tag{7}$$

If m is chosen so that

$$m > \sum a_i' \quad , \tag{8}$$

then (7) implies that S' is equal to $\Sigma x_i * a_i'$ in integer arithmetic as well as mod m. This knapsack is easily solved for $\mathbf{x}$, which is also the solution to the apparently difficult, but trapdoor knapsack problem $S = \mathbf{a} * \mathbf{x}$.

To help make these ideas clearer, we give a small example with n = 5. Taking m = 8443, $\mathbf{a}' = (171,196,457,1191,2410)$, and w = 2550 (so $w^{-1} = 3950$), then $\mathbf{a} = (5457,1663,216,6013,7439)$. Given S = 1663 + 6013 + 7439 = 15115, the designer computes

$$S' = w^{-1} * S \bmod m \tag{9}$$

$$= 3950 * 15115 \bmod 8443 \tag{10}$$

$$= 3797 \quad . \tag{11}$$

Because $S' > a_5'$, he determines that $x_5 = 1$. Then using (2) for the $\mathbf{a}'$ vector, he determines that $x_4 = 1$, $x_3 = 0$, $x_2 = 1$, $x_1 = 0$, which is also the correct solution to $S = \mathbf{a} * \mathbf{x}$.

Anyone who does not know m, $\mathbf{a}'$, and w has great difficulty in solving for x in $S = \mathbf{a} * \mathbf{x}$ even though the general method used for generating the trapdoor knapsack vector $\mathbf{a}$ is known by the public. The code breaker's task can be further complicated by scrambling the order of the a_i and by adding different random multiples of m to each of the a_i.

The example given was extremely small in size and was only intended to illustrate the technique. Using n = 100, which is the bottom end of the usable range for secure systems, we would suggest that m be chosen uniformly from the numbers between $2^{201} + 1$ and $2^{202} - 1$, that a_1' be chosen uniformly from the range $[1, 2^{100}]$, that a_2' be chosen uniformly from $[2^{100} + 1, 2 * 2^{100}]$, that a_3' be chosen uniformly from $[(2^{i-1} - 1) * 2^{100} + 1, 2^{i-1} * 2^{100})]$, that a_{100}' be chosen uniformly from $[(2^{99} - 1) * 2^{100} + 1, 2^{99} * 2^{100}]$, and that w' be chosen uniformly from $[2, m - 2]$ and then divided by the greatest common divisor of w' and m to yield w.

These choices ensure that (8) holds and that an opponent has at least 2^{100} possibilities for each parameter and hence cannot even search over one of them. Note that each a_i will be pseudo-randomly distributed between 1 and m - 1 and hence will require a 202-bit representation. Since S requires a 209-bit representation, there is a 2.09:1 data expansion from **x** to S.

III. Multiplicative Trapdoor Knapsacks

A multiplicative knapsack is easily solved if the vector entries are relatively prime. Given $\mathbf{a}' = (6,11,35,43,169)$ and P = 2838, it is easily determined that P = 6 * 11 * 43 because 6, 11, and 43 evenly divide P but 35 and 169 do not. A multiplicative knapsack is transformed into an additive knapsack by taking logarithms. To make both vectors have reasonable values, the logarithms are taken over GF(m) where m is a prime number [7].

A small example is again helpful. Taking n = 4, m = 257, $\mathbf{a}' = (2,3,5,7)$, and the base of the logarithms to be b = 131 results in $\mathbf{a} = (80,183,81,195)$. That is, $131^{80} = 2 \bmod 257$, $131^{183} = 3 \bmod 257$, etc. Finding logarithms over GF(m) is relatively easy if m - 1 has only small prime factors [7]. (On a computer, the current upper limit on small is in the range 10^6 to 10^{12}.)

Now suppose we are given S = 183 + 81 = 264 and are asked to find the solution to S = $\mathbf{a} * \mathbf{x}$. Knowing the trapdoor information m, $\mathbf{a}'$, and b, we are able to compute

$$
\begin{aligned}
S' &= b^S \bmod m \\
&= 131^{264} \bmod 257 \\
&= 15 \\
&= (2^0) * (3^1) * (5^1) * (7^0) \qquad (12)
\end{aligned}
$$

which implies that x = (0,1,1,0). This is because

$$b^S = b^{(\Sigma a_i * x_i)}$$
$$= \Pi b^{(a_i * x_i)}$$
$$= \Pi a_i'^{x_i} \bmod m \quad . \tag{13}$$

It is now necessary that

$$\prod_{i=1}^{n} a_i' < m \tag{14}$$

to ensure that $\Pi a_i' x_i$ mod m equals $\Pi a_i' x_i$ in arithmetic over the integers.

An opponent who knows the public information **a**, but who does not know the trapdoor information m, **a**$'$, and b, again appears to face an impossible computational problem.

The example given was again small and only intended to illustrate the technique. Taking n = 100, if each a_i' is a random 100-bit prime number, then m would have to be approximately 10,000 bits long to ensure that (14) is met. While a 100:1 data expansion is acceptable in certain applications, such as secure key distribution over an insecure channel [4], [8], it is probably not necessary for an opponent to be so uncertain of the a_i'. It may even be possible to use the first n primes for the a_i', in which case m could be as small as 730 bits long when n = 100 and still meet condition (14). There is a possible trade-off between security and data expansion.

IV. An Iterative Method

This section discusses techniques for improving the security and utility of the basic methods.

In the first method we transformed a hard and apparently very difficult knapsack problem **a** into a very simple and easily solved knapsack problem $\mathbf{a}'$ by means of the transformation

$$a_i' = w^{-1} * a_i \bmod m \quad . \tag{15}$$

We could solve a knapsack involving $\mathbf{a}$ because we could solve a knapsack involving $\mathbf{a}'$. Notice though that it does not matter *why* we are able to solve knapsacks involving $\mathbf{a}'$; all that matters is that we *can* solve them. Rather than requiring that $\mathbf{a}'$ satisfy (1), we could require that $\mathbf{a}'$ be transformable into a new problem $\mathbf{a}''$ by the transformation

$$a_i'' = w'^{-1} * a_i' \bmod m' \tag{16}$$

where the new problem $\mathbf{a}''$ satisfies (1) or is otherwise easy to solve. Having done the transformation twice, there is no problem in doing it a third time. That is, we select an $\mathbf{a}''$ that is easy to solve, not because it satisfies (1), but because it can be transformed into $\mathbf{a}'''$, which *is* easy to solve, by

$$\mathbf{a}_i''' = w''^{-1} * \mathbf{a}_i'' \bmod m'' \quad . \tag{17}$$

It is clear that we can repeat this process as often as we wish.

With each successive transformation, the structure in the publicly known vector $\mathbf{a}$ becomes more and more obscure. In essence, we are encrypting the simple knapsack vector by the repeated application of a transformation that preserves the basic structure of the problem. The final result $\mathbf{a}$ appears to be a collection of random numbers. The fact that the problem can be easily solved has been totally obscured.

The effect of repeating the process several times is very different from that obtained with certain ciphers, such as a simple substitution. A simple substitution cipher is not strengthened by repetition because the composition of two substitution ciphers is yet another substitution cipher. The (w,m) transformations do not have this closure property. The following example shows that the repetition of two (w,m) transforms need not be equivalent to a single (w,m) transform.

If $w = 3$, $m = 89$, $w' = 17$, $m' = 47$, and $\mathbf{a}'' = (5,10,20)$, then $\mathbf{a}' = (38,29,11)$ and $\mathbf{a} = (25,87,33)$. Assume there exists $\hat{w}$ and $\hat{m}$ such that

$$\mathbf{a} = \hat{w} * \mathbf{a}'' \bmod \hat{m} \quad . \tag{18}$$

Then $a_1 = 25$ and $a_1'' = 5$ imply that

$$25 = \hat{w} * 5 \bmod \hat{m} \quad . \tag{19}$$

From this we have

$$2 * 25 = \hat{w} * 2 * 5 \bmod \hat{m} \tag{20}$$

or

$$50 = \hat{w} * 10 \bmod \hat{m} \quad . \tag{21}$$

But now the relation between $a_2 = 87$ and $a_2'' = 10$ implies that

$$87 = \hat{w} * 10 \bmod \hat{m} \tag{22}$$

so $87 = 50 \bmod \hat{m}$ or $37 = 0 \bmod \hat{m}$, which implies that $\hat{m} = 37$. Equation (19) then becomes

$$25 = \hat{w} * 5 \bmod 37 \tag{23}$$

so $\hat{w} = 5$. However, if $\hat{w} = 5$ and $\hat{m} = 37$, then (18) for $a_3 = 33$ and $a_3'' = 20$ becomes

$$33 = 5 * 20 \bmod 37 \tag{24}$$

or $33 = 26 \bmod 37$, a contradiction. We conclude that no such $\hat{w}$ and $\hat{m}$ can exist.

The original easy-to-solve knapsack vector can meet any condition, such as (1), that guarantees it is easy to solve.

For example, it could be a multiplicative trapdoor knapsack. In this way it is possible to combine both of the trapdoor knapsack methods into a single method, which is presumably harder to break.

It is important to consider the rate of growth of **a** because this rate determines the data expansion involved in transmitting the n-bit vector **x** as the larger quantity S. The rate of growth depends on the method of selecting the numbers, but with n = 100, each a_i need be at most seven bits larger than the corresponding a_i', each a_i' need be at most seven bits larger than a_i'', and so on. Each successive stage of the transformation needs to increase the size of the problem by only a small fixed amount. Repeating the transformation 20 times will add at most 140 bits to each a_i. If each a_i is 200 bits long to begin with, then they need only be 340 bits long after 20 stages, and S is representable in 347 bits. The data expansion is then only 3.47:1.

V. Compressing the Public File

As described above, the Ith user must place his trapdoor knapsack vector **a**(I) in a public file. The Jth user can then look up **a**(I) and send a message **x** to I, hidden as S = **a**(I) * **x**. To avoid storing the rather large vector **a**(I), J could ask I to transmit **a**(I) to him. But, unless J has some method for testing **a**(I), user K might fool J by sending him **a**(K) and saying it was **a**(I). J would then mistakenly tell all his secrets to K. A method is needed for J to convince himself that he was really sent **a**(I). With a public file, each user can make one personal appearance when depositing his vector, and after identifying himself to the system, he could identify (authenticate) himself to any user by his ability to decipher messages hidden with his vector. The file itself must be protected, but this is relatively easy because only write protection is needed.

To preserve this authentication benefit of the public file, but to reduce its size (potentially 20 or more kilobits per user), we suggest storing a 100-bit one-way hash total $h[\mathbf{a}(I)]$ instead of $\mathbf{a}(I)$ itself. When J receives $\mathbf{a}(I)$ from I, he computes $h[\mathbf{a}(I)]$ and checks this against the value I stored in the public file. The hash function h must be a one-way function [4,9,10,11], so that K cannot generate a new vector $\mathbf{a}(K)$ such that $h[\mathbf{a}(K)] = h[\mathbf{a}(I)]$, without having to perform a computationally impossible feat.

Allowing 100 bits for storing the user's name and address, (or phone number) the public file now contains 200 bits, instead of over 20 kbit/user. A system with a million users requires a 200 million bit, instead of a 20 billion bit, public file. Transmission costs are comparable for both implementations.

A 100-bit number can be coded as 20 alphanumeric characters, which is small enough to fit in a telephone book. A typical entry would look like this:

Joe Smith......497-1573
KSDJR E6K65 3GFVM OMK4K .

The second line is the one-way hash total of Smith's trapdoor knapsack vector $\mathbf{a}$(Smith). With this information we can call up Smith and hold a secure conversation with him that no one else can understand. We do not need to have met Smith previously to know we are talking with him or for him to know he is talking with us.

Transmitting 20 kbits on a high-speed 50 kbit/s link takes 0.4 s, but on a low-speed 300 bit/s link, it takes more than a minute. The transmitted data can be reduced by a factor of five to about 4 kbits, which takes less than 15 s to transmit at 300 bit/s, by cutting the number of a_i to $n = 20$. The vector $\mathbf{x}$, however, now has only 20 binary elements, which is small enough to allow solution by exhaustive search. To maintain security, the information in the **x** vector must be increased to about 100 bits while keeping $n = 20$. This can be done by allowing each element x_i to take on values in the set $\{0,1,2,3,\cdots,31\}$ instead of just in $\{0,1\}$. Specifying each x_i takes 5 bits and specifying the whole vector **x** takes 100 bits. Equation (1) must now be modified to

$$a_i > 31 * \sum_{j=1}^{i-1} a_j \quad . \tag{25}$$

If n is reduced to 1 and the single element of the **x** vector assumes a value in $\{0,1,2,\cdots,2^{100} - 1\}$, then the system is easily broken because

$$x = S/a \quad . \tag{26}$$

When $n = 2$, the system can also be broken easily by an algorithm similar in spirit to the greatest common divisor algorithm. It seems that small values of n weaken the system, and further research is needed to determine how small n can be while still preserving security.

VI. Signatures

As discussed in [4], the need for a digital equivalent of a written signature is a major barrier to the replacement of physical mail by teleprocessing systems. Usual digital authenticators protect against third party forgeries but cannot be used to settle disputes between the transmitter and receiver as to what message, if any, was sent. A true digital signature allows the recipient to prove that a particular message was sent to him by a particular person. Obviously it must be impossible for the recipient to alter the contents of the message and generate the corresponding signature, but it must be easy for him to check the validity of a signature for any message from any user. A digital signature can also be used to generate receipts. The recipient signs a message saying, "I have received the following message: TEXT." This section describes how trapdoor knapsacks can be used to generate such signatures and receipts.

If every S in some large fixed range had an inverse image $\mathbf{x}$, then it could be used to provide signatures. When the Ith user wanted to send the message m, he would compute and transmit $\mathbf{x}$ such that $\mathbf{a}(I) * \mathbf{x} = m$. The recipient could easily compute m from $\mathbf{x}$ and by checking a date/time field (or some other redundancy in m) determine that the message was authentic. Because the recipient could not generate such an $\mathbf{x}$, he saves $\mathbf{x}$ as proof that the Ith user sent him the message m.

This method of generating signatures can be modified to work when the density of solutions (the fraction of S between 0 and Σa_i that have solutions to $\mathbf{x} * \mathbf{a} = S$) is less than 1, provided it is not too small. The message m is sent in plaintext form or encrypted if eavesdropping is a threat, and a sequence of one-way functions [4], [9], [10], [11] $y_1 = F_1(m)$, $y_2 = F_2(m), \cdots$ are computed. The transmitter then seeks inverse images for $y_1, y_2, \cdots$ until one is found and appends the corresponding $\mathbf{x}$ to m as a signature. The receiver computes $y = \mathbf{a} * \mathbf{x}$ and checks that y is equal to y_k with k not too large, for example, at most 10 times the expected value of k.

The sequence of functions $F_i(*)$ can be as simple as

$$F_i(m) = F(m) + i \tag{20a}$$

or

$$F_i(m) = F(m+i) \tag{20b}$$

where F(*) is a one-way function. It is necessary that the range of F(*) have at least 2^{100} values to foil trial and error attempts at forgery. If the message is much longer than 100 bits, the expansion caused by the addition of a 100-bit authentication field is unimportant.

If the trapdoor knapsack vector were generated as suggested at the end of Section II, the solution density would be less than $1/2^{100}$, and more than $2^{100} y_k$ would have to be tried on the average before one with a solution is found. The multiplicative method of Section III has an even smaller solution density. It is possible, however, to use the iterative method of Section IV to obtain a solution density of approximately $1/10^4$ with two iterations or $1/10^6$ with three iterations when n = 100. First, a knapsack vector $\mathbf{a}''$ with a solution density near 1 is selected. If $\mathbf{a}'' = (1,2,4,8,\cdots, 2^{99})$ then the solution density is 1, but increasing some of the larger a_i'' need not greatly reduce the solution density. For example, (1,2,4,8,17,35,68,142) has a solution density of 0.92 and still satisfies (1). Such choices may not be necessary, but they provide an additional margin of safety at almost no additional cost.

After selecting $\mathbf{a}''$, parameters m′ and w′ are chosen such that $m' > \Sigma a_i''$ and $w^{-1\prime}$ exists modulo m′. The weak trapdoor knapsack vector

$$\mathbf{a}' = w' * \mathbf{a}'' \quad \text{mod } m' \tag{27}$$

is then computed. New parameters $m > \Sigma \mathbf{a}'_i$ and w (with w^{-1} existing mod m) are chosen, and the more secure trapdoor knapsack vector

$$\mathbf{a} = w * \mathbf{a}' \quad \text{mod } m \tag{28}$$

is computed. The process can be iterated more than twice to obtain the final vector $\mathbf{a}$, but the solution density typically decreases by a factor of n/2 with each iteration. When used for hiding information this decrease is of little importance, but when used for signatures several iterations are all that can be afforded because of the need for a high solution density. With so few iterations, it is possible for two adjacent a_i to be in the same ratio (usually 2:1) as they were in the $\mathbf{a}$ vector. This weakness can be overcome by adding multiples of m′ (or m) to a subset of the a_i' (or a_i) that suffer from this problem. This decreases the solution density somewhat and accounts for our $1/10^4$ and $1/10^6$ estimates for two and three iterations when n = 100.

A small example is again helpful in illustrating the method. Starting with

$$\mathbf{a}'' = (1,2,4,8,17,35,68,142) \tag{29}$$

whose components sum to 277, we choose m′ = 291 and w′ = 176 (w'^{-1} = 167) resulting in

$$\mathbf{a}' = (176,61,122,244,82,49,37,257) \quad . \tag{30}$$

The second, third, and fourth components are in the ratio of 2:1, which can be hidden by adding m′ to the third component to obtain the new vector

$$\mathbf{a}' = (176,61,413,244,82,49,37,257) \tag{31}$$

whose components sum to 1319. Choosing m = 1343, w = 498 (w^{-1} = 925) yields

$$\mathbf{a} = (353,832,195,642,546,228,967,401) \tag{32}$$

whose components sum to 4164. The density of solutions using $\mathbf{a}$ is 256/4164 = 0.061 so approximately 16 attempts are needed on the average to obtain a signature. This agrees well with the estimated range of $n^2/4$ = 16 to n^2 = 64.

The density of solutions can be increased by restricting the y_k to lie near the middle of the range $(0, \Sigma \mathbf{a}_i)$, say between 1000 and 3000 in this example. The law of large numbers indicates that for most $\mathbf{x}$ the sum $\mathbf{a} * \mathbf{x}$ will lie in this range.

Merkle and Reeds [12] have developed another approach to obtaining high-density knapsacks. Empirical results indicate densities of approximately 20 percent when n = 100.

VII. Discussion

We have shown that it is possible to construct trapdoor knapsack problems and that information and signatures can be hidden in them for transmission over an insecure channel. Conventional cryptographic systems also can hide information and authenticators during transmission over an insecure channel but have the disadvantage that first a "key" must be exchanged via courier service or some other secure means. Also in conventional cryptography, the authenticator only prevents third party forgeries and cannot be used to settle disputes between the transmitter and receiver as to whether a message was actually sent.

We have not proved that it is computationally difficult for an opponent who does not know the trap information to solve the problem. Indeed, proofs of security are not yet available for normal cryptographic systems, and even the general knapsack problem has not been *proved* difficult to solve. The theory of computational complexity has not yet reached the level of development where such proofs are feasible. The best published algorithm for solving the knapsack problem is exponential, taking $O(2^{n/2})$ time and space [1]. Schroeppel [2] has devised an algorithm that takes $O(2^{n/2})$ time and $O(2^{n/4})$ space. Faith in the security of these systems must therefore rest on intuition and on the failure of concerted attempts to break them.

Attempts to break the system can start with simplified problems (e.g., assuming m is known). If even the most favored of certificational attacks is unsuccessful, then there is a margin of safety against cleverer, wealthier, or luckier opponents. Or, if the favored attack is successful, it helps establish where the security really must reside. For example, if knowledge of m allows solution, then an opponent's uncertainty about m must be large.

As noted, the techniques suggested in this paper generalize to x_i in the set $\{0,1,2,3,\cdots,N\}$. The advantages and weaknesses of such systems deserve further study. Further work with knapsack-based methods is in progress, and research oriented toward placing trapdoors in other combinatorial problems also appears promising.

Other techniques for securely communicating over an insecure channel have been proposed in [4], [8] and [13]. The method described in [4] involved exponentiation mod q. The techniques proposed in this paper appear to be significantly more secure and allow the direct transfer of information **x** generated by the transmitter. The technique proposed in [4] allows the transmitter and receiver to generate a common piece of information K which they then use as the key in a normal cryptographic system, but K cannot be predetermined by either party. Merkle's technique [8] was generalized to the first public key cryptosystem and is quite secure but computationally expensive. The current work describes a computationally efficient public key cryptosystem.

Recently, Rivest, Shamir, and Adleman [13] have proposed another public key cryptosystem that yields signatures more directly because the density of solutions in their problem is one. Their system also requires a smaller key (apparently 600 bits versus 20 kbits). Neither system's security has been adequately established, but when iterated, the trapdoor knapsack appears less likely to possess a chink in its armor. When used for obtaining signatures the trapdoor knapsack appears to be the weaker of the two. Both public key systems clearly need further certification and study.

References

[1] E. Horowitz and S. Sahni, "Computing partitions with applications to the knapsack problem," JACM, vol. 21, no. 2, pp. 277-292, Apr. 1974.

[2] R. Schroeppel, unpublished work.

[3] A. V. Aho, J. E. Hopcroft, and J. D. Ullman, The Design and Analysis of Computer Algorithms. Reading, MA: Addison-Wesley, 1974.

[4] W. Diffie and M. E. Hellman, "New directions in cryptography," IEEE Trans. Inform. Theory, vol. IT-22, Nov. 1976, pp. 644-654.

[5] O. H. Ibarra and C. E. Kim, "Fast approximation algorithms for the knapsack and sum of subset problems," JACM, vol. 22, no. 4, pp. 463-468, Oct. 1975.

[6] E. L. Lawler, "Fast approximation algorithms for knapsack problems," Electronics Research Laboratory, College of Eng. U.C. Berkeley Memorandum UCB/ERL M77/45 21, June 1977.

[7] S. C. Pohlig and M. E. Hellman, "An improved algorithm for computing logarithms over GF(P) and its cryptographic significance," IEEE Trans. Inform. Theory, vol. IT-24, pp. 106-110, Jan. 1978.

[8] R. Merkle, "Secure communications over insecure channels," Commun. ACM, vol. 21, no. 4, pp. 294-299.

[9] M. V. Wilkes, Time-Sharing Computer Systems. New York: Elsevier, 1972.

[10] A. Evans, Jr., W. Kantrowitz, and E. Weiss, "A user authentication system not requiring secrecy in the computer," Commun. ACM, vol. 17, no. 8, Aug. 1974, pp. 437-442.

[11] G. B. Purdy, "A high security log-in procedure," Commun. ACM, vol. 17, no. 8, Aug. 1974, pp. 442-445.

[12] R. Merkle and J. Reeds, unpublished work.

[13] R. L. Rivest, A. Shamir, and L. Adleman, "A method for obtaining digital signatures and public-key cryptosystems," Commun. ACM, vol. 21, no. 2, pp. 120-126, Feb. 1978.

[14] R. M. Karp, "Reducibility among combinatorial problems," in Complexity of Computer Computations, R. E. Miller and J. W. Thatcher, Eds., New York: Plenum, (1972), pp. 85-104.

Ronald L. Rivest, Adi Shamir,
Leonard M. Adleman

9. A Method for Obtaining Digital Signatures and Public Key Cryptosystems

Abstract

An encryption method is presented with the novel property that publicly revealing an encryption key does not thereby reveal the corresponding decryption key. This has two important consequences:

1. Couriers or other secure means are not needed to transmit keys, since a message can be enciphered using an encryption key publicly revealed by the intended recipient. Only he can decipher the message, since only he knows the corresponding decryption key.
2. A message can be "signed" using a privately held decryption key. Anyone can verify this signature using the corresponding publicly revealed encryption key. Signatures cannot be forged, and a signer cannot later deny the validity of his signature. This has obvious applications in "electronic mail" and "electronic funds transfer" systems. A message is encrypted by representing it as a number M, raising

This research was supported by National Science Foundation grant MCS76-14294, and the Office of Naval Research grant number N00014-67-A-0204-0063.

M to a publicly specified power e, and then taking the remainder when the result is divided by the publicly specified product, n, of two large secret prime numbers p and q. Decryption is similar; only a different, secret, power d is used, where $e * d \equiv 1(\text{mod}(p-1) * (q-1))$. The security of the system rests in part on the difficulty of factoring the published divisor, n.

I. Introduction

The era of "electronic mail" [10] may soon be upon us; we must ensure that two important properties of the current "paper mail" system are preserved: (a) messages are *private*, and (b) messages can be *signed*. We demonstrate in this paper how to build these capabilities into an electronic mail system.

At the heart of our proposal is a new encryption method. This method provides an implementation of a "public-key cryptosystem", an elegant concept invented by Diffie and Hellman [1]. Their article motivated our research, since they presented the concept but not any practical implementation of such a system. Readers familiar with [1] may wish to skip directly to Section V for a description of our method.

II. Public-Key Cryptosystems

In a "public-key cryptosystem" each user places in a public file an encryption procedure E. That is, the public file is a directory giving the encryption procedure of each user. The user keeps secret the details of his corresponding decryption procedure D. These procedures have the following four properties:

(a) Deciphering the enciphered form of a message M yields M. Formally,

$$D\big(E(M)\big) = M \quad . \tag{1}$$

(b) Both E and D are easy to compute.

(c) By publicly revealing E the user does not reveal an easy way to compute D. This means that in practice only he can decrypt messages encrypted with E, or compute D efficiently.

(d) If a message M is first deciphered and then enciphered, M is the result. Formally,

$$E\big(D(M)\big) = M \quad . \tag{2}$$

An encryption (or decryption) procedure typically consists of a *general method* and an *encryption key*. The general method, under control of the key, enciphers a message M to obtain the enciphered form of the message, called the *ciphertext* C. Everyone can use the same general method; the security of a given procedure will rest on the security of the key. Revealing an encryption algorithm then means revealing the key.

When the user reveals E he reveals a very *inefficient* method of computing D(C): testing all possible messages M until one such that E(M) = C is found. If property (c) is satisfied the number of such messages to test will be so large that this approach is impractical.

A function E satisfying (a)-(c) is a "trap-door one-way function;" if it also satisfies (d) it is a "trap-door one-way permutation." Diffie and Hellman [1] introduced the concept of trap-door one-way functions but did not present any examples. These functions are called "one-way" because they are easy to compute in one direction but (apparently) very difficult to compute in the other direction. They are called "trap-door" functions since the inverse functions are in fact easy to compute once certain private "trap-door" information is known. A trap-door one-way function which also satisfies (d) must be a permutation: every message is the ciphertext for some other message and every ciphertext is itself a permissible message. (The mapping is "one-to-one" and "onto"). Property (d) is needed only to implement "signatures".

The reader is encouraged to read Diffie and Hellman's excellent article [1] for further background, for elaboration of the concept of a public-key cryptosystem, and for a discussion of other problems in the area of cryptography. The ways in which a public-key cryptosystem can ensure privacy and enable "signatures" (described in Sections III and IV below) are also due to Diffie and Hellman.

For our scenarios we suppose that A and B (also known as Alice and Bob) are two users of a public-key cryptosystem. We will distinguish their encryption and decryption procedures with subscripts: E_A, D_A, E_B, D_B.

III. Privacy

Encryption is the standard means of rendering a communication private. The sender enciphers each message before transmitting it to the receiver. The receiver (but no unauthorized person) knows the appropriate deciphering function to apply to the received message to obtain the original message. An eavesdropper who hears the transmitted message hears only "garbage" (the ciphertext) which makes no sense to him since he does not know how to decrypt it.

The large volume of personal and sensitive information currently held in computerized data banks and transmitted over telephone lines makes encryption increasingly important. In recognition of the fact that efficient, high-quality encryption techniques are very much needed but are in short supply, the National Bureau of Standards has recently adopted a "Data Encryption Standard" [13,14], developed at IBM. The new standard does not have property (c), needed to implement a public-key cryptosystem.

All classical encryption methods (including the NBS standard) suffer from the "key distribution problem." The problem is that before a private communication can begin, *another* private transaction is necessary to distribute corresponding encryption and decryption keys to the sender and receiver, respectively. Typically a private courier is used to carry a key from the sender to the receiver. Such a practice is not feasible if an electronic mail system is to be rapid and inexpensive. A public-key cryptosystem needs no private couriers; the keys can be distributed over the insecure communications channel.

How can Bob send a private message M to Alice in a public-key cryptosystem? First, he retrieves E_A from the public file. Then he sends her the enciphered message $E_A(M)$. Alice deciphers the message by computing $D_A\left(E_A(M)\right) = M$. By property (c) of the public-key cryptosystem only she can decipher $E_A(M)$. She can encipher a private response with E_B, also available in the public file.

Observe that no private transactions between Alice and Bob are needed to establish private communication. The only "setup" required is that each user who wishes to receive private communications must place his enciphering algorithm in the public file.

Two users can also establish private communication over an insecure communications channel without consulting a public file. Each user sends his encryption key to the other. Afterwards all messages are enciphered with the encryption key of the recipient, as in the public-key system. An intruder listening in on the channel cannot decipher any messages, since it is not possible to derive the decryption keys from the encryption keys. (We assume that the intruder cannot modify or insert messages into the channel.) Ralph Merkle has developed another solution [5] to this problem.

A public-key cryptosystem can be used to "bootstrap" into a standard encryption scheme such as the NBS method. Once secure communications have been established, the first message transmitted can be a key to use in the NBS scheme to encode all following messages. This may be desirable if encryption with our method is slower than with the standard scheme. (The NBS scheme is probably somewhat faster if special-purpose hardware encryption devices are used; our scheme may be faster on a general-purpose computer since multiprecision arithmetic operations are simpler to implement than complicated bit manipulations.)

IV. Signatures

If electronic mail systems are to replace the existing paper mail system for business transactions, "signing" an electronic message must be possible. The recipient of a signed message has proof that the message originated from the sender. This quality is stronger than mere authentication (where the recipient can verify that the message came from the sender); the recipient can convince a "judge" that the signer sent the message. To do so, he must convince the judge that he did not forge the signed message himself! In an authentication problem the recipient does not worry about this possibility, since he only wants to satisfy *himself* that the message came from the sender.

An electronic signature must be *message*-dependent, as well as *signer*-dependent. Otherwise the recipient could modify the message before showing the message-signature pair to a judge. Or he could attach the signature to any message whatsoever, since it is impossible to detect electronic "cutting and pasting."

To implement signatures the public-key cryptosystem must be implemented with trap-door one-way permutations (i.e. have property (d)), since the decryption algorithm will be applied to unenciphered messages.

How can user Bob send Alice a "signed" message M in a public-key cryptosystem? He first computes his "signature" S for the message M using D_B:

$$S = D_B(M) \quad .$$

(Deciphering an unenciphered message "makes sense" by property (d) of a public-key cryptosystem: each message is the ciphertext for some other message.) He then encrypts S using E_A (for privacy), and sends the result $E_A(S)$ to Alice. He need not send M as well; it can be computed from S.

Alice first decrypts the ciphertext with D_A to obtain S. She knows who is the presumed sender of the signature (in this case, Bob); this can be given if necessary in plaintext attached to S. She then extracts the message with the encryption procedure of the sender, in this case E_B (available on the public file):

$$M = E_B(S) \quad .$$

She now possesses a message-signature pair (M,S) with properties similar to those of a signed paper document.

Bob cannot later deny having sent Alice this message, since no one else could have created $S = D_B(M)$. Alice can convince a "judge" that $E_B(S) = M$, so she has proof that Bob signed the document.

Clearly Alice cannot modify M to a different version M', since then she would have to create the corresponding signature $S' = D_B(M')$ as well.

Therefore Alice has received a message "signed" by Bob, which she can "prove" that he sent, but which she cannot modify. (Nor can she forge his signature for any other message.)

An electronic checking system could be based on a signature system such as the above. It is easy to imagine an encryption device in your home terminal allowing you to sign checks that get sent by electronic mail to the payee. It would only be necessary to include a unique check number in each check so that even if the payee copies the check the bank will only honor the first version it sees.

Another possibility arises if encryption devices can be made fast enough: it will be possible to have a telephone conversation in which every word spoken is signed by the encryption device before transmission.

When encryption is used for signatures as above, it is important that the encryption device not be "wired in" between the terminal (or computer) and the communications channel, since a message may have to be successively enciphered with several keys. It is perhaps more natural to view the encryption device as a "hardware subroutine" that can be executed as needed.

We have assumed above that each user can always access the public file reliably. In a "computer network" this might be difficult; an "intruder" might forge messages purporting to be from the public file. The user would like to be sure that he actually obtains the encryption procedure of his desired correspondent and not, say, the encryption procedure of the intruder. This danger disappears if the public file "signs" each message it sends to a user. The user can check the signature with the public file's encryption algorithm E_{PF}. The problem of "looking up" E_{PF} itself in the public file is avoided by giving each user a description of E_{PF} when he first shows up (in person) to join the public-key cryptosystem and to deposit his public encryption procedure. He then stores this description rather than ever looking it up again. The need for a courier between every pair of users has thus been replaced by the requirement for a single secure meeting between each user and the public-file manager when the user joins the system. Another solution is to give each user, when he signs up, a book (like a telephone directory) containing all the encryption keys of users in the system.

V. Our Encryption and Decryption Methods

To encrypt a message M with our method, using a public encryption key (e,n), proceed as follows. (Here e and n are a pair of positive integers.)

First, represent the message as an integer between 0 and n - 1. (Break a long message into a series of blocks, and represent each block as such an integer.) Use any standard representation. The purpose here is not to encrypt the message but only to get it into the numeric form necessary for encryption.

Then, encrypt the message by raising it to the eth power modulo n. That is, the result (the ciphertext C) is the remainder when M^e is divided by n.

To decrypt the ciphertext, raise it to another power d, again modulo n. The encryption and decryption algorithms E and D are thus:

$$C \equiv E(M) \equiv M^e \pmod{n}, \text{ for a message } M \ .$$
$$D(C) \equiv C^d \pmod{n}, \text{ for a ciphertext } C \ .$$

Note that encryption does not increase the size of a message; both the message and the ciphertext are integers in the range 0 to n - 1.

The *encryption key* is thus the pair of positive integers (e,n). Similarly, the *decryption key* is the pair of positive integers (d,n). Each user makes his encryption key public, and keeps the corresponding decryption key private. (These integers should properly be subscripted as in n_A, e_A, and d_A, since each user has his own set. However, we will only consider a typical set, and will omit the subscripts.)

How should you choose your encryption and decryption keys, if you want to use our method?

You first compute n as the product of two primes p and q:

$$n = p * q \quad .$$

These primes are very large, "random" primes. Although you will make n public, the factors p and q will be effectively hidden from everyone else due to the enormous difficulty of factoring n. This also hides the way d can be derived from e.

You then pick the integer d to be a large, random integer which is relatively prime to (p-1) * (q-1). That is, check that d satisfies:

$$\gcd\left(d,\ (p-1) * (q-1)\right) = 1$$

("gcd" means "greatest common divisor").

The integer e is finally computed from p, q, and d to be the "multiplicative inverse" of d, modulo (p-1) * (q-1). Thus we have

$$e * d \equiv 1 \left(\bmod\ (p-1) * (q-1)\right) \quad .$$

We prove in the next section that this guarantees that (1) and (2) hold, i.e. that E and D are inverse permutations. Section VII shows how each of the above operations can be done efficiently.

The aforementioned method should not be confused with the "exponentiation" technique presented by Diffie and Hellman [1] to solve the key distribution problem. Their technique permits two users to determine a key in common to be used in a normal cryptographic system. It is not based on a trap-door one-way permutation. Pohlig and Hellman [8] study a scheme related to ours, where exponentiation is done modulo a prime number.

VI. The Underlying Mathematics

We demonstrate the correctness of the deciphering algorithm using an identity due to Euler and Fermat [7]: for any integer (message) M which is relatively prime to n,

$$M^{\varphi(n)} \equiv 1 \pmod{n} \quad . \tag{3}$$

Here $\varphi(n)$ is the Euler totient function giving the number of positive integers less than n which are relatively prime to n. For prime numbers p,

$$\varphi(p) = p-1 \quad .$$

In our case, we have by elementary properties of the totient function [7]:

$$\begin{aligned} \varphi(n) &= \varphi(p) * \varphi(q) \quad , \\ &= (p-1) * (q-1) \\ &= n - (p+q) + 1 \quad . \end{aligned} \tag{4}$$

Since d is relatively prime to $\varphi(n)$, it has a multiplicative inverse e in the ring of integers modulo $\varphi(n)$:

$$e * d \equiv 1 \left(\bmod\ \varphi(n)\right) \quad . \tag{5}$$

We now prove that equations (1) and (2) hold (that is, that deciphering works correctly if e and d are chosen as above). Now

$$\begin{aligned} D\big(E(M)\big) &\equiv \big(E(M)\big)^d \equiv (M^e)^d \equiv M^{e*d} \pmod{n} \\ E\big(D(M)\big) &\equiv \big(D(M)\big)^e \equiv (M^d)^e \equiv M^{e*d} \pmod{n} \end{aligned}$$

and

$$M^{e*d} \equiv M^{k*\varphi(n)+1} \pmod{n} \quad \text{(for some integer } k) \ .$$

From (3) we see that for all M such that p does not divide M

$$M^{p-1} \equiv 1 \pmod{p}$$

and since (p-1) divides $\varphi(n)$

$$M^{k*\varphi(n)+1} \equiv M \pmod{p} \quad .$$

This is trivially true when $M \equiv 0 \pmod{p}$, so that this equality actually holds for *all* M. Arguing similarly for q yields

$$M^{k*\varphi(n)+1} \equiv M \pmod{q} \quad .$$

Together these last two equations imply that for all M,

$$M^{e*d} \equiv M^{k*\varphi(n)+1} \equiv M \pmod{n} \quad .$$

This implies (1) and (2) for all M, $0 \leq M < n$. Therefore E and D are inverse permutations. (We thank Rich Schroeppel for suggesting the above improved version of the authors' previous proof.)

VII. Algorithms

To show that our method is practical, we describe an efficient algorithm for each required operation.

A. How to Encrypt and Decrypt Efficiently

Computing $M^e \pmod{n}$ requires at most $2 * \log_2(e)$ multiplications and $2 * \log_2(e)$ divisions using the following procedure (decryption can be performed similarly using d instead of e):

Step 1. Let $e_k e_{k-1} \cdots e_1 e_0$ be the binary representation of e.

Step 2. Set the variable C to 1.

Step 3. Repeat steps 3a and 3b for $i = k, k-1, \cdots, 0$:

Step 3a. Set C to the remainder of C^2 when divided by n.

Step 3b. If $e_i = 1$, then set C to the remainder of C * M when divided by n.

Step 4. Halt. Now C is the encrypted form of M.

This procedure is called "exponentiation by repeated squaring and multiplication." This procedure is half as good as the best; more efficient procedures are known. Knuth [3] studies this problem in detail.

The fact that the enciphering and deciphering are identical leads to a simple implementation. (The whole operation can be implemented on a few special-purpose integrated circuit chips.)

A high-speed computer can encrypt a 200-digit message M in a few seconds; special-purpose hardware would be much faster. The encryption time per block increases no faster than the cube of the number of digits in n.

B. How to Find Large Prime Numbers

Each user must (privately) choose two large random prime numbers p and q to create his own encryption and decryption keys. These numbers must be large so that it is not computationally feasible for anyone to factor n = p * q. (Remember that n, but not p or q, will be in the public file.) We recommend using 100-digit (decimal) prime numbers p and q, so that n has 200 digits.

To find a 100-digit "random" prime number, generate (odd) 100-digit random numbers until a prime number is found. By the prime number theorem [7], about $(\ln 10^{100})/2 = 115$ numbers will be tested before a prime is found.

To test a large number b for primality we recommend the elegant "probabilistic" algorithm due to Solovay and Strassen [12]. It picks a random number a from a uniform distribution on $\{1,\cdots,b-1\}$, and tests whether

$$\gcd(a,b) = 1 \quad \text{and } J(a,b) \equiv a^{(b-1)/2} \pmod{b} \quad , \tag{6}$$

where J(a,b) is the Jacobi symbol [7]. If b is prime (6) is always true. If b is composite (6) will be false with probability at least 1/2. If (6) holds for 100 randomly chosen values of a then b is almost certainly prime; there is a (negligible) chance of one in 2^{100} that b is composite. Even if a composite were accidentally used in our system, the receiver would probably detect this by noticing that decryption didn't work correctly. When b is odd, $a \leq b$, and gcd(a,b) = 1, the Jacobi symbol J(a,b) has a value in $\{-1,1\}$ and can be efficiently computed by the program:

$$
\begin{aligned}
J(a,b) = \ & \textbf{if } a = 1 \textbf{ then } 1 \textbf{ else} \\
& \textbf{if } a \text{ is even } \textbf{then } J(a/2,b) * (-1)^{(b^2-1)/8} \\
& \textbf{else } J\big(b \pmod{a},\ a\big) * (-1)^{(a-1)*(b-1)/4}
\end{aligned}
$$

(The computations of J(a,b) and gcd(a,b) can be nicely combined, too.) Note that this algorithm does *not* test a number for primality by trying to factor it. Other efficient procedures for testing a large number for primality are given in [6,9,11].

To gain additional protection against sophisticated factoring algorithms, p and q should differ in length by a few digits, both (p-1) and (q-1) should contain large prime factors, and gcd(p-1, q-1) should be small. The latter condition is easily checked.

To find a prime number p such that (p-1) has a large prime factor, generate a large random prime number u, then let p be the first prime in the sequence $i * u + 1$, for $i = 2,4,6,\cdots$. (This shouldn't take too long.) Additional security is provided by ensuring that (u-1) also has a large prime factor.

A high-speed computer can determine in several seconds whether a 100-digit number is prime, and can find the first prime after a given point in a minute or two.

Another approach to finding large prime numbers is to take a number of known factorization, add one to it, and test the result for primality. If a prime p is found it is possible to *prove* that it really is prime by using the factorization of p - 1. We omit a discussion of this since the probabilistic method is adequate.

C. How to Choose d

It is very easy to choose a number d which is relatively prime to $\varphi(n)$. For example, any prime number greater than max(p,q) will do. It is important that d should be chosen from a large enough set so that a cryptanalyst cannot find it by direct search.

D. How to Compute e from d and $\varphi(n)$

To compute e, use the following variation of Euclid's algorithm for computing the greatest common divisor of $\varphi(n)$ and d. (See exercise 4.5.2.15 in [3].) Calculate $\gcd(\varphi(n),d)$ by computing a series $x_0, x_1, x_2, \cdots$, where $x_0 = \varphi(n)$, $x_1 = d$, and $x_{i+1} \equiv x_{i-1} (\text{mod } x_i)$, until an x_k equal to 0 is found. Then $\gcd(x_0,x_1) = x_{k-1}$. Compute for each x_i numbers a_i and b_i such that $x_i = a_i * x_0 + b_i * x_1$. If $x_{k-1} = 1$ then b_{k-1} is the multiplicative inverse of x_1 (mod x_0). Since k will be less than $2 * \log_2(n)$, this computation is very rapid.

If e turns out to be less than $\log_2(n)$, start over by choosing another value of d. This guarantees that every encrypted message (except M = 0 or M = 1) undergoes some "wrap-around" (reduction modulo n).

VIII. A Small Example

Consider the case p = 47, q = 59, n = p * q = 47 * 59 = 2773, and d = 157. Then $\varphi(2773) = 46 * 58 = 2668$, and e can be computed as follows:

$$\begin{aligned} x_0 &= 2668, & a_0 &= 1, & b_0 &= 0, \\ x_1 &= 157, & a_1 &= 0, & b_1 &= 1, \\ x_2 &= 156, & a_2 &= 1, & b_2 &= -16 \text{ (since } 2668 = 157 * 16 + 156\text{)}, \\ x_3 &= 1, & a_3 &= -1, & b_3 &= 17 \text{ (since } 157 = 1 * 156 + 1\text{)}. \end{aligned}$$

Therefore e = 17, the multiplicative inverse (mod 2668) of d = 157.

With n = 2773 we can encode two letters per block, substituting a two-digit number for each letter: blank = 00, A = 01, B = 02, ···, Z = 26. Thus the message

ITS ALL GREEK TO ME

(Julius Caesar, I, ii, 288, paraphrased) is encoded:

0920 1900 0112 1200 0718 0505 1100 2015 0013 0500

Since e = 10001 in binary, the first block (M = 920) is enciphered:

$$M^{17} = \left(\left(\left(\left((1)^2 * M\right)^2\right)^2\right)^2\right)^2 * M \equiv 948 \pmod{2773} \quad .$$

The whole message is enciphered as:

0948 2342 1084 1444 2663 2390 0778 0774 0219 1655 .

The reader can check that deciphering works: $948^{157} \equiv 920 \pmod{2773}$, etc.

IX. Security of the Method: Cryptanalytic Approaches

Since no techniques exist to *prove* that an encryption scheme is secure, the only test available is to see whether anyone can think of a way to break it. The NBS standard was "certified" this way; seventeen manyears at IBM were spent fruitlessly trying to break that shceme. Once a method has successfully resisted such a concerted attack it may for practical purposes be considered secure. (Actually there is some controversy concerning the security of the NBS method [2].)

We show in the next sections that all the obvious approaches for breaking our system are at least as difficult as factoring n. While factoring large numbers is not provably difficult, it is a well-known problem that has been worked on for the last three hundred years by many famous mathematicians. Fermat (1601?-1665) and Legendre (1752-1833) developed factoring algorithms; some of today's more efficient algorithms are based on the work of Legendre. As we shall see in the next section, however, no one has yet found an algorithm which can factor a 200-digit number in a reasonable amount of time. We conclude that our system has already been partially "certified" by these previous efforts to find efficient factoring algorithms.

In the following sections we consider ways a cryptanalyst might try to determine the secret decryption key from the publicly revealed encryption key. We do not consider ways of protecting the decryption key from theft; the usual physical security methods should suffice. (For example, the encryption device could be a separate device which could also be used to *generate* the encryption and decryption keys, such that the decryption key is never printed out (even for its owner) but only used to decrypt messages. The device could erase the decryption key if it was tampered with.)

A. Factoring n

Factoring n would enable an enemy cryptanalyst to "break" our method. The factors of n enable him to compute $\varphi(n)$ and thus d. Fortunately, factoring a number seems to be much more difficult than determining whether it is prime or composite.

A large number of factoring algorithms exist. Knuth [3, Section 4.5.4] gives an excellent presentation of many of them. Pollard [9] presents an algorithm which factors a number n in time $O(n^{1/4})$.

The fastest factoring algorithm known to the authors is due to Richard Schroeppel (unpublished); it can factor n in approximately

$$\exp\left(\text{sqrt}\left(\ln(n) * \ln\left(\ln(n)\right)\right)\right) = n^{\text{sqrt}(\ln(\ln(n))/\ln(n))}$$
$$= \left(\ln(n)\right)^{\text{sqrt}(\ln(n)/\ln(\ln(n)))}$$

steps (here ln denotes the natural logarithm function). Table I gives the number of operations needed to factor n with Schroeppel's method, and the time required if each operation uses one microsecond, for various lengths of the number n (in decimal digits):

We recommend that n be about 200 digits long. Longer or shorter lengths can be used depending on the relative importance of encryption speed and security in the application at hand. An 80-digit n provides moderate security against an

Table I.

Digits	Number of operations	Time
50	1.4×10^{10}	3.9 hours
75	9.0×10^{12}	104 days
100	2.3×10^{15}	74 years
200	1.2×10^{23}	3.8×10^{9} years
300	1.5×10^{29}	4.9×10^{15} years
500	1.3×10^{39}	4.2×10^{25} years

attack using current technology; using 200 digits provides a margin of safety against future developments. This flexibility to choose a key-length (and thus a level of security) to suit a particular application is a feature not found in many of the previous encryption schemes (such as the NBS scheme).

B. Computing $\varphi(n)$ Without Factoring n

If a cryptanalyst could compute $\varphi(n)$ then he could break the system by computing d as the multiplicative inverse of e modulo $\varphi(n)$ (using the procedure of Section VII D).

We argue that this approach is no easier than factoring n since it enables the cryptanalyst to easily factor n using $\varphi(n)$. This approach to factoring n has not turned out to be practical.

How can n be factored using $\varphi(n)$? First, $(p+q)$ is obtained from n and $\varphi(n) = n - (p+q) + 1$. Then $(p-q)$ is the square root of $(p+q)^2 - 4n$. Finally, q is half the difference of $(p+q)$ and $(p-q)$.

Therefore breaking our system by computing $\varphi(n)$ is no easier than breaking our system by factoring n. (This is why n must be composite; $\varphi(n)$ is trivial to compute if n is prime.)

C. Determining d Without Factoring n or Computing $\varphi(n)$

Of course, d should be chosen from a large enough set so that a direct search for it is unfeasible.

We argue that computing d is no easier for a cryptanalyst than factoring n, since once d is known n could be factored easily. This approach to factoring has also not turned out to be fruitful.

A knowledge of d enables n to be factored as follows. Once a cryptanalyst knows d he can calculate $e * d - 1$, which is a multiple of $\varphi(n)$. Miller [6] has shown that n can be factored using any multiple of $\varphi(n)$. Therefore if n is large a cryptanalyst should not be able to determine d any easier than he can factor n.

A cryptanalyst may hope to find a d′ which is equivalent to the d secretly held by a user of the public-key cryptosystem. If such values d′ were common then a brute-force search could break the system. However, all such d′ differ by the least common multiple of (p-1) and (q-1), and finding one enables n to be factored. (In (3) and (5), $\varphi(n)$ can be replaced by lcm(p-1, q-1).) Finding any such d′ is therefore as difficult as factoring n.

D. Computing D in Some Other Way

Although this problem of "computing e^{th} roots modulo n without factoring n" is not a well-known difficult problem like factoring, we feel reasonably confident that it is computationally intractable. It may be possible to prove that any general method of breaking our scheme yields an efficient factoring algorithm. This would establish that any way of breaking our scheme must be as difficult as factoring. We have not been able to prove this conjecture, however.

Our method should be certified by having the above conjecture of intractability withstand a concerted attempt to disprove it. The reader is challenged to find a way to "break" our method.

X. Avoiding "Reblocking" when Encrypting a Signed Message

A signed message may have to be "reblocked" for encryption since the signature n may be larger than the encryption n (every user has his own n). This can be avoided as follows. A threshold value h is chosen (say $h = 10^{199}$) for the public-key cryptosystem. Every user maintains two public (e,n) pairs, one for enciphering and one for signature-verification, where every signature n is less than h, and every enciphering n is greater than h. Reblocking to encipher a signed message is then unnecessary; the message is blocked according to the transmitter's signature n.

Another solution uses a technique given in [4]. Each user has a single (e,n) pair where n is between h and 2h, where h is a threshold as above. A message is encoded as a number less than h and enciphered as before, except that if the ciphertext is greater than h, it is repeatedly re-enciphered until it is less than h. Similarly for decryption the ciphertext is repeatedly deciphered to obtain a value less than h. If n is near h re-enciphering will be infrequent. (Infinite looping is not possible, since at worst a message is enciphered as itself.)

XI. Conclusions

We have proposed a method for implementing a public-key cryptosystem whose security rests in part on the difficulty of factoring large numbers. If the security of our method proves to be adequate, it permits secure communications to be established without the use of couriers to carry keys, and it also permits one to "sign" digitized documents.

The security of this system needs to be examined in more detail. In particular, the difficulty of factoring large numbers should be examined very closely. The reader is urged to find a way to "break" the system. Once the method has withstood all attacks for a sufficient length of time it may be used with a reasonable amount of confidence.

Our encryption function is the only candidate for a "trap-door one-way permutation" known to the authors. It might be desirable to find other examples, to provide alternative implementations should the security of our system turn out someday to be inadequate. There are surely also many new applications to be discovered for these functions.

Acknowledgments

We thank Martin Hellman, Richard Schroeppel, Abraham Lempel, and Roger Needham for helpful discussions, and Wendy Glasser for her assistance in preparing the initial manuscript. Xerox PARC provided support and some marvelous text-editing facilities for preparing the final manuscript.

References

1. Diffie, W., and Hellman, M. New directions in cryptography. IEEE Trans. Inform. Theory IT-22, 6 (Nov. 1976), 644-654.

2. Diffie, W., and Hellman, M. Exhaustive cryptanalysis of the NBS data encryption standard. Computer 10 (June 1977), 74-84.

3. Knuth, D. E. The Art of Computer Programming, Vol. 2: Seminumerical Algorithms. Addison-Wesley, Reading, Mass., 1969.

4. Levine, J., and Brawley, J. V. Some cryptographic applications of permutation polynomials. Cryptologia 1 (Jan. 1977), 76-92.

5. Merkle, R. Secure communications over an insecure channel. Submitted to Comm. ACM.

6. Miller, G. L. Riemann's hypothesis and tests for primality. Proc. Seventh Annual ACM Symp. on the Theory of Comptng. Alguquerque, New Mex., May 1975, pp. 234-239; extended vers. available as Res. Rep. CS-75-27, Dept. of Comptr. Sci., U. of Waterloo, Waterloo, Ont., Canada, Oct. 1975.

7. Niven, I., and Zuckerman, H. S. An Introduction to the Theory of Numbers, Wiley, New York, 1972.

8. Pohlig, S. C., and Hellman, M. E. An improved algorithm for computing logarithms over GF(p) and its cryptographic significance. To appear in IEEE Trans. Inform. Theory, 1978.

9. Pollard, J. M. Theorems on factorization and primality testing. Proc. Camb. Phil. Soc. 76 (1974), 521-528.

10. Potter, R. J., Electronic mail. Science 195, 4283 (March 1977), 1160-1164.

11. Rabin, M. O., Probabilistic algorithms. In Algorithms and Complexity, J. F. Traub, Ed., Academic Press, New York, 1976, pp. 21-40.

12. Solovay, R., and Strassen, V. A fast Monte-Carlo test for primality. SIAM J. Comptng. 6 (March 1977), 84-85.

13. Federal Register, Vol. 40, No. 52, March 17, 1975.

14. Federal Register, Vol. 40, No. 149, August 1, 1975.

Gustavus J. Simmons

10. Symmetric and Asymmetric Encryption

Abstract

All cryptosystems currently in use are symmetric in the sense that they require the transmitter and receiver to share, in secret, either the same piece of information (key) or one of a pair of related keys easily computed from each other; the key is used in the encryption process to introduce uncertainty to an unauthorized receiver. Not only is an asymmetric encryption system one in which the transmitter and receiver keys are different, but in addition it is computationally infeasible to compute at least one from the other. Asymmetric systems make it possible to authenticate messages whose contents must be revealed to an opponent or allow a transmitter whose key has been compromised to communicate in privacy to a receiver whose key has been kept secret -- neither of which is possible using a symmetric cryptosystem.

This paper opens with a brief discussion of encryption principles and then proceeds to a comprehensive discussion of the asymmetric encryption/decryption channel and its application in secure communications.

This article was sponsored by the U. S. Department of Energy under Contract DE-AC04-76DP00789.

Introduction

The object of secure communications has been to provide privacy or secrecy, i.e., to hide the contents of a publicly exposed message from unauthorized recipients. In contemporary commercial and diplomatic applications, however, it is frequently of equal or even greater concern that the receiver be able to verify that the message has not been modified during transmission or that it is not a counterfeit from an unauthorized transmitter. In at least one important class of problems message authentication is needed at the same time that the message itself is revealed.

In this paper secure communications are discussed with emphasis on applications that cannot be satisfactorily handled by present cryptographic techniques. Fortunately, an entirely new concept -- the asymmetric encryption/decryption channel -- solves the new requirements in secure communications. For perspective, the reader should keep in mind that all current cryptosystems are *symmetric* in the sense that either the same piece of information (key) is held in secret by both communicants, or else that each communicant holds one from a pair of related keys where either key is easily derivable from the other. These secret keys are used in the encryption process to introduce uncertainty (to the unauthorized receiver), which can be removed in the process of decryption by an authorized receiver using his copy of the key or the "inverse key." This means, of course, that if a key is compromised, further secure communications are impossible with that key. The new cryptosystems are *asymmetric* in the sense that the transmitter and receiver hold different keys at least one of which it is computationally infeasible to derive from the other.

It is possible to communicate in secrecy and to "sign" digital messages using either symmetric or asymmetric techniques if both the receiver and transmitter keys can be secret. One of these functions can be accomplished with an asymmetric system even though the transmitter or the receiver key has been revealed. It is also possible to communicate privately without a prior covert exchange of keys and to authenticate messages even when the contents cannot be concealed from an opponent -- neither of which is possible with a symmetric cryptosystem. The current revolution in secure communications is based on the ability to secure communications even when one terminal (and the key) is located in a physically unsecured installation.

1. Classical Cryptography

Classical cryptography seeks to prevent an unauthorized (unintended) recipient from determining the content of the message. In this section we illustrate the concepts of all cryptosystems, such as key, stream or block ciphers, and unicity point. A more detailed account can be found in the paper by Lempel [Lemp79] and in Kahn's encyclopedic The Codebreakers, the Story of Secret Writing [Kahn67].

A primitive distinction among cryptosystems is the structural classification into stream and block ciphers. The plaintext message is a sequence of symbols from some alphabet $\mathcal{C}$ (letters or numbers). A stream cipher operates on the plaintext symbol by symbol to produce a sequence of cipher symbols from an alphabet C. (C and $\mathcal{C}$ are frequently the same.) Symbolically, if π is a nonsingular mapping $\pi : \mathcal{C} \to C$, and M is a plaintext message

$$M = (a_1 a_2 \cdots a_k | a_i \in \mathcal{C}) \quad ,$$

then the stream cipher $C = \pi(M)$ is given by

$$C = \left(\pi(a_1), \pi(a_2), \cdots, \pi(a_k) | \pi(a_i) \in C\right) \quad .$$

The mapping π is commonly a function of previous inputs -- as in the rotor cryptomachines of the World War II period. The various versions of Vigenére encryption to be discussed shortly are all examples of stream ciphers, some of which use a fixed mapping and others, such as the running key and autokey systems, a usage-dependent mapping.

In a block cipher a block of symbols from $\mathcal{G}$ is operated on jointly by the encryption algorithm, so that in general one may view a block cipher as a nonsingular[1] mapping from the set of plaintext n-tuples $\mathcal{G}^n$ into the set of cipher n-tuples $\mathcal{C}^n$. For cryptosystems which use the same key repeatedly, block ciphers are cryptographically stronger than stream ciphers. Consequently, most contemporary cryptosystems are block ciphers, although one-time key systems are used in applications where the very highest security is required. Examples of block ciphers are the Playfair digraph substitution technique, the Hill linear transformation scheme, and the NBS Data Encryption Standard (DES). The distinction between block and stream ciphers is more apparent than real since a block cipher on n-tuples from $\mathcal{G}$ is equivalent to a stream cipher over the enlarged alphabet $\mathcal{G}^n$.

Since much of the discussion relies on the concept of a "key" in the cryptosystem, we shall present several examples that illustrate keys and possible attacks to discover them.

In the most general terms possible, an encryption system must combine two elements: some information -- called the *key* -- known only to the authorized communicants, and an *algorithm* which operates on this key and the message (plaintext) to produce the cipher. The authorized receiver, knowing the key, must be able to recover the message (decrypt the cipher); an unauthorized receiver should not be able to deduce either the message or the unknown key. The key as defined here is very general: It is the total equivocation of

---

[1]Nonsingular simply means that every cipher decrypts to a unique message. In Section 6.2 an example of a singular cryptomapping is described.

everything that is kept secret from an opposing cryptanalyst. By this definition, a key can be much longer than the bit stream serving as the key in some cryptodevices.

The encryption algorithm must be so constructed that even if it becomes known to the opponent, it gives no help in determining either the plaintext messages or the key. This principle, first formulated by Kerchoffs in 1883, is now universally assumed in determining the security of cryptosystems.

Preprocessing a text by encoding into some other set of symbols or symbol groups by an unvarying rule is not considered to be a part of the encryption process, even though the preprocessing may complicate the cryptanalyst's task. For example, The Acme Commercial Code [Acme23] replaces entire phrases and sentences by five-letter groups; the preprocessed text EJEHS OHAOR CZUPA, which is derived from (BUDDY) (CAN YOU SPARE) ((A) DIME(S)), would be as baffling to the cryptanalyst as a cipher. Continued use of fixed preprocessing codes, however, destroys this apparent cryptosecurity, which is therefore considered to be nonexistent from the beginning. Common operations which compress text by deleting superfluous symbols or expand text with null symbols are considered to be part of the encoding of the text rather than part of the encryption process.

The encryption process itself consists of two primary operations and their combinations, *substitution* and *transposition.*[2] A substitution cipher or *cryptogram* simply replaces each plaintext symbol by a cipher symbol; the key specifies the mapping. An example is the Caesar cipher, in which each letter is replaced by the letter occurring k places later in the alphabet (considered cyclically); when k = 3,

---

[2]Kahn [Kahn67, p. 764] has analogized substitution and transposition ciphers with continuous and batch manufacturing processes, respectively.

COMPUTING SURVEYS = FRPSXWLQJ VXUYHBV .

Simple transposition permutes symbols in the plaintext. The permutation is the key. For example, if the permutation (15327468)[3] is applied to the two blocks of eight symbols above,

COMPUTING SURVEYS = NMUICPOTS UVYGRSE .

In either of these simple cases the frequency of occurrence of symbols is unaffected by the encryption operation. The cryptanalyst can get a good start toward breaking the code by a frequency analysis of cipher symbols [Kull76]. In secure systems complicated usage-dependent combinations of the two primitive encryption operations are used to cause all cipher symbols to occur with equal frequency.

It might seem that such simple systems would offer reasonable cryptosecurity since there are $26! \approx 4 \times 10^{26}$ substitutions possible on the 26 alphabetic characters in the first case and n! permutations on n-symbol blocks in the second. But the redundancy of English (indeed, any natural language) is so great that the $\log_2(26!) \approx 88.4$ bits of equivocation introduced by the encryption algorithm can be resolved by a cryptanalyst, using frequency of occurrence counts on symbols, with approximately 25 symbols of cipher text! This illustrates how deceptive the appearance of large numbers of choices to the cryptanalyst can be in judging the cryptosecurity of a cryptosystem.

An obvious means of strengthening substitution ciphers is to use not one but several monoalphabetic substitutions, with the key specifying which substitution is to be used for each symbol of the cipher. Such systems are known as polyalphabetics. The best known are the simple Vigenére ciphers

[3]This notation means: move the first symbol to the fifth place, the fifth symbol to the third place, the third symbol to the second place, and so on.

wherein the substitutions are taken as the mod 26 sum of a symbol of the message m_i and a symbol of the key k_i, with the convention A = 0,···,Z = 25. Depending on the complexity of the substitution rule (key) chosen, the equivocation of such a Vigenére-type system can be made as great as desired, as we see later in examining the random key Vernam-Vigenére system. The following examples illustrate how the key complexity can affect the security of a cryptosystem.

In the simplest Vigenére-type systems, the key is a word or phrase repeated as many times as necessary to encrypt the message; for example, if the key is COVER and the message is THE MATHEMATICS OF SECRECY, the resulting cipher is

```
Message  THE MATHEMATICS OF SECRECY
Key      COV ERCOVERCOVE RC OVERCOV
Cipher   VVZ RQVVZRQVWXW FH GZGIGQT  .
```

Kasiski's general solution of repeated key Vigenére ciphers starts from the fact that like pairings of message and key symbols produce the same cipher symbols; these repetitions are recognizable to the cryptanalyst [Kahn67]. The example above shows the group VVZRQ repeated twice; the length of the repeated group reveals that the key length is five. The cipher symbols would then be partitioned into five monoalphabets each of which is solved as a substitution cipher.

To avoid the problems of the preceding example, one can use a nonrepeating text for the key. The result is called a running-key Vigenére cipher. The running key prevents the periodicity exploited by the Kasiski solution. However, there are two basic types of solution available to the cryptanalyst in this case [Kahn66]. One can apply statistical analysis by assuming that both cipher text and key have the same frequency distributions of symbols. For example, E encrypted with E occurs with a frequency of ≈ 0.0169 and T by T occurs only half as often. A much longer segment of cipher test is required to decrypt a running-key Vigenére cipher;

however, the methods, based on recurrence of like events, are similar.

The other technique for attacking running-key ciphers is the so-called *probable word* method in which the cryptanalyst "subtracts" from the cipher words that are considered likely to occur in the text until fragments of sensible key text are recovered; these are then expanded using either of the two techniques just discussed. The vital point is that although the equivocation in the running text can be made as large as desired, the redundancy in the language is so high that the number of bits of information communicated per bit of cipher exceeds the rate at which equivocation is introduced by the running key. Therefore, given sufficient cipher text, the cryptanalyst will eventually have enough information to solve the cipher.

The most important of all key variants to the Vigenére system was proposed in 1818 by the American engineer G. S. Vernam [Vern26]. Messages for transmission over the AT&T teletype system were at that time encoded in Baudot code, a binary code consisting of marks and spaces. Vernam recognized that if a random sequence of marks and spaces were added mod 2 to the message, then all of the frequency information, inter-symbol correlation, and periodicity, on which earlier successful methods of attack against various Vigenére systems had been based, would be totally lost to the cryptanalyst. In this judgment Vernam's intuition was absolutely right, as would be proved two decades later by another AT&T scientist, Claude Shannon [Shan49]. Vernam proposed to introduce uncertainty at the same rate at which it was removed by redundancy among symbols of the message. Unfortunately, this ideal requires exchanging impractical amounts of key in advance of communication, i.e., one symbol of key must be provided for every symbol of message. In Vernam's invention the keys were made up in the form of punched paper tapes which were read automatically as each symbol was typed at the keyboard of a teletypewriter and encrypted "on line" for transmission. An inverse operation at the receiving teletype decrypted the cipher using a copy of the tape. Vernam at first thought that a short random key could safely be used over and over; however, the resulting periodicity of the key permits a simple Kasiski-type solution. A second proposed solution was to compute a key of n_1n_2 bits in length by forming the logical sum, bit by bit, of two shorter key tapes of relatively prime lengths n_1 and n_2, so that the resulting key stream would not repeat until n_1n_2 bits of key had been generated. This form of Vernam system was used for a time by the U.S. Army.

The greatest contribution of the two-tape Vernam system came from its successful cryptanalysis, which led to the recognition of the unconditional cryptosecurity of one-time keys or pads. Major J. O. Mauborgne of the U.S. Army Signal Corps showed that cipher produced from key generated by the linear combination of two or more short tapes could be successfully analyzed by techniques essentially the same as those used against running-key systems. The unavoidable conclusion was that the Vernam-Vigenère system with either a repeating single key tape or with linear combinations of repeating short tapes to form a long key sequence were both insecure. The truly significant conclusion was arrived at by Friedman and Mauborgne: The key in an unconditionally secure stream cipher[4] must be *incoherent* (the uncertainty, or entropy, of each key symbol must be at least as great as the average information content per symbol of the message). Such a crypto-

[4]This condition applies to both block and stream ciphers, although at the time the conditions were stated, block ciphers were not considered because of the difficulty of manual implementation.

system is referred to as a random one-time key or pad.[5] In other words, the system is unconditionally secure -- not because the equivocation faced by the cryptanalyst leaves an irresolvable number of choices for key or plaintext message. While it is often stated that a Vernam-Vigenére cryptosystem with a nonrepeating random key is unconditionally secure, it necessary to add the qualification that each symbol of the key introduce at least as much uncertainty as is removed by a symbol of the cipher.

An interesting example of the need for the key to introduce uncertainty, even with a nonrepeating random key, appears in a recent article by Deavours on the unicity point[6] of various encryption systems [Deav77]. In Deavours' example, the key introduces exactly 1 bit per symbol using the random binary stream 0011001100100000101110111··· to encipher a message in the Vigenére scheme with B as key if $k_i = 0$ and C as key if $k_i = 1$. Deavours' cipher is

TPOGD JRJFS UBSFC SQLGP COFUQ NFDSF CLVIF TONWG T.

The first four letters, for example, would decrypt sensibly to either SOME or ROME, etc., but the reader should have no difficulty determining the intended message to be: SOME CIPHERS ARE BROKEN AND SOME BREAK THEMSELVES.

---

[5] One needs to clearly distinguish between two kinds of undecipherability. In one kind the equivocation is too high even if the analyst makes perfect use of all available information. This may be because of the brevity of cipher or of a lost key, as with the famous Thomas Jefferson Beale book ciphers, numbers 1 and 3 [Hart64]. In the other, the code can be deciphered in principle but not in practice, as is probably the case with the MIT challenge cipher [Gard77].

[6] The unicity point was defined by Shannon to be the length of cipher beyond which only a single plaintext message could have produced the cipher, i.e., the point of zero equivocation to the cryptanalyst [Shan49].

All of the preceding examples are of stream ciphers, illustrating the way in which the key equivocation appears in each case, and also the concepts of unicity point and one-time pad or key. We turn now to block ciphers, of which we will describe two. Block ciphers attempt to deny to the cryptanalyst the frequency statistics which have proved so useful against stream ciphers. One way to accomplish this is to operate on pairs of symbols (digraphs), triples (trigraphs), or, in general, on blocks (polygraphs). For manageability, manual block cryptosystems are limited to digraph substitutions. The best known manual digraph system is Wheatstone's Playfair cipher, in which a 25-symbol alphabet[7] is written in a 5 x 5 array with a simple geometric rule [Gain56] specifying the cipher digraph to be substituted for each digraph in the message.

The cornerstone of modern mathematical cryptography was laid by Hill [Hill29, Hill31, Albe41] in 1929. Hill recognized that nearly all the existing cryptosystems could be formulated in the single model of linear transformations on a message space. Hill identified a message n-tuple with an n-tuple of integers and equated the operations of encryption and decryption with a pair of inverse linear transformations. The simplest representation for such transformations is multiplication of an n-tuple (message) by a nonsingular n x n matrix to form the cipher and by the inverse matrix to decrypt and recover the message. For example, let the digits zero-nine be represented by the numbers 0-9, blank by 10, and the 26 letters of the alphabet by 11-36. The number of symbols, 37, is a prime; the encoding and decoding can be carried out with arithmetic modulo 37. If the encrypting matrix is

[7]The letter J is usually dropped in the Playfair cipher since it occurs infrequently and can almost always be filled in by context or by substituting I in the text.

$$\mathcal{E} = \begin{pmatrix} 7 & 6 \\ 3 & 11 \end{pmatrix}$$

and the decrypting matrix is

$$\mathcal{E}^{-1} = \begin{pmatrix} 19 & 30 \\ 15 & 2 \end{pmatrix} .$$

then the message LULL = (22, 31, 22, 22) would encrypt to the cipher

$$\begin{pmatrix} 7 & 6 \\ 3 & 11 \end{pmatrix}\begin{pmatrix} 22 & 31 \\ 22 & 22 \end{pmatrix} = \begin{pmatrix} 27 & 16 \\ 12 & 2 \end{pmatrix}$$

(all computations mod 37).

Similarly, the cipher (27, 16, 12, 2) decrypts to yield the message LULL by,

$$\begin{pmatrix} 19 & 30 \\ 15 & 2 \end{pmatrix}\begin{pmatrix} 27 & 16 \\ 12 & 2 \end{pmatrix} = \begin{pmatrix} 22 & 31 \\ 22 & 22 \end{pmatrix} \pmod{37} .$$

Note that the three L's in LULL encipher into different symbols. This illustrates the cryptographic advantage of polygraphic systems: The raw frequency-of-occurrence statistics for blocks up to size n are obscured in the encryption process; in the limit (with n), they are lost completely.

Table 1

Letter	Number of Occurrences	Letter	Number of Occurrences	Letter	Number of Occurrences
E	540	C	212	Y	57
T	479	M	177	B	44
O	384	D	168	U	42
A	355	H	145	K	33
N	354	U	136	Q	11
I	326	P	114	X	7
R	317	F	87	Z	4
S	308	G	67	J	1
L	219	W	65		

Table 1 shows the number of occurrences of each letter in 4652 letters of an English language computing science article. These patterns, which survive any monographic substitution, are invaluable clues to the cryptanalyst. For instance, he knows that T is one of the most frequently occurring letters and can be quite sure that T is one of the eight most frequently seen letters. Figure 1 shows the frequency-of-occurrence data for single symbols in the cipher, for a simple monographic encryption, and for polygraphic encryption distributions with matrix sizes 2×2, 3×3, and 4×4. A perfect encryption system would have a flat distribution for all n-tuples; i.e., all possible n-tuples would be equally likely.[8]

Tuckerman [Tuck70] in his analysis of Vigenére-Vernam cryptosystems has shown that Vigenére systems using nonrandom transformations are always subject to statistical attack. This is to be expected since the initial equivocation to the opponent must eventually be eroded by usage. Tuckerman provides the neat proof of this intuitive statement.

The reader wishing a more complete treatment is referred to [Gain56, Kahn67, or Brig77] for further details of cryptanalysis. In a later section we take up current cryptotechnology, which has developed since World War II.

---

[8] Hill's system using an nth-order transformation resists simple statistical methods of cryptanalysis based on the frequency of occurrence of i-tuples in the cipher for i less than n; however, if the cryptanalyst has two ciphers resulting from the encryption of a single message with two involutory transformations $\mathcal{Q}_1$ and $\mathcal{Q}_2$ in $\mathcal{C}^n$ so that for all messages $M \in \mathcal{C}^n$, $\mathcal{Q}_1(\mathcal{Q}_1(M)) = \mathcal{Q}_2(\mathcal{Q}_2(M)) = M$, and if he knows $\mathcal{C}$, he can recover $\mathcal{Q}_1$ and $\mathcal{Q}_2$. It was not this cryptanalytic weakness, however, which prevented the adoption of Hill's cryptosystem, but rather the difficulty of carrying out the manual encryption/decryption operations he had defined.

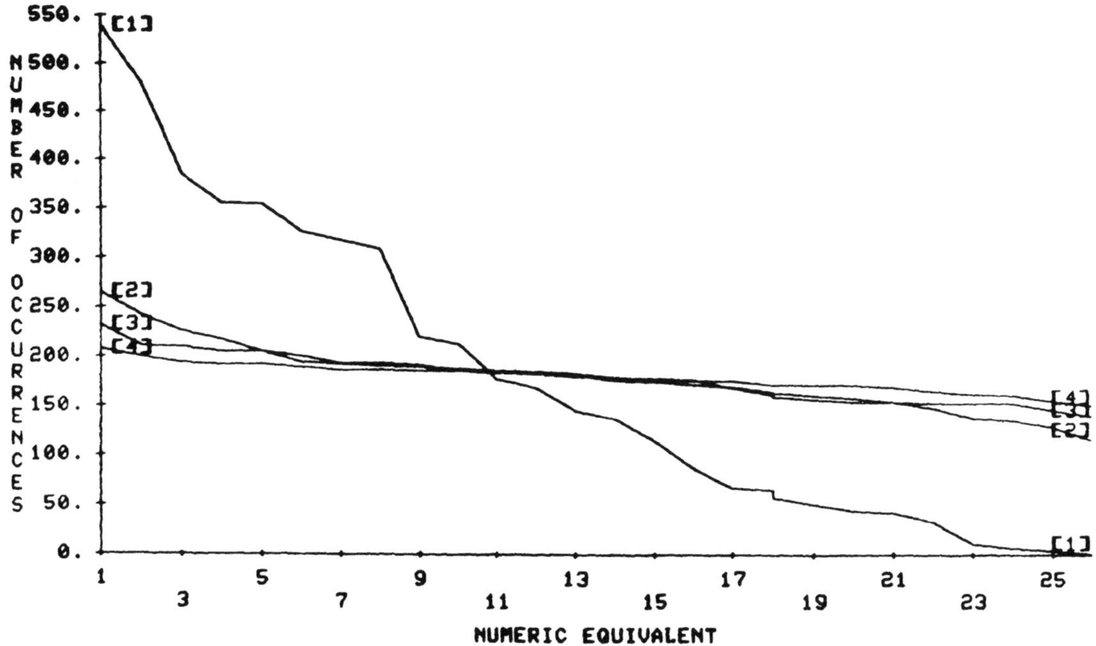

Figure 1. [1] Monographic substitution; [2] polygraphic substitution, matrix size 2 x 2; [3] polygraphic substitution, matrix size 3 x 3; [4] polygraphic substitution, matrix size 4 x 4.

2. Reader's Guide

Because of the unavoidable length and detail of the subsequent sections, a brief outline of the development is given here. First a parallel between the classical noisy communications channel and the general encryption/decryption channel is drawn. The reason for doing this is that error detecting and correcting codes and message or transmitter authentication are mathematically dual problems. In both cases redundancy, i.e., extra symbols, is introduced in the message, but the way in which this redundancy is used to communicate through the channel is different in the two applications. This is true whether the cryptosystem is symmetric or asymmetric.

Second, computationally infeasible problems are the source of cryptosecurity for both symmetric and asymmetric systems. One of the important points to this paper is to make clear how these computationally complex problems are embedded in an encryption/decryption process. To illustrate this, a frequently rediscovered encryption scheme dependent on maximal length linear feedback shift registers (LFSRs) is discussed to show how computational feasibility can destroy cryptosecurity. In the discussion of asymmetric encryption two examples of computationally infeasible problems are described in detail.

Linear feedback shift registers provide not only a simple illustration of the relationship between cryptosecurity and computational feasibility, but they also illustrate how redundancy is used in error detecting and correcting codes. The main text emphasizes these points, while a brief discussion of these devices is given in the appendix.

The ultimate objective of the paper is to impart to the reader a clear perception of how secrecy and authentication are accomplished in both symmetric and asymmetric encryption

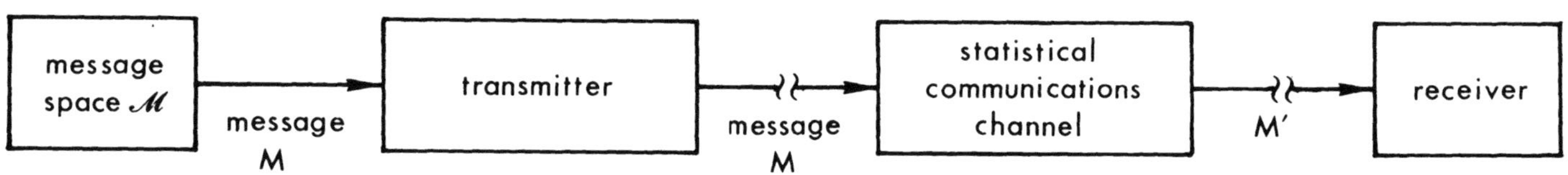

Figure 2. Classical communications channel.

systems. This implies a clear understanding of which forms of secure communication can only be realized through asymmetric techniques, and which forms can be realized by either symmetric or asymmetric cryptosystems.

3. The Communications Channel

A transmitter draws a message M from a space of possible messages $\mathfrak{M}$ and sends it to a receiver over a noisy communications channel. It is possible that some $M' \neq M$ may be received. In 1948 Shannon [Shan48] proposed the concept of the *entropy* of a message, which measures its information content. He showed how to introduce redundancy by means of a code; the extra symbols could be used to detect (and correct) errors in the received message M'. For example, Hamming codes add $2k + 1$ bits for each k errors to be detected [MacW77]. How this redundancy is introduced and utilized is a function of the way in which the errors occur in transmission, i.e., the statistics of the communications channel shown schematically in Figure 2. Essentially one wishes to impose a metric on the message space $\mathfrak{M}$ so that the set of messages most apt to result from errors in the transmission of a given message M is also the one "closest" to M in $\mathfrak{M}$. For example, if the errors in the binary symmetric channel are independent and uniformly distributed, the Hamming metric is a natural one to use; however, if adjacent symbol errors are more apt to occur, Berlekamp [Berl68] has shown the Lee metric[9] to be preferable. Coding theory is concerned with finding a partitioning of $\mathfrak{M}$ into a collection of disjoint subsets (ideally

[9]Whereas the Hamming metric is the number of symbol differences between two words, the Lee metric is the sum of the absolute differences of the symbols: for $W_1 = (0,1,2)$ and $W_2 = (2,0,1)$, $H(W_1,W_2) = 3$ and $L(W_1,W_2) = 4$. For binary code words the Hamming and Lee metrics are identical.

"spheres") with all points in the ith set less than some specified distance from a central point C_i in the set. The code then consists of the labels (code words) of the collection of central points in the subsets of $\mathfrak{M}$, with the maximum likelihood error correction rule being to decode any received point in $\mathfrak{M}$ as the central point of the class that it belongs to in the partition.

Since we shall later wish to contrast the partitioning of $\mathfrak{M}$ for message authentication to the kind of partitioning useful for error detection and correction -- where the objective in both instances is to detect an incorrect message -- we give in Table 2 an example of a Hamming code that adds three extra bits to each 4-bit block of message code [Mass69]. This code can be generated by taking as code words the 7-bit subsequences having the 4-bit messages in the low-order bit positions from the output of the linear feedback shift register (see appendix). If any single bit of the 7-bit code word is altered in transmission, the receiver can recover the message correctly by finding the code word that differs from the received block in the fewest number of bits.

Table 2

Message	Code Word
0000	000,0000
0001	011,0001
0010	110,0010
0011	101,0011
0100	111,0100
0101	100,0101
0110	001,0110
0111	010,0111
1000	101,1000
1001	110,1001
1010	011,1010
1011	000,1011
1100	010,1100
1101	001,1101
1110	100,1110
1111	111,1111

Figure 3 is a schematic diagram of the Shannon channel. The codes in C are so designed that the likelihood of an altered message being misinterpreted by the receiver is minimum. In the case of error correction, the code is designed to maximize the likelihood that the receiver will be able to transform the received message to the message actually sent correctly.

4. The Encryption/Decryption Channel

The encryption channel also consists of a transmitter who wishes to send a message M to a receiver. But now the channel is assumed to be under surveillance by a hostile opponent. Cryptographic theory seeks to devise codes that cannot systematically be distinguished from purely random bit strings by the opponent. The statistical communications channel of the coding/decoding model has been replaced by a game-theoretic channel; nature has been replaced by an intelligent opponent. The opponent can have one or more of the following purposes:

a) To determine the message M.
b) To alter the message M to some other message M′ and have M′ accepted by the receiver as the message actually sent.
c) To impersonate the transmitter.

Thwarting a), i.e., ensuring secrecy, is the best known purpose of cryptographic systems, but modern data processing systems with controlled log-in and access to business files are greatly concerned with authenticating the "transmitter" (thwarting c)) and ensuring the integrity of the received messages (thwarting b)) [Feis73, Hoff77, Lipt78, Mart73]. In many cases the privacy or secrecy of communications is a secondary objective. An intelligent opponent could easily defeat the fixed strategies underlying error detecting codes by making improbable changes such that the received code words would be interpreted as incorrect messages. Moreover the

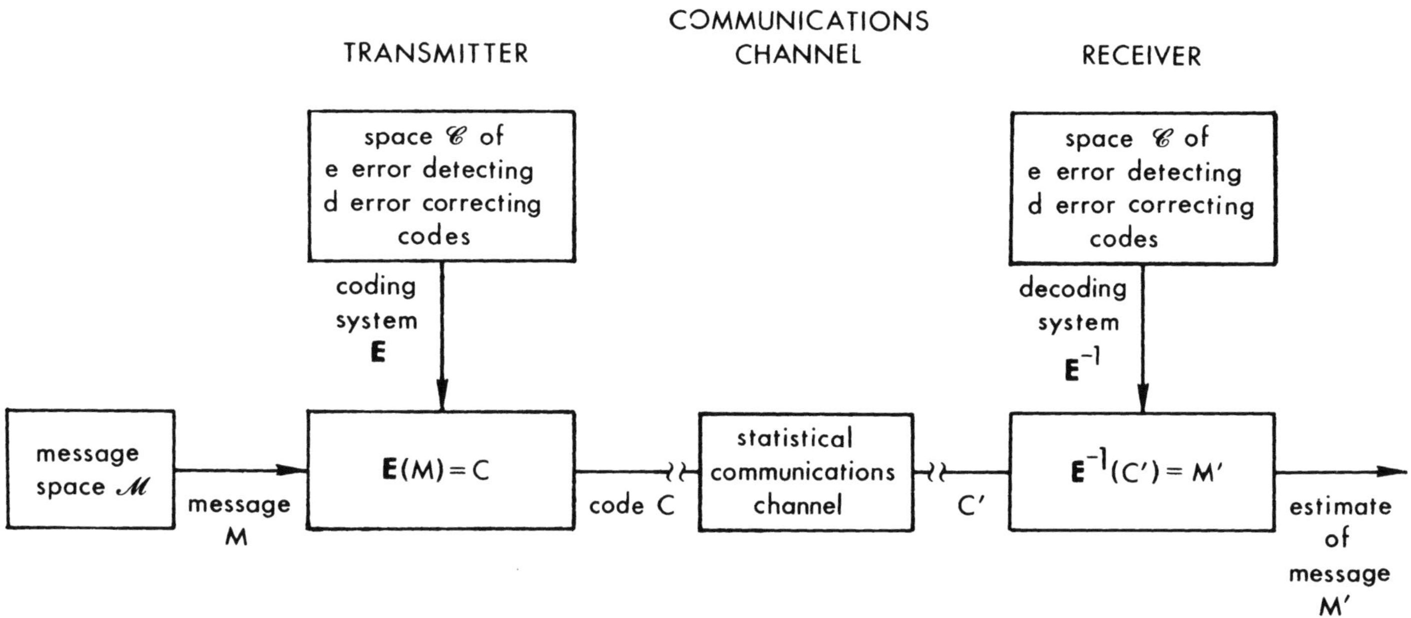

Figure 3. Functional schematic for the Shannon coding/decoding channel.

opponent's task of "breaking" the code is not difficult because the code space is partitioned into spheres, which reduces the search. A perfectly secure code is one in which each cipher symbol is produced with equal probability by any message symbol when averaged over all possible keys. Deavour's example [Deav77] was not secure because each cipher symbol could have been produced by only two message symbols rather than all 26 message symbols.

To be perfectly secure, an encryption system should randomly map the message space onto itself such that the opponent must consider all points in $\mathfrak{M}$ to be equally likely candidates for the plaintext corresponding to the received ciphertext. Whereas a satisfactory "random" number generator need not be a good encryption function (as we shall see in an example a little later), a good encryption system is necessarily a good random number generator. In fact, Gait [Gait77] has used the DES algorithm for random number generation with considerable success.

As Shannon pointed out [Shan49], this implies that a perfect encryption scheme is equivalent to a latin square where rows correspond to messages, entries to keys, and columns to ciphers. However, a perfect cryptosystem may be unable to authenticate messages. Suppose that $\mathfrak{M}$ is the space of *all* n-bit binary numbers, and that encryption consists in adding, modulo 2, a random n-bit binary number. In this case every proposed decipherment produces an acceptable message. When there is no redundancy in the messages, there is no basis on which to deduce the authenticity of a received cipher. An authentication system must introduce redundancy such that the space of ciphers is partitioned into the images (encryptions) of the messages in $\mathfrak{M}$ and a class of unacceptable ciphers. If authentication is to be perfect, then the encryption scheme must consist of a family of partitions of the cipher space such that on learning any message -- cipher

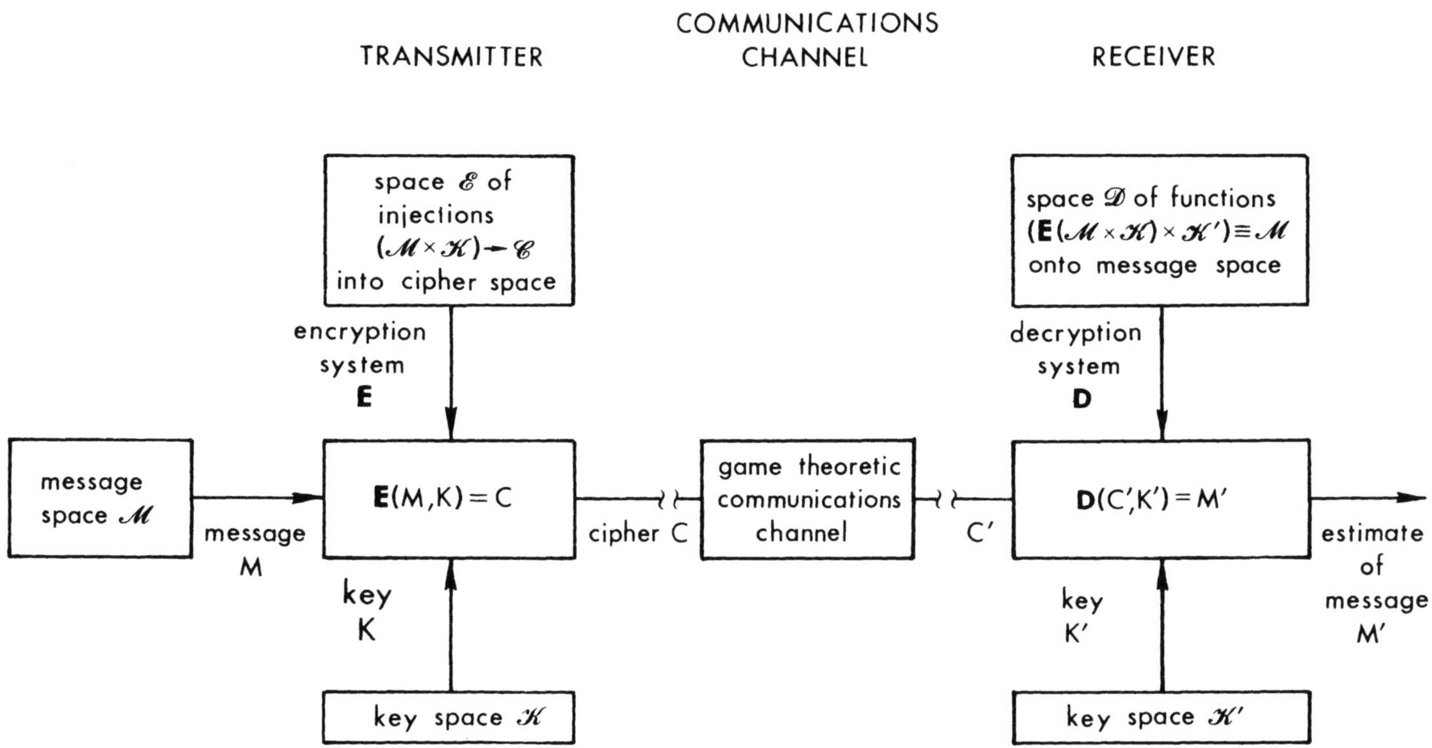

Figure 4. Functional schematic for the general encryption/decryption channel.

pair, the opponent who does not know the key will be unable to do any better than pick a cipher at random from the cipher space. In other words, the objective is to diffuse the unacceptable ciphers throughout the entire cipher space. This is precisely the opposite of the error defeating code's objective, which is the *clustering* of the incorrect codes about an acceptable (correct) code.

Figure 4 is a schematic diagram of the abstract encryption/decryption channel. The parallel with the Shannon coding/decoding channel is apparent. Figure 4 is more general than the secrecy systems described by Shannon [Shan49], Albert [Albe41], or Feistel [Feis73]; Shannon's and Albert's models were concerned only with secrecy, and Feistel's model dealt with a restricted form of message authentication. The model of Figure 4 encompasses all the objectives for secure communications. It should be noted that a cipher can be encoded to allow for the detection and correction of errors in transmission. This requires that the receiver first decode and correct errors before decrypting. In fact, such compound encryption/encoding is routinely used with satellite communications systems.

In encryption/decryption systems, the functions **E** and **D** (encryption and decryption) are assumed known to the opponent. If the system were to depend completely on **E** and **D**, the opponent would have sufficient information to defeat it. Therefore, something must be unknown if the opponent is to be unable to duplicate the actions performed by the authorized receiver. The unknown information is called the cryptographic *key*. The authorized receiver can use his secret deciphering key K' to decrypt the encrypted message.

An encryption system can be described formally with the help of the message space $\mathfrak{M}$, the key spaces $\mathcal{K}$ and $\mathcal{K}'$, the cipher space $\mathcal{C}$, a space $\mathcal{E}$ of mappings from $\mathfrak{M} \times \mathcal{K}$ into $\mathcal{C}$, and a related space $\mathcal{D}$ of inverse mappings. For a particular mapping **E** from $\mathcal{E}$, M from $\mathfrak{M}$, and K from $\mathcal{K}$, **E**(M,K) = C is the encipherment of message M by key K. There must be a deciphering function $\mathbf{D}_E$ corresponding to **E** and a key K′ corresponding to K such that messages can be uniquely recovered:

$$M = \mathbf{D}_E\big(\mathbf{E}(M,K),\ K'\big)$$
$$= \mathbf{D}_E(C,K') \quad \text{for all} \quad M \quad . \tag{1}$$

By itself (1) does not describe a secure encryption system. For example, if $\mathfrak{M} \equiv \mathcal{C}$ and **E** is the identity function, then (1) is trivially satisfied with C = M for all M; obviously there is no cryptosecurity for any choice of K. Shannon [Shan49] defines a secrecy system **E** to be perfect (unconditionally secure) if an opponent knowing **E** and arbitrarily much cipher C is still left with a choice from among all possible messages M from $\mathfrak{M}$. For this to be true, there must be as many keys as there are messages. Moreover the uncertainty about the key K must be essential: The opponent's uncertainty about messages must be at least as great as his uncertainty about the key. In Shannon's model $\mathcal{K} \equiv \mathcal{K}'$ and $\mathcal{E} \equiv \mathcal{D}$, and only objective a), secrecy, is considered. Under these constraints, **E** is a mapping from the message space $\mathfrak{M}$ into the cipher space $\mathcal{C}$, and **D** is $\mathbf{E}^{-1}$, the inverse function to **E**; the key K then acts as an index for a pair (**E**,**D**). Perfect security is achieved by having one key for each possible (**E**,**D**) pair. Contemporary cryptosystems seldom realize this level of unconditional security. In fact, most of current cryptology deals with systems which are secure in the sense that exploiting the available information is computationally infeasible; but these systems are not unconditionally secure in Shannon's sense. The important exceptions include the Washington-Moscow hot line and various high-level command circuits. In the remainder of this paper, we are concerned with computationally secure systems, but not unconditionally secure ones.

5. Computational Complexity and Symmetric Encryption

A fundamental change in the practice of cryptography began in the early 1950s. We have already pointed out that a perfectly secure cryptosystem requires impractical quantities of key for most applications. Almost all of cryptography has been devoted to finding ways of "diffusing" smaller, manageable amounts of uncertainty in order to approximate longer keys, that is, keys which appear to have come from a key space with greater uncertainty. This is usually done with an easily computed function of an input sequence, the true key, which produces as output a much longer sequence, the pseudokey. The pseudoky is used as K in Figure 4.

If such a procedure is to be cryptosecure, it must be infeasible to invert the function to recover the true key from the pseudokey; that is, it must be intractable to compute the future output of the function even though the function itself is known and lengthy observations of the output are available. From World War II until the early 1950s these objectives were met on an ad hoc basis through the intuitive judgment of cryptosystem designers. However, electronic computing and the theory of computational complexity transformed the idea of "diffusing" a limited amount of uncertainty into an analytical design question.

In Figure 4 the key spaces $\mathcal{K}$ and $\mathcal{K}'$ represent the equivocation to the opponent of the system at any given stage in its operation. For example, in an English alphabet one-time pad of n equally likely symbols $|\mathcal{K}| = 26^n$; each point in $\mathcal{K}$ represents about $\log_2(26)^n \approx 4.7n$ bits of information, and so a 1000-symbol one-time "key" would be represented as a point in a binary space of 2^{4700} possible sequences. Because keys are as voluminous as the messages they secure, one-time keys are impractical for large-volume communications. In the early 1950s cryptologists recognized that if a (true) key K

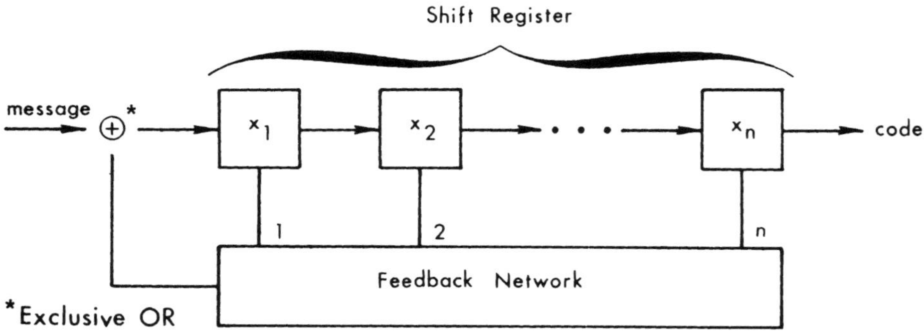

Figure 5.

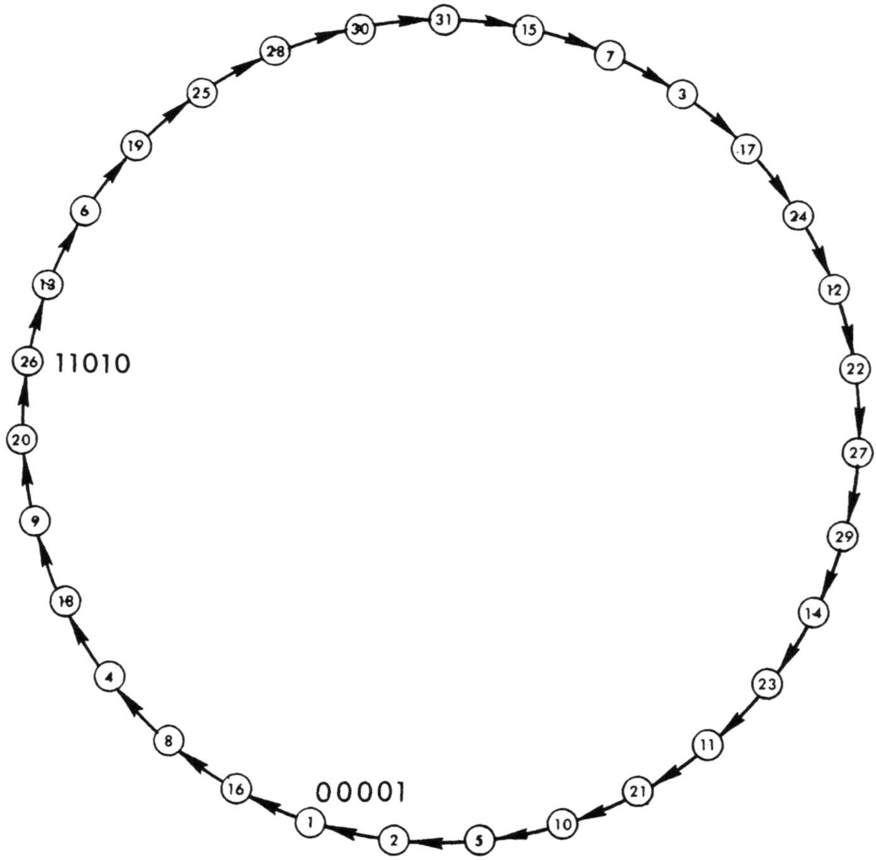

Figure 6.

from a smaller dimensional key space $\mathcal{K}$ was used to generate a much longer (pseudo) key $\hat{K}$ using an algorithm whose inversion was sufficiently complex computationally, then the cryptanalyst would be unable to compute either K or $\hat{K}$. Modern cryptology rests largely on the implementation of this principle.

In terms of Figure 4, the "diffusing" of uncertainty is defined by this condition: For nearly all encryption/decryption pairs (**E**,**D**) and keys K and K′, it is computationally infeasible to compute K (or K′) from a knowledge of **E**, **D**, C, and M. A system in which either K = K′ or one of K and K′ is easily computed from knowledge of the other is called a *symmetric* system.

All the examples in the introduction are of symmetric systems. For a one-time key, the two communicants must each have a copy of the same key; K = K′ in this case. Similarly the simple Vigenére and Vernam-Vigenére systems both have K ≡ K′. On the other hand, in the Hill linear transformation system, described in Section 1, the receiver must have $\mathbf{E}^{-1}$, not **E**, although it is easy to compute $\mathbf{E}^{-1}$ from a knowledge of **E**.

Maximal length linear feedback shift registers (LFSRs), which are used for error detecting and correcting codes, illustrate that one must take great care in choosing key functions. Some apparently complex functions are not so. Because the (2^n-1)-bit sequence from a maximal length LFSR satisfies many tests for randomness, e.g., the runs property [Golo67] and lack of intersymbol correlation up to the register length n, numerous suggestions have been made to use these sequences either as key in a Vernam-Vigenére stream cipher mode, as shown in Figure 5, or as block encryption devices on n-bit blocks of message bits [Brig76, Geff73, Golo67, Meye72]. The feedback network, i.e., the coefficients of the feedback polynomial, and the starting state of the register serve as the key.

Assuming that the cryptanalyst can by some means, such as probable word analysis, recover bits of the cipher (which need not be consecutive), he can set up and solve a system of at most 2n linear equations with which to duplicate the future output of the original sequence generator. Berlekamp [Berl68] and Massey [Mass69] have found efficient algorithms for doing this in at most 2n steps. Thus the problem of finding K is only of linear complexity (in n); hence K is not well concealed despite the apparently large number of possible feedback functions. A more complete description of LFSRs is given in the appendix.

Another proposed mode of crypto use for LFSRs is for block ciphers: The register is loaded with an n-bit block of plaintext, it is stepped for k > n steps, and the resulting register state is taken as the cipher. Figure 6 (p. 266) shows an example of the state diagram for such an LFSR. Using k = 7. for example, the message 00001 encrypts to 11010. To decrypt, one uses the "inverse feedback function," which reverses the stepping order of the state diagram of Figure 6, when a 00001 would be the register state resulting from stepping the register seven steps from the starting point (cipher) of 11010. In this example K (forward stepping) and K′ (reverse stepping) are easily computable from each other. Although the output is sufficiently random to be useful as a pseudorandom bit sequence generator, the inversion to find K′ or K is only of linear computational complexity.

The National Bureau of Standards Data Encryption Standard (DES) provides a widely recognized example of a symmetric encryption/decryption whose keys are well concealed by computational complexity. Roberts [Robe75] states that

> The algorithm is designed to encipher and decipher blocks of data consisting of 64 bits under control of a 64-bit key.[10] Deciphering must be accomplished by using the same key as for enciphering, but with the schedule of addressing the key bits altered so that the deciphering process is the reverse of the enciphering process. A block to be enciphered is subjected to an initial permutation IP, then to a complex key-dependent computation and finally to a permutation which is the inverse of the initial permutation IP^{-1}

This shows clearly that the system is symmetric. It indicates that the "complex key-dependent computation" conceals the key. The encryption function used in the DES is known as a product cipher [Morr77]; it comprises 16 successive repetitions of a nonlinear substitution (to provide "confusion") alternating with permutations (to provide "diffusion"). There is considerable controversy[11] about the cryptosecurity of the DES [Diff77, Morr77] centering on the possible brute force attack of a system by enumerating all the keys for the present 56-bit key; yet no one has proposed an inversion of the encryption function itself, which thus far appears to be as computationally complex as its designers believed it to be.

6. Computational Complexity and Asymmetric Encryption

In symmetric cryptosystems, the keys at the transmitter and receiver, K and K′, respectively, either are the same or can be easily computed from each other. We now consider

[10]Actually only 56 bits rather than the stated 64, since 8 bits are used for a parity check.

[11]The controversy is centered on Hellman's accusation that the National Security Agency has deliberately chosen the DES key to be of a size that it can break. The pros [Hell79a, Davi79] and cons [Tuch79, Bran79] of this argument are summarized in the recent editorial debate in the IEEE Spectrum [Suga79].

cryptosystems in which this is not the case. There are three possibilities.

a) *Forward asymmetric:* The receiver's key (K′) cannot easily be computed given the transmitter's key (K).

b) *Backward asymmetric:* The transmitter's key (K) cannot easily be computed given the receiver's key (K′).

c) *Bidirectional asymmetric:* Neither K nor K′ can be computed given the other.

As usual, the enemy is assumed to know **E**, **D**, M, and C. The term "asymmetric system" refers to all three cases.

The primary applications of (bidirectional) asymmetric encryption systems derive from these two properties:

1) Secure (i.e., secret) communication is possible even if the transmitter's key is compromised.

2) Authentication of the transmitter (message) is possible even if the receiver's key is compromised.

Note that 1) applies to the forward asymmetric encryption system and 2) to the backward encryption system.

Whereas symmetric cryptosystems have been in use for many years, asymmetric encryption systems are a recent development in cryptography. In 1976 Diffie and Hellman [Diff76] published a conceptual scheme for this kind of cryptosystem, which they called a *public-key cryptosystem* because no pair of potential communicants had to exchange a key secretly in advance. It is essential, however, that the key exchange be secure, so that the communicants can be confident of the keys' owners -- otherwise authentication is not possible. Merkle [Merk78a] contemporaneously discovered a related principle that allows the communicants to exchange a key with work $O(n)$, while requiring the opponent to face work $O(n^2)$ to determine the key from monitoring the communicants' exchange. Merkle discovered a forward asymmetric encryption system.

In terms of Figure 4, these conditions must be satisfied by an asymmetric encryption scheme:

1) The keys are concealed by a computationally complex problem from the plaintext and cipher.
2) It is easy to compute matched pairs of keys (K,K′) such that

$$\mathbf{D}_E(\mathbf{E}(M,K),K') = M \quad .$$

3) The encryption and decryption functions, **E** and **D** are implemented by fast algorithms.
4) At least one of the keys (K and K′) is concealed from a knowledge of the other key by a computationally complex problem.
5) For almost all messages it must be infeasible to find cipher/key pairs that yield that message. That is, the opponent is forced to find the "true" (M,K) that encrypted to the cipher C at hand.

These conditions differ slightly from those imposed on public-key cryptosystems [Diff76]. Condition 1) is the basic requirement for a practical privacy system; we state it explicitly to exhibit one of the two places in the abstract encryption channel where computational complexity is essential. The public-key cryptosystem was formulated as a two-way communications channel by its inventors, so that the keys are interchangeable: $\mathbf{E}(\mathbf{D}_E(M,K'),\ K) = M = \mathbf{D}(\mathbf{E}(M,K),\ K')$ [Adle78, Hell78]. Condition 5) enables detecting deception: The opponent cannot easily find alternate keys giving the same ciphertext [Gilb74].

As of 1979, no one had exhibited functions that provably satisfied these conditions. The working approach toward constructing such functions has been to take some problem, known or believed to be exceedingly complex, and make the "obvious" method of finding the keys equivalent to solving the hard problem. Examples of hard problems are factoring a product of very large prime factors, the general knapsack problem, and finding the logarithm of an element in a large field with respect to a primitive element. What is hoped for in such a scheme is that the converse is also true; i.e., decryption is equivalent to solving the hard problem. The first results toward this crucial step in "proving" the cryptosecurity of any asymmetric system were obtained by Rabin [Rabi79] and Williams [Will79B]; they showed that the factorization problem for large moduli is equivalent to decryption for almost all ciphers in Rabin's encryption scheme. We will return to this point later.

6.1 The Knapsack Trapdoor

One of the best known proposals for a forward asymmetric system was made by Merkle and Hellman [Merk78b], who suggested basing asymmetric encryption on the knapsack (or subset sum) problem. The *knapsack problem* is to determine whether a weight S can be realized as the sum of some subset of a given collection of n weights w_i -- i.e., to determine whether there exists a binary vector $\mathbf{s}$ for which $S = \mathbf{s} \cdot \mathbf{w}$.[12] Without restrictions on $\mathbf{w}$, solutions need not exist or there may be several. For example, S = 515 has three solutions, while S = 516 has no solution in the 10-weight knapsack appearing in Hellman's paper [Hell78].[13] The time to verify whether a given vector $\mathbf{s}$ is a solution is O(n). In contrast, the time needed to find a solution vector $\mathbf{s}$ is believed to be of exponential complexity. Horowitz and Sahni [Horo74] have published a search algorithm for the knapsack problem requiring $O(2^{n/2})$

[12] If $\mathbf{s} = (s_1, \cdots, s_n)$ and $\mathbf{w} = (w_1, \cdots, w_n)$, then the dot product $\mathbf{s} \cdot \mathbf{w} = \sum_{i=1}^{n} s_i w_i$. The vector $\mathbf{s}$, where $s_i = 0$ or 1 such that $S = \mathbf{s} \cdot \mathbf{w}$, selects some of the "objects" to fill a "knapsack" of capacity S.

[13] $\mathbf{w} = (14,28,56,82,90,132,197,284,341,455)$, and $\mathbf{s} =$ (1001111000), (0110100010), or (1100010010) for S = 515.

time and $O(2^{n/2})$ memory; and more recently Schroeppel and Shamir [Schr79] have devised an algorithm of the same time complexity but requiring only $O(2^{n/4})$ memory. The knapsack problem is an NP-complete problem [Karp72].

It is important to remember that the computational complexity of NP-complete problems is measured by the difficulty of solving the worst cases, whereas cryptosecurity is measured by the expected difficulty over all members of the class. Suppose, for example, that the knapsack vector **w** is chosen with the w_i in strict dominance, i.e., $w_i > \Sigma_{j=1}^{i-1} w_j$. In this case **s** can either be found or shown not to exist in at most n subtractions: $s_i = 1$ if and only if $S - S_{i-1} \geq w_i$, where S_{i-1} is the partial sum of the first i - 1 components of the dot product. Another example is $w_i = 2^{i-1}$, in which case the problem reduces to finding the binary representation of $0 \leq S \leq 2^n - 1$. Both these examples illustrate how simple a knapsack problem can be for special **w.** An encryption system based on such a simple **w** would not be secure.

Merkle and Hellman defined two special classes of vectors **w**, which they call *trapdoor knapsacks*; with a trapdoor knapsack the designer can easily compute the subset vector **s**, while the opponent is faced with solving a hard $(O(2^{n/2})?)$ problem. The simplest scheme is an "additive trapdoor knapsack," in which the designer starts with any strictly dominating weight vector **w** containing n weights, as described above, and derives a related weight vector **v**, which is believed to be a hard knapsack. This is done by choosing a modulus n and a multiplier e which is relatively prime with respect to n, and then computing the n weights v_i of **v** by the rule $ew_i \equiv v_i \pmod m$. Since e is relatively prime with respect to m, there exists a d, easily computed using the Euclidean algorithm, such that $ed \equiv 1 \pmod n$. The numbers d and m are the receiving key K′, and the "hard" knapsack weight vector $\mathbf{v}$ is the transmitting key K. A binary message is broken into n-bit blocks. Each n-bit block becomes a vector $\mathbf{s}$ for the knapsack problem: the transmitter computes the cipher $S' = \mathbf{s} \cdot \mathbf{v}$. Since the cryptanalyst only knows S' and $\mathbf{v}$, he is forced to solve the knapsack problem for $\mathbf{v}$. The authorized receiver, however, computes $dS' \equiv S \pmod{m}$; he then solves the simple knapsack $(S, \mathbf{w})$ in $O(n)$ time because $\mathbf{w}$ is of the dominating form. If m is chosen to strictly dominate the sum of all the weights, then the computations may be done in integer arithmetic as well as in the modular arithmetic.

To further illustrate this simple trapdoor knapsack, use the easy knapsack weight vector $\mathbf{w} = (1,2,4,8)$; choose $m = 17 > 1+2+4+8 = 15$ and $e = 5$. Then $d = 7$ and $\mathbf{v} = (5,10,3,6)$. In this system the subset vector $\mathbf{s} = (0,1,0,1)$ would be transmitted as $S' = \mathbf{s} \cdot \mathbf{v} = 16$. The receiver finds $S = 7 \cdot 16 = 10 \pmod{17}$; since he also knows $\mathbf{w}$, the authorized receiver can solve for $\mathbf{s}$ in three subtractions. The same principles apply to realistic implementations, which use $n = 100$ or larger.

Note that it has not yet been *proved* that the modular derivation of $\mathbf{v}$ from the easy knapsack $\mathbf{w}$ results in a hard knapsack. Shamir and Zippel [Sham78] have shown that if the opponent knows m as well as $\mathbf{v}$, he can employ a simple algorithm whose output is $\mathbf{w}$ with high probability.

6.2 The Factorization Trapdoor

Another asymmetric system is the public-key encryption scheme proposed by Rivest, Shamir, and Adleman [Rive78]. The trapdoor in the scheme is based on the difference in computational difficulty in finding large primes as opposed to factoring large numbers. The best algorithms known at the present can find a d-digit prime number in time $O(d^3)$, while the complexity of factoring a large number n exceeds any polynomial bound, currently $O\left(n^{(\ln(\ln n)/\ln n)^{1/2}}\right)$. In the proposed system, one chooses a pair of primes p and q so large that factoring $n = pq$ is beyond all projected computational capabilities. One also chooses a pair of numbers e and d, where $(e, \varphi(n)) = 1$,[14] and $ed \equiv 1 \bmod \varphi(n)$; $\varphi(n) = (p-1)(q-1)$. In other words, e and d are multiplicative inverses in the group of residue classes modulo $\varphi(n)$. When used as a public-key cryptosystem, e and n are published in the public-key directory and d is kept secret. Because the receiver (designer) knows p and q, the system is forward asymmetric.

A variant of this scheme illustrates a bidirectional asymmetric encryption system. Assume that a higher level of command designs the system, e.g., chooses p, q, and e, computes d, and then gives (e,n) and (d,n) to two subordinate commands that require an asymmetric encryption channel between them. Since computing the multiplicative inverse d of e from a knowledge of e and n is essentially the same as factoring n or determining $\varphi(n)$, d is secure from an opponent knowing only n and e. Conversely, computing e from a knowledge of d and n is of the same difficulty. The two keys (e,n) and (d,n) are separated by a computationally difficult problem. Obviously, the "higher level of command" can be replaced by a volatile memory computing device so that no single party is in possession of the information which could compromise the system.

A message $M \in \mathfrak{M}$ is encrypted in this system to the cipher C by the transmitter using key $K = (e,n)$ by the rule

$$M^e \equiv C \pmod{n} \quad ,$$

and C is decrypted by the authorized receiver using $K = (d,n)$ by the rule

[14] $\varphi(n)$ is the Euler totient; it is simply the number of integers less than n and relatively prime with respect to n. $(e, \varphi(n)) = 1$ is a notation indicating that e and $\varphi(n)$ are relatively prime.

$$C^d \equiv M \pmod{n} \quad .$$

For example, if p = 421 and q = 577 so that n = pq = 242,917 and $\varphi(n)$ = 241,920, then for e = 101, d = 9581. Using these values K = (101:242,917) and K′ = (9581:242,917) so that the message M = 153,190 encrypts by

$$C = 153{,}190^{101} \equiv 203{,}272 \pmod{242{,}917} \quad ,$$

and C decrypts by

$$M = 203{,}272^{9581} \equiv 153{,}190 \pmod{242{,}917} \quad .$$

Much effort has been devoted to the investigation of whether the scheme just described is secure and whether decryption (for almost all ciphers) is as hard as the factorization of n. Several authors [Herl78, Simm77, Will79a] have investigated the restrictions on the primes p and q that must be imposed to ensure cryptosecurity; they conclude that it is not difficult to choose the primes so that the known cryptoweaknesses are avoided [Will79a]. It is probable that these same steps are also sufficient to ensure that decryption of almost all ciphers is as hard as the factorization of n. However, this crucial result has not been proved. Instead, Rabin [Rabi79] has shown that if instead of the encryption function $C = M^e$ one uses

$$C \equiv M(M+b) \pmod{n} \quad , \qquad b \geq 0 \quad ,$$

which is effectively the same as e = 2 where n = pq, as in the Rivest et al. scheme, then decryption to an unauthorized user is not simply a consequence of being able to factor n but is actually equivalent. Unfortunately, even the authorized user is left with an ambiguity among four potential messages in this scheme. Williams has completed this work by proving that for suitably chosen primes p and q the ambiguity is removed and that decryption of almost all messages is equivalent to factoring n [Will79b]. (Ron Rivest has pointed out that this statement is precisely true for ciphertext-only attack and that it does not hold for chosen-plaintext attack [Brig77].)

For example, using the same primes and message as above in the simple Rabin scheme, p = 421, q = 577, and M = 153,190, and letting b = 0, one obtains the cipher

$$C = 153{,}190^2 \equiv 179{,}315 \pmod{242{,}917}.$$

Four messages from $\mathfrak{M}$ have C as their square mod n: M, of course, and -M = 089,727, as well as M′ = 022,788 and -M′ = 220,129.

The important point is that these results are persuasive evidence of equivalence between decryption for almost all messages and the factorization of n in these schemes.

A common misconception is that asymmetric encryption/ decryption (public-key encryption) is more secure than its (symmetric) predecessors. For example, Gardner [Gard77] suggests that public-key cryptosystems are more cryptosecure than existing systems, and a lengthy editorial in the Washington Post, July 9, 1978, was entitled "The New Unbreakable Codes -- Will They Put NSA Out of Business?" [Shap78]. The discussion in the two previous sections on symmetric and asymmetric encryption demonstrates clearly that asymmetric cryptosecurity depends on precisely the same mathematical condition as most high-quality symmetric cryptosystems -- computational work factor. Basing cryptosystems on NP-hard problems opens new worlds of codes which may be as secure as traditional codes. But the new systems are not necessarily more or less secure than existing cryptosystems.

7. Authentication

The asymmetric encryption channel serves two functions:

1) Secret communication is possible even if the transmitter's key (K) is public.

2) Authentication of messages is possible by anyone who knows the receiver's key (K′), assuming that K and K′ are not easily computed from each other.

The separation of secrecy and authentication in asymmetric systems has a natural counterpart in the different security concerns of the transmitter and receiver: The transmitter wishes assurances that the message cannot be disclosed or altered, whereas the receiver is primarily concerned that the message could only have come from the transmitter.

The different security concerns of transmitter and receiver are well illustrated by the concerns of the various parties involved in a transaction by check. The person writing the check (the transmitter) is not concerned with its authenticity, but he is concerned that no one will be able to alter the amount shown on his signed draft. The person accepting the check (the receiver) is primarily concerned with the authenticity of the check. An intermediate party accepting the check as a second-party draft is concerned with both of these aspects: that the check is unaltered and authentic. The ultimate receiver, the bank, keeps signature cards on file to help verify (if needed) the identity of the person who wrote the check, but its concerns are the same as those of the other intermediate receivers.

Authentication is closely related to error detecting codes. The message $\mathcal{M}$ is partitioned into two classes, acceptable and unacceptable messages, similar to the classes comprising the most probably correct and incorrect messages in the previous case. To realize authentication despite an intelligent opponent, it is essential to conceal these classes in the ciphers. Using an unconditionally secure cryptosystem to encrypt the messages from $\mathcal{M}$ into ciphers from $\mathcal{C}$, every cipher $C \in \mathcal{C}$ would with equiprobability over $\mathcal{K}$ be the encryption of any message in $\mathcal{M}$. But in this ideal case, if the opponent substituted another cipher C′ for the correct cipher C, the probability that it would decrypt to a message in the class of acceptable messages would be simply $|\mathfrak{a}|/|\mathfrak{m}|$, where $\mathfrak{a}$ is the class of acceptable messages. For example, if $\mathfrak{m}$ is the set of $26^4 = 456{,}976$ four-letter alphabetic sequences and $\mathfrak{a}$ is the set of four-letter English words in Webster's Unabridged International Dictionary, then the probability that a randomly chosen four-letter cipher will decrypt to an English word is very close to 1/7. In other words, the equivocation to the opponent of this "natural" authentication system is ≈ 2.81 bits.

The point is that authentication is only achievable by introducing redundancy into the message -- exactly as is done to achieve an error detecting or correcting capability. Simply having the required level of redundancy is not sufficient. The redundancy must be diffused throughout the cipher, lest the signature information be separated from the proper message and appended to another message.

The bidirectional public-key encryption system proposed by Rivest, Shamir, and Adleman can be used by two subscribers, A and B, as a means of authenticating (signing) messages. Assume that A wishes to send a message M to B; B must later be able to prove to a third party (observer or judge) that M originated with A. For example, A is ordering B (his broker) to make a large stock sale which B fears A may disavow if the market value of the stock should increase. A has entered his public-key (e_A,n_A) into the public directory. Similarly B has entered (e_B,n_B). A computes

$$M^{d_A} \equiv C_A \pmod{n_A}$$

using his secret key (d_A,n_A) and then computes

$$C_A^{e_B} \equiv C \pmod{n_B}$$

using B's public key. This cipher can only be decrypted by B; A is therefore assured of the secrecy of his message. On receiving C, B computes

$$C^{d_B} \equiv C_A \pmod{n_B}$$

using his secret key and saves C_A as his "signed" version of the message. He then computes

$$C_A^{e_A} \equiv M \pmod{n_A}$$

using A's public key. Since this later step can be duplicated by any observer given C_A by using A's public information, the claim is that M could only have come from A.[15]

It has been argued that since M, C_A, and C are all the same length, say k bits, there is no apparent redundancy, as is required for authentication. But this is not true: Suppose that M were perfectly encoded, i.e., a random (equiprobable) k-bit binary number. Now the observer has no way of rejecting any k-bit number as not having been originated by A. A must therefore include in M identifiers, such as his name or ID number, time of day, or transaction number, which serve only to distinguish acceptable from unacceptable messages. The security of the authenticator is still measured by the degree of signature redundancy introduced.

Authentication is possible using either symmetric or asymmetric channels. We noted earlier that with DES, a symmetric block ciphering system, messages can be authenticated using Feistel's block chaining [Feis73] technique. In this approach successive blocks of 56 bits of the text are used as keys to successively encrypt the ciphers from the preceding step, with one 56-bit initial key unknown to the opponent.

---

[15]There is a significant difference between digital signatures and a signature to a document. Once the signer affixes his signature to a document, there is nothing he can do that will interfere with the future verification of the authenticity of the signature. In the digital signature scheme described above, however, A can deliberately expose his secret key d_A and thereby make the authenticity of all digital signatures attributed to him questionable.

The resulting cipher is a "function" of every bit in the message and is resistant to inversion even against a known plaintext attack. The appended authenticator must match an "acceptable" message, usually in a natural language to be accepted.

The unique feature of asymmetric encryption systems for authentication is that a receiver can decrypt but not encrypt; one terminal of the communications link can be intentionally exposed without compromising the other terminal. This is not possible in a symmetric system.

8. Secure Communications

Despite the different concerns of the transmitter, the receiver, or the intermediary in authentication, the objective is always an authentication system whose cryptosecurity is equivalent to the security of the transmitter's encryption key. This means that the transmitter can purposely introduce redundancy in such forms as message identifiers prior to encryption, or else he can depend on redundancy inherent in the message format or language to allow the authorized receiver to reject bogus messages. The cryptosystem may be either symmetric if all communications terminals are secure, or asymmetric if one of the communications terminals is at a physically unsecured site.

There are four possible combinations of security concerns. They are listed in Table 3. Each corresponds to a class of real communications systems.

Table 3

Class	Message/Transmitter Authentication	Secrecy
I	No	No
II	No	Yes
III	Yes	No
IV	Yes	Yes

Class I corresponds to normal, nonsecure communications. We call this the *public channel*.

Class II is the classical case of secret or private communications. We call this the *private channel*. This channel is realizable with symmetric or asymmetric techniques. In the symmetric case a compromise of the key at either end of the communications channel precludes all further secret communications. In a forward asymmetric system secret communications are still possible even if the transmitter's key is public.

The necessity for communicants' using symmetric systems to provide a secure way to exchange keys in advance is a severe restriction. A commercial cryptonet, for example, could have many thousands of subscribers, any pair of whom might wish to communicate. Clearly the number of keys to support symmetric encryption would be unmanageable. In a forward asymmetric encryption system, however, a subscriber S_i could publish his encryption pair E_i and K_i in a public directory. Anyone wishing to communicate a secret message M to S_i in secrecy transmits $E_i(M,K_i)$, which can only be deciphered by S_i. It is this application that led to the name "public-key cryptosystem." It is essential, however, that the transmitter be certain that E_i and K_i are the key entries for S_i. In other words, while a secret exchange of keys is no longer (in an asymmetric system as opposed to a symmetric one) needed, an authenticated exchange of keys is still required! This is an important point since it is frequently said -- incorrectly -- that there is no key distribution problem for public-key systems.

Class III is an unusual communications system that could not exist in a symmetric cryptosystem. In a system of this type, message and transmitter authentication is required, but secrecy cannot be tolerated. We call this a *signature channel*. An application of this channel for treaty verification has been developed at Sandia Laboratories [Simm79].

Assume that the United States and the Soviet Union sign a comprehensive test ban treaty in which each party agrees to stop all underground testing of nuclear weapons. Each side wishes to verify that the other is complying, that is, is not surreptitiously carrying out underground tests. One of the most reliable techniques for detecting underground tests uses medium-distance seismic observatories that measure the ground motions resulting from an underground detonation. These techniques are highly reliable; either nation could have confidence in the output message from seismic instruments suitably located in the host (other) nation's territory. It is not difficult to secure the instruments physically in subsurface emplacements; only the data stream sent through an open communications channel is subject to attack. If the host nation could successfully substitute innocuous seismic records for the incriminating records of underground tests, it could cheat undetected. This problem is solvable using either symmetric or asymmetric encryption techniques. The receiver (nation to which the seismic installation belongs) need only encrypt the seismic data along with as many identifiers -- station ID number, date, or clocks -- as might be needed for authentication. This method of authentication is as secure as the encryption system used to produce the cipher. However this solution would almost certainly be unacceptable to the host nation (in whose territory the seismic observatory is placed), which would be ignorant of the contents of the enciphered messages; it would fear that the cipher contains information other than the agreed-upon seismic data. If the host nation were given the key to a symmetric encryption system (so that it could decrypt the cipher and verify the message content), it would also, by definition, be able to generate counterfeit ciphers. A compromise solution is to form an authenticator much shorter than the entire message; the authenticator depends on all of the symbols in the message through some hashing function. The authenticator is also encrypted. (The block chaining technique was implemented in such a solution in the late 1960s for a similar application.) The shorter authenticator (cipher) is of course still inscrutable to the host nation, but its smaller size means that less information could be concealed in each transmission. Periodically, the hashing algorithm and key could be changed; the hashing algorithm and key used in the previous period would be given to the host, which could then verify that the authenticators had not concealed unauthorized information in the previous period. After satisfying itself that the system had not been misused, the host would renew the license to operate for one more period. This compromise is not completely satisfying to both parties because the host nation still must trust the other nation not to begin concealing information in the current authenticators.

The problem can be solved completely with either a forward or a bidirectional asymmetric encryption system. The message M and the cipher $\mathbf{E}(M,K)$ are given to the host nation, which has already been given $\mathbf{D}_E$ and K' but not K. The host would compare $\mathbf{D}_E(\mathbf{E}(M,K), K')$ with the purported message M. If the two agree, the host is assured of the content of the message. The other nation also compares $\mathbf{D}_E(\mathbf{E}(M,K), K')$ and M to determine if the message is authentic.

Class IV is typified by commercial transactions in which it is essential to be certain both that the message came from the purported transmitter and that it has not been altered in transmission -- and also to ensure that outsiders are not privy to the communication. Since all the secure communications objectives are met in such a system, we call this the *secure channel*.

There are many business applications in which a secure channel is desirable, for example, the remote automatic bank teller or the control of access to a computer's unsecured data files. In these cases the user would like to be certain that no one can wiretap the communication link while he is authenticating himself and then later be able to impersonate him to the bank's computer or to the CPU. Secure log-in computer systems require the user to identify himself before granting him access to the operating computer system [Hoff77, Mart73], but these systems may be complex. Many low-security systems simply store all user numbers and the corresponding passwords in a file normally inaccessible to users. Anyone gaining (illegal) access to this file could then impersonate any system user. The most common defense is the one-way cipher [Evan74, Purd74, Wilk68], which does not store the user's password W_i, but rather a function $\mathbf{E}(W_i)$, where $\mathbf{E}$ is chosen to be computationally infeasible to invert. Anyone gaining access to the password file would know $\mathbf{E}(W_i)$ for all the authroized users but would be unable to determine any W_i and hence unable to impersonate any user. Obviously, there are requirements other than the difficulty of inverting $\mathbf{E}$; for instance, the file can contain only a vanishingly small fraction of the total number of possible passwords; otherwise the opponent could simply choose a random collection of W_i, form the corresponding $\mathbf{E}(W_i)$, and if a match were found in the file, use that identity. This type of system has generally been adopted by the banking industry for "window identification" of passcard holders for savings accounts.

The requirement for a full-fledged secure channel arises with the brokerage house that responds to either a very large buy or sell order. The house wants the highest possible level of secrecy concerning the details of the order lest it disturb the market. The house also wants full authentication of the giver of the order. Private commercial codes were once used for precisely these purposes; these codes, however, provide little cryptosecurity.

As further illustration of the requirements on secure channels, consider a military commander who sends scouting patrols into enemy territory. A two-way radio communication link exists between each patrol and the command post, and all the patrols use the same asymmetric system. Before the mission is completed, some of the patrols may have been captured and their cryptosystems divulged. Communication from the uncompromised patrols to headquarters remains secret because only the transmitter's key has been compromised. Moreover, the enemy cannot impersonate the commander's messages because it knows only a receiver's key.

Now, suppose that a hybrid cryptosystem is used. The first communication over the asymmetric channel from a patrol to the commander could be a key, for example, a 56-bit random number for the DES symmetric cryptosystem. This communication is in secret since only the transmitter key could have been compromised for this channel. Thereafter the commander and patrol can engage in a secure two-way communication over the symmetric channel using the new "session" key. This is not possible using the asymmetric system alone because the commander's ciphers may be legible to the enemy. This system is not foolproof, however, because the commander has no way to authenticate the patrol initiating the communication. Some other concealed information, such as a sign or countersign, could be used, but this additional information would be considered to be a part of the key according to the strict definition given earlier and hence may have been divulged to the enemy.

The foregoing discussion assumes that the sender and receiver are sure of each other's identity and keys -- for example, a higher level commander has generated the keys, or each user has generated his own pair of keys. Needham and Schroeder [Need78] have shown that the secure distribution of keys is essential to cryptosecurity and is the same for symmetric and asymmetric systems. The following example illustrates the possibility that completely anonymous communicants can enter into a private conversation. Let $\mathcal{E}$ be a class of commutative encryption functions,[16] i.e., $\mathbf{E}_A, \mathbf{E}_B \in \mathcal{E}$ implies $\mathbf{E}_A(\mathbf{E}_B(M,K_B), K_A) = \mathbf{E}_B(\mathbf{E}_A(M,K_A), K_B)$. If A wishes to communicate a message M to B in secrecy where no advance arrangements such as key distribution or public-key disclosure have been made, A chooses $\mathbf{E}_A$, $\mathbf{D}_A$, and K_A and K'_A. He then transmits the cipher $\mathbf{E}_A(M,K_A)$ to B, who cannot decrypt the cipher. Now B chooses $\mathbf{E}_B$, $\mathbf{D}_B$, and K_B and K'_B from the family of commutative encryption functions and transmits the cipher $\mathbf{E}_B(\mathbf{E}_A(M,K_A), K_B)$ to A. A computes $\mathbf{D}_A\big(\mathbf{E}_B(\mathbf{E}_A(M,K_A), K_B), K'_A\big)$, which reduces to $\mathbf{E}_B(M,K_B)$ because $\mathbf{D}_A$ "undoes" $\mathbf{E}_A$. Then A relays this cipher back to B, who computes $\mathbf{D}_B(\mathbf{E}_B(M,K_B), K'_B)$ to recover M. On the surface it appears that an impossible result has been accomplished because the keys were kept secret all through the exchange. In fact, A has communicated in secret to whomever responded to his original transmission of the cipher $\mathbf{E}_A(M,K_A)$, but A cannot establish the identity of his receiver. In other words, A can only be certain that he has a private communication with an unknown party.

Perhaps the most intriguing example of this paradox of initiating secret communications between two parties who cannot establish each other's identities occurs in Shamir, Rivest,

---

[16] An example of a commutative cryptosystem is a variant of the Pohlig-Hellman log-antilog scheme over large finite fields [Pohl78]. Let $\mathfrak{M} = \{GF(2^{127})/\{0,1\}\}$ be the message space known to everyone. A selects an exponent $2 \leq e \leq 2^{127} - 2$ and encrypts M as M^e in $GF(2^{127})$. B chooses an exponent d similarly and relays $(M^e)^d$ (also in $GF(2^{127})$), which A then raises to the e^{-1} power to get $M^d = ((M^e)^d)^{e^{-1}}$, which is retransmitted to B who computes $(M^d)^{d^{-1}}$ to obtain M. An opponent will have seen M^e, M^d and will know the space $\mathfrak{M}$, so he is faced with the "known plaintext" decryption problem with the twist that he knows two messages which encrypt to a common cipher.

and Adleman's protocol for playing mental poker [Sham79]. In this case the names of the cards are encrypted by player A and the resulting ciphers passed to B who chooses a random subset (deal), etc., to relay to B using a commutative encryption function as described in the preceding paragraph. The resulting game is self-consistent in the sense that the players can verify that a game of poker is being played fairly -- but with an unknown opponent.

The point of the preceding three paragraphs is to illustrate an essential point about asymmetric encryption systems. It *is not true* that "in a public-key cryptosystem[17] there is no need of a secure channel for the distribution of keys" [Hell79b]. What is true is that whereas the secure key distribution system must be able to certify the secrecy of the delivered key for use in symmetric systems, it need only be able to certify the authenticity of the key for asymmetric systems. There is implicit in this statement a distinction between a passive wiretapper (eavesdropper) who only listens to but does not originate ciphers and an active wiretapper who may alter or originate ciphers. An eavesdropper listening to the microwave scatter from a microwave link illustrates the first threat, while a wiretapper in a central switching office illustrates the second. In the case of the active wiretapper, the only way to avoid the "postal chess ploy"[18] is to have the keys delivered securely, either in a face-to-face exchange by the transmitter and receiver or by trusted couriers, etc.

---

[17]Read asymmetric cryptosystem.

[18]In this scheme a third party interposes himself simply to relay moves in the correspondence of two postal chess players with a guarantee of either drawing against both or else winning against one while losing to the other, irrespective of his chess playing abilities.

Summary and Conclusion

The primary objectives in this paper have been to develop the concept of the asymmetric encryption/decryption channel and to show some real problems that can only be solved by using such a channel. A secondary objective has been to draw analogies between coding theory and encryption theory in order to clarify the concepts of secrecy and authentication.

Cryptosystems are naturally classified into two classes, symmetric or asymmetric, depending only on whether the keys at the transmitter and receiver are easily computed from each other. The only well-tested operational cryptosystems in 1979 were symmetric. All depend on the computational intractability of working backward from a knowledge of the cipher, plaintext, and encryption/decryption function for their cryptosecurity. Asymmetric cryptosystems are inherently neither more nor less secure than symmetric cryptosystems. Both kinds of system depend on the high "work factor" associated with a computationally infeasible problem to provide computational cryptosecurity. An essential difference between symmetric and asymmetric cryptosystems is that one of the transmitter or receiver keys can be compromised in the asymmetric system with some secure communications still possible. In some instances, such as the public-key cryptosystem, the exposure may be deliberate; in others it cannot be insured against simply because of the physical exposure of one end of the communications link. If in an asymmetric system the receiver key is concealed from a knowledge of the transmitter key, it is still possible to communicate in secrecy even after the transmitter key is exposed. Conversely, if the transmitter key is concealed from a knowledge of the receiver key, it is possible for the transmitter to authenticate himself even though the receiver key is known to an opponent. These unique capabilities of asymmetric systems distinguish them from symmetric systems.

Two vital points need to be restated. First, it is false that key protection and secure key dissemination are unnecessary in an asymmetric system. As Needham and Schroeder [Need78] have shown for network authentication, the protocols are quite similar, and the number of protocol messages which must be exchanged is comparable using either symmetric or asymmetric encryption techniques. At the end of the section on secure communications we illustrated an anomaly, the establishing of a secret link with a party whose identity cannot be verified, which can arise in the absence of key dissemination. For this reason asymmetric techniques can be used to disseminate a key which is then used in a symmetric system.

The second point is that asymmetric systems are not a priori superior to symmetric ones. The particular application determines which system is appropriate. In the 1979 state of the art, all the proposed asymmetric systems exact a high price for their asymmetry: The higher amount of computation in the encryption/decryption process significantly cuts the channel capacity (bits per second of message information communicated). No asymmetric scheme known to the author has a capacity better than $C^{1/2}$, where C is the channel capacity of a symmetric channel having the same cryptosecurity and using the same basic clock or bit manipulation rate. Under these conditions, the higher overhead of asymmetric encryption is warranted only for applications in which one of the communications terminals is physically insecure.

Appendix

The following brief discussion of LFSRs is included for the benefit of readers who may not be familiar with the inner workings of these devices. Given an nth-order nonhomogeneous polynomial, i.e., $P^n(x) = \Sigma_{i=0}^{n} c_i x^i$, where $c_0 = c_n = 1$, with binary coefficients,[19] we define an associated n-stage linear feedback shift register by the rules

$$x_1^t = \sum_{i=1}^{n} c_i x_i^{t-1}$$

and

$$x_i^t = x_{i-1}^{t-1} \quad , \qquad i > 1$$

where x_i^t is the state of the ith stage of the register on the tth step and $\sum$ is the modulo 2 sum (binary arithmetic). For example, if $P^4(x) = x^4 + x^3 + x^2 + x + 1$, the shift register is of the form shown in Figure 7 and the sequence of states of the register (depending on the initial fill) is one of four cycles:

0000	1000	0100	1110
	0001	1001	1101
	0011	0010	1011
	0110	0101	0111
	1100	1010	1111

In this case the 16 possible 4-bit binary numbers are divided into three cycles of length 5 and one of length 1. The explanation is that $x^4 + x^3 + x^2 + x + 1$ divides $x^5 + 1$ evenly; i.e.,

$$(x+1)(x^4 + x^3 + x^2 + x + 1) = x^5 + 1 \quad .$$

Note: Remember that the coefficients are treated as residues modulo 2.

A well-known result from algebra says that $P^n(x)$ always divides $x^{2^n - 1} + 1$, but that $P^n(x)$ may also divide $x^d + 1$ where d is a divisor of $2^n - 1$, in which case the maximum period of the sequences from the associated LFSR is also a

---

[19] Modulo 2 using the rules

+	0	1
0	0	1
1	1	0

×	0	1
0	0	0
1	0	1

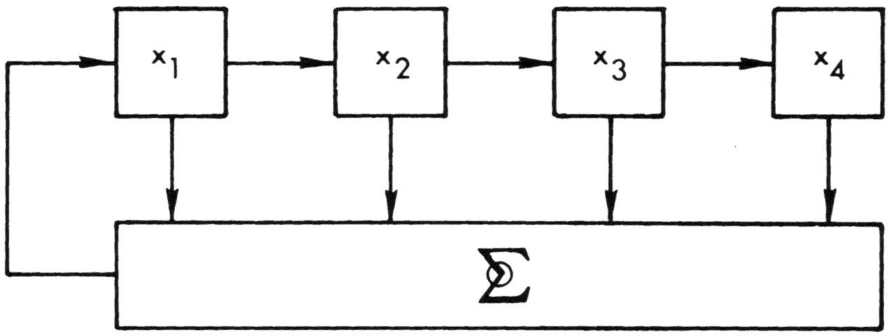

Figure 7.

proper divisor of $2^n - 1$. If the polynomial $P^n(x)$ has no factors and does not divide $x^d + 1$ for any proper divisor d of $2^n - 1$, then $P^n(x)$ is said to be primitive. The important point is that the nonzero cycle generated by the associated linear feedback shift register for any primitive polynomial has the maximum possible period of $2^n - 1$:00 ... 0 is always in a cycle by itself. For example, $P^4(x) = x^4 + x + 1$ divides $x^{15} + 1$ but not $x^d + 1$ for any $d < 15$; hence $P^4(x)$ is primitive and the maximal length nonzero cycle generated by the associated LFSR is:

```
1000   0101
0001   1011
0011   0110
0111   1100
1111   1001
1110   0010
1101   0100
1010
```

Linear feedback shift registers based on primitive polynomials are therefore said to be maximal length, and the resulting bit sequences have been shown to satisfy many tests for randomness [Golo67, Taus65]. For example, 0, 1 and 00, 01, 10, 11, etc. (up to n-tuples), are as nearly uniform in their probability of occurrence as is possible; i.e., since the all-zero n-tuple is not in the cycle, the all-zero k-tuple will occur one time less than do the other k-tuples. Because of these very useful properties and also because of the ease of implementing maximal length LFSRs in either hardware or software, a voluminous literature exists on the subject -- including extensive tables of the primitive polynomials [Golo67, Pete72] needed to compute the feedback functions. An especially simple class of primitive polynomial [Zier68, Zier69], both to analyze and to implement, is the trinomials, $x^n + x^a + 1$, which require only two stages of the feedback shift register to be tapped and combined by an Exclusive OR

⊕	0	1
0	0	1
1	1	0

to compute the feedback sum.

Acknowledgments

The author wishes to acknowledge the many and valuable contributions of M. J. Norris to the ideas presented here. He is also grateful to D. Kahn and H. Bright for careful reviews of a first draft of the manuscript and to the anonymous referees whose detailed suggestions materially shaped the present form of the paper. Finally, he wishes to express his appreciation to R. J. Hanson and P. J. Denning whose assistance has made it possible for this material to be published in Computing Surveys.

References

Acme23 Acme commodity and phrase code, Acme Code Co., San Francisco, Calif., 1923.

Adle78 Adleman, L. M., and Rivest, R. L. "The use of public-key cryptography in communication system design," IEEE Trans. Commun. COM-16, 6 (Nov. 1978), 20-23.

Albe41 Albert, A. A. "Some mathematical aspects of cryptography," presented at the AMS 382nd Meeting, Manhattan, Kans., Nov. 22, 1941.

Berl68 Berlekamp, E. R. Algebraic coding theory, McGraw-Hill, New York, 1968.

Bran79 Branstad, D. "Hellman's data does not support his conclusion," IEEE Spectrum 16, 7 (July 1979), 41.

Brig76 Bright, H. S., and Enison, R. L. "Cryptography using modular software elements," in Proc. AFIPS 1976 NCC, Vol. 45, AFIPS Press, Arlington, Va., pp. 113-123.

Brig77 Bright, H. S. "Cryptanalytic attack and defense: ciphertext-only, known-plaintext, chosen-plaintext," Cryptologia 1, 4 (Oct. 1977), 366-370.

Davi79 Davida, G. I. "Hellman's scheme breaks DES in its basic form," IEEE Spectrum 16, 7 (July 1979), 39.

Deav77 Deavours, C. A. "Unicity points in cryptanalysis," Cryptologia 1, 1 (Jan. 1977), 46-68.

Diff76 Diffie, W., and Hellman, M. E. "New directions in cryptography," IEEE Trans. Inform Theory IT-22, 6 (Nov. 1976), 644-654.

Diff77 Diffie, W., and Hellman, M. E. "Exhaustive cryptanalysis of the NBS data encryption standard," Computer 10, 6 (June 1977), 74-84.

Evan74 Evans, A., Jr., and Kantrowitz, W. "A user authentication scheme not requiring secrecy in the computer," Commun. ACM 17, 8 (Aug. 1974), 437-442.

Feis73 Feistel, H. "Cryptography and computer privacy," Sci. Am. 228, 5 (May 1973), 15-23.

Gain56 Gaines, H. F. Cryptanalysis: a study of ciphers and their solution, Dover, New York, 1956.

Gait77 Gait, J. "A new nonlinear pseudorandom number generator," IEEE Trans. Softw. Eng. SE-3, 5 (Sept. 1977), 359-363.

Gard77 Garner, M. Mathematical games (section), Sci. Am. 237, 2 (Aug. 1977), 120-124.

Geff73 Geffe, P. R. "How to protect data with ciphers that are really hard to break," Electronics 46, 1 (Jan. 4, 1973), 99-101.

Gilb74 Gilbert, E. N., MacWilliams, F. J., and Sloane, N. J. A. "Codes which detect deception," Bell Syst. Tech. J. 53, 3 (March 1974), 405-423.

Golo67 Golomb, S. W. Shift register sequences, Holden-Day, San Francisco, Calif., 1967.

Hart64 Hart, G. L. The Beale papers, Roanoke Public Library, Roanoke, Va., 1964.

Hell78 Hellman, M. E. "An overview of public-key cryptography," IEEE Trans. Commun. COM-16, 6 (Nov. 1978), 24-32.

Hell79a Hellman, M. E. "DES will be totally insecure within ten years," IEEE Spectrum 16, 7 (July 1979), 32-39.

Hell79b Hellman, M. E. "The mathematics of public-key cryptography," Sci. Am. 241, 3 (Aug. 1979), 146-157.

Herl78 Herlestam, T. "Critical remarks on some public-key cryptosystems," BIT 18 (1978), 493-496.

Hill29 Hill, L. S. "Cryptography in an algebraic alphabet," Am. Math. Monthly 36 (June-July 1929), 306-312.

Hill31 Hill, L. S. "Concerning certain linear transformation apparatus of cryptography," Am. Math. Monthly 38 (March 1931), 135-154.

Hoff77 Hoffman, L. J. Modern methods for computer security and privacy, Prentice-Hall, Englewood Cliffs, N. J., 1977.

Horo74 Horowitz, E., and Sahni, S. "Computing partitions with applications to the knapsack problem," J. ACM 21, 2 (April 1974), 277-292.

Kahn66 Kahn, D. "Modern cryptology," Sci. Am. 215 (July 1966), 38-46.

Kahn67 Kahn, D. The codebreakers, the story of secret writing, MacMillan, New York, 1967.

Karp72 Karp, R. M. "Reducibility among combinatorial problems," in Complexity of computer computations, R. E. Miller and J. W. Thatcher (Eds.), Plenum Press, New York, 1972, pp. 85-104.

Kull76 Kullback, S. Statistical methods in cryptanalysis, Aegean Park Press, Laguna Hills, Calif., 1976.

Lemp79 Lempel, A. "Cryptology in transition: a survey," Comput. Surv. 11, 4 (Dec. 1979), 285-304.

Lipt78 Lipton, S. M., and Matyas, S. M. "Making the digital signature legal -- and safeguarded," Data Commun. 7, 2 (Feb. 1978), 41-52.

MacW77 MacWilliams, F. J., and Sloane, N. J. A. The Theory of error-correcting codes, Vols. I and II, North-Holland, New York, 1977.

Mart73 Martin, J. Security, accuracy and privacy in computing systems, Prentice-Hall, Englewood Cliffs, N. J., 1973.

Mass69 Massey, J. L. "Shift-register synthesis and BCH decoding," IEEE Trans. Inform. Theory IT-15, 1 (Jan. 1969), 122-127.

Merk78a Merkle, R. C. "Secure communications over insecure channels," Commun. ACM 21, 4 (April 1978), 294-299.

Merk78b Merkle, R. C., and Hellman, M. E. "Hiding information and signatures in trapdoor knapsacks," IEEE Trans. Inform. Theory IT-24, 5 (Sept. 1978), 525-530.

Meye72 Meyer, C., and Tuchman, W. "Pseudo-random codes can be cracked," Electron. Des. 23 (1972), 74-76.

Morr77 Morris, R., Sloane, N. J. A., and Wyner, A. D. "Assessment of the National Bureau of Standards proposed federal Data Encryption Standard," Cryptologia 1, 3 (July 1977), 281-291.

Need78 Needham, R. M., and Schroeder, M. D. "Using encryption for authentication in large networks of computers," Commun. ACM 21, 12 (Dec. 1978), 993-999.

Pete72 Peterson, W. W., and Weldon, E. J. Error correcting codes, 2nd ed., MIT Press, Cambridge, Mass., 1972.

Pohl78 Pohlig, S. C., and Hellman, M. E. "An improved algorithm for computing logarithms over GF(p) and its cryptographic significance," IEEE Trans. Inform. Theory IT-24, 1 (Jan. 1978), 106-110.

Purd74 Purdy, G. B. "A high security log-in procedure," Commun. ACM 17, 8 (Aug. 1974), 442-445.

Rabi79 Rabin, M. O. Digitalized signatures and public-key functions as intractable as factorization, Tech. Rep. MIT/LCS/TR-212, MIT Lab. Comput. Sci., Cambridge, Mass., Jan. 1979.

Rive78 Rivest, R., Shamir, A., and Adleman, L. "A method for obtaining digital signatures and public-key cryptosystems," Commun. ACM 21, 2 (Feb. 1978), 120-126.

Robe75 Roberts, R. W. Encryption algorithm for computer data encryption," (NBS) Fed. Reg. 40, 52 (March 17, 1975), 12134-12139.

Schr79 Schroeppel, R., and Shamir, A. "A $T \cdot S^2 = O(2^n)$ time/space tradeoff for certain NP-complete problems," to appear as MIT Lab. Comput. Sci. Rep.

Sham78 Shamir, A., and Zippel, R. E. On the security of the Merkle-Hellman cryptographic scheme, Tech. Rep. MIT/LCS/TM-119, MIT Lab. Comput. Sci., Cambridge, Mass., Dec. 1978.

Sham79 Shamir, A., Rivest, R. L., and Adleman, L. M. Mental Poker, Tech. Rep. MIT/LCS/TM-125, MIT Lab. Comput. Sci., Cambridge, Mass., Feb. 1979.

Shan48 Shannon, C. E. "A mathematical theory of communication," Bell Syst. Tech. J. 27 (July 1948), 379-423; (Oct. 1948), 623-656.

Shan49 Shannon, C. E. "Communication theory of secrecy systems," Bell Syst. Tech. J. 28 (Oct. 1949), 656-715.

Shap78 Shapley, D. "The new unbreakable codes -- will they put NSA out of business?," The Washington Post, Outlook, sec. B1, July 9, 1978.

Simm77 Simmons, G. J., and Norris, M. J. "Preliminary comments on the MIT public-key cryptosystem," Cryptologia 1, 4 (Oct. 1977), 406-414.

Simm79 Simmons, G. J. "Cryptology: the mathematics of secure communication," Math. Intell. 1, 4 (Jan. 1979), 233-246.

Suga79 Sugarman, R. "On foiling computer crime," IEEE Spectrum 16, 7 (July 1979), 31-32.

Taus65 Tausworthe, R. C. "Random numbers generated by linear recurrence modulo two," Math. Comput. 19 (1965), 201-209.

Tuch79 Tuchman, W. "Hellman presents no shortcut solutions to the DES," IEEE Spectrum 16, 7 (July 1979), 40-41.

Tuck70 Tuckerman, B. A study of the Vigenére-Vernam single and multiple loop enciphering systems, Rep. RC-2879 (#13538), IBM T. J. Watson Res. Ctr., Yorktown Heights, N.Y., May 14, 1970.

Vern26 Vernam, G. S. "Cipher printing telegraph systems for secret wire and radio telegraphic communications," J. AIEE 45 (Feb. 1926), 109-115.

Wilk68 Wilkes, M. V. Time-sharing computer systems, American Elsevier, New York, 1968.

Will69a Williams, H. C., and Schmid, B. Some remarks concerning the M.I.T. public-key cryptosystem, Rep. 91, U. of Manitoba Dep. of Comput. Sci., May 22, 1979.

Will79b Williams, H. C. A modification of the RSA public-key encryption procedure, Rep. 92, U. of Manitoba Dep. of Comput. Sci., 1979.

Zier68 Zierler, N., and Brillhart, J. "On primitive trinomials (mod 2)," Inform. Control 13 (1968), 541-554.

Zier69 Zierler, N., and Brillhart, J. "On primitive trinomials (mod 2, II)," Inform. Control 14 (1969), 566-569.

Part 3

The Future

Whitfield Diffie

11. Cryptographic Technology: Fifteen-Year Forecast

Abstract

This paper examines the forces driving public development of cryptography today and projects the course of the field over the next fifteen years with attention to the possible influence of government regulation.

Summary

The emergence of cryptography into technical and political prominence during the 1970's has disquieted its traditional practitioners and led to calls for public regulation of the new field. An essential ingredient in deciding how if at all such regulation is to be carried out is a baseline prediction of the future of cryptography which identifies the areas in which government regulation might be significant.

The past five years have witnessed two major developments: the promulgation of a federal Data Encryption Standard (DES) by the National Bureau of Standards and the devel-

This paper was prepared, under contractual arrangements to CRC Systems, in support of the Commerce Department National Telecommunications and Information Administration (NTIA) Special Project Office activity to formulate a national policy for cryptography. The NTIA activity was in response to a White House Office of Science and Technology Policy request that the Secretaries of the Departments of Commerce and Defense propose a national policy on cryptography.

opment of a new variety of cryptographic systems, public key cryptography, by academic researchers. DES products are now available from many of the major electronics manufacturers and public key systems, with their "digital signature" capability, have been implemented for specialized applications. Major corporations have responded by beginning to study both their own security requirements and the business opportunities, but so far sales of the new equipment have been sluggish.

Trends in modern communications and computing which are expected to influence cryptography include:

- Increasing importance of communication coupled with the increasing vulnerability of communication channels to unauthorized interception or manipulation.
- Developments in computer science which will make cryptography cheaper and easier to apply.
- Rapid development of public key cryptography.
- Inroads into the traditional secrecy that surrounds the practice of cryptography.
- Decline of a government monopoly in the practice of cryptography and an increasing academic and commercial interest in the field.
- A likely need to replace DES before the turn of the century.

These influences may be affected to varying degrees by government regulation.

The report concludes with scenarios for each of the next three five-year periods.

- 1980-1985 DES, implemented in the current LSI technology, will remain viable. Public key products and the first secure computer operating systems will appear.

- 1985-1990 Use of VLSI and secure computing, will markedly decrease the cost of cryptography, while similarly decreased cost of eavesdropping will increase the demand.

  Public key cryptography will be entering its second decade and the development of new, higher performance, systems is likely.

  Diminished security of DES will make multiple encryption a *de facto* standard for higher security applications.

- 1990-1995 New technology and new threats will lead to major changes in communication security. Replacement of DES, either by a more secure system based on current technology or by a new product of 1980's research, is virtually certain and unification of the techniques used for protecting classified and unclassified information is likely.

Preface

Though aware that prophecy is always an uncertain business, I have not allowed this awareness to influence my use of English. In expressing my degrees of certainty, I have used the overconfident "will" as readily as the unassailable "may." The reader must weigh the strength of my conviction together with my arguments and references in forming his own opinion.

Introduction

Cryptography has developed during the past decade from a little known technical aspect of military and intelligence operations to a widely discussed and much studied adjunct of data communication and storage. Where a decade ago cryptography was almost completely secret, and the government agencies responsible for its practice avoided identification whenever possible, today it is discussed regularly in the nation's leading newspapers and news magazines as well as scientific magazines and technical journals.

This sudden prominence has had a disquieting effect on the conventional practitioners of the subject who fear that the actions of the new civilian cryptographic community will upset the flow of intelligence information and have an ill effect on the security of the United States. Although the instinctive desire of this community is to discourage the new cryptographers, the soundness of such a course of action is placed in doubt by evidence that American well being is also jepardized by lack of security in our own civilian communications -- a lack of security which can in large part be blamed on the lack of civilian awareness and understanding of communications intelligence and security which was the rule until very recently.

The conflict in views between those who disparage and those who support development of an unclassified cryptographic technology for application to commercial communications has lead to a need for a considered governmental policy on how, if at all, the new wave of cryptographic activity is to be regulated.

An indispensible input to the formulation of any such policy is a projection of probable developments in communication security and an analysis of the effects that proposed government policies might have.

The following report will attempt to provide a baseline projection of the direction and impact of communication security research and practice and where possible identify the areas in which government regulation might be influential.

Cryptography Today

Cryptography is the technique of protecting data by transforming it from a usable and comprehensible "plaintext" form to a scrambled and incomprehensible "ciphertext" form, from which the plaintext can only be recovered by use of a secret "key." The mechanism which performs this transformation is known as a cryptographic system or cryptosystem and the transformations are known as "encryption" and "decryption" respectively.

If the plaintext can, despite the efforts of the designers, be recovered from the ciphertext without the use of the key, the process is called "cryptanalysis" and the system so defeated is said to have been "broken" or "read." The two problems to which cryptography can be applied are called "privacy" and "authentication." The former is the problem of guaranteeing that the contents of a message will not be revealed to any unauthorized party while it is being transmitted from a sender to a receiver. The latter is the problem of guaranteeing that the message which reaches the receiver is actually one transmitted by the sender and that it has arrived unaltered and on time.

Until recently, the study and use of cryptography were practiced almost entirely by the military, diplomatic, and intelligence communities. During the past decade, however, the vastly increased use of computer operated telecommunications systems has extended interest in cryptography to communications companies, computer manufacturers, banks, and universities, among others.

The two most conspicuous results of this expanded interest have been the promulgation of a cryptographic standard by the National Bureau of Standards and the development of public key cryptography by university researchers.

In 1975, the National Bureau of Standards, published a proposed standard algorithm for data protection. In 1977, after two years of public controversy over its security, this algorithm was adopted as Federal Information Processing Standard 46, the Data Encryption Standard (DES)[4]. Both the publication of the standard and the controversy over its adoption have focused new attention on cryptography in the technical community.

The Data Encryption Standard, in its basic form, is a "block" cryptosystem; it transforms 64 bits (eight characters) of plaintext into 64 bits of ciphertext under the control of a 56 bit key. The encryption takes place in sixteen rounds. During each round, the left 32 bits are combined in a reversible way with the result of a complex substitution and transposition of the right 32 bits. The new left half is then interchanged with the old (unaltered) right half and the two halves play opposite roles in the next round. The substitution and transposition operation on the right half is controlled by a 48 bit subset of the key bits, which varies from round to round.

In the three and one half years since its adoption as a standard, DES has enjoyed great success with manufacturers, making a sweeping change in the availability of cryptographic products. Where before these were available only from a few specialized companies, now approximately a dozen major computer and electronics manufacturers are producing equipment ranging from individual DES chips to stand alone link encryption units to cryptographically protected automated teller machines.

The second recent development, public key cryptography [6], is almost exactly the same age as DES and has been prospering within its own sphere. This proposal for cryptographic systems in which some of the keying material could be made public in such a way as to permit both freer and more secure communication has developed into such a thriving area of research that it has often been confused for a competing product.

A public key cryptosystem is one in which the conversion of plaintext to ciphertext and the conversion of ciphertext to plaintext are done using different keys. Furthermore, given one of the keys, it is just as difficult to discover the other as it would be to discover the plaintext given only a sample of the ciphertext. This separation of the keys for encrypting and decrypting makes it possible to disclose one (the public key) while retaining the other (the secret key).

Because the public key can be revealed without compromising the secret key, the process of providing suitable keys to the sender and receiver ("key distribution") can be made both freer and more secure. Public key cryptosystems also make possible a new form of authentication called a "digital signature." A message that has been encrypted with a secret key could only have been created by the holder of that secret key. The identity of the creator can, however, be verified by anyone who has the corresponding public key. This property (creatable by only one person but recognizable by many) allows the digital signature to play much the same role in electronic communication that a written signature plays in paper communication.

Public key cryptography was discovered in the spring of 1975 and the first paper on the subject appeared in June 1976 [5]. In the intervening four years two major approaches, drawn from different areas of mathematics, have been found for implementing it.

The first of these [19], called the RSA system after its inventors initials, is drawn from number theory. It is based on the concept of a prime number (a number that cannot be evenly divided by any numbers except itself and one) and on the relative ease with which a pair of primes can be multiplied together compared with the difficulty of factoring their product to discover the two primes. Like DES, the RSA system is a block system, though in this case the blocks must be five to ten times as long for the system to be secure. A block of plaintext is encrypted by exponentiation in a finite arithmetic structure. The exponent in this operation together with the product of the primes comprise the public key. The inverse operation can be performed only by those who know the pair of primes (the secret key). Because this cryptosystem requires dozens of multiplications of numbers hundreds of digits in length, its operation is quite slow. The fastest versions so far constructed can process thousands of bits per second as compared with millions for some DES implementations.

The second public key system [15], called the "trapdoor knapsack system," has its roots in field called combinatorial mathematics. Here the trick is that given a list of numbers it is easy to add up the whole list or any specified subset, but given instead a list of numbers and a sum it is extremely difficult to discover a subset which totals to exactly that sum. The name is imaginatively derived from the notion of attempting to choose just the right set of rods from those in a box so that when packed into a long thin knapsack, the rods would fit tightly and not rattle. In order to do encryption in this system, the input block is treated as a specification of which numbers are to be selected from a list and added up; the output is their sum. The trapdoor knapsack system is based on Merkle's discovery that if the list of numbers is constructed correctly, certain details of that construction constitute a secret key which allows the constructor to take the sum and discover which members of the list were added. Unlike the RSA system, knapsack systems are quite fast. Unfortunately, the public key is a list of approximately one hundred numbers, each of about thirty digits in length, which is quite unwieldy.

Although these first approaches fall short of conventional cryptographic systems in performance (speed or storage requirements), both have already found application [21,16].

At present, the most active area of communication security is the development and standardization of protocols for the use of cryptography in modern data communication systems. Experiments in cryptographic network security are being carried out at various laboratories [16,20] and an effort to set standards has been underway over the past two years in the American National Standards Institute and such governmental bodies as the National Bureau of Standards, the National Communication System, and the National Security Agency.

At present, despite substantial research activity and study by "Fortune 500" companies of their security requirements [11], the market for the new cryptographic products has been sluggish. Many feel, however, that as electronics funds transfer and other developments in communications progress the cryptographic market will improve dramatically [2,14].

Trends and Influences

Increasing Threats to Communications

Two major trends in modern communication technology combine to make communications increasingly vulnerable to eavesdropping.

- The use of microwave radio and satellite relay to replace cables allows an eavesdropper to intercept with a mobile or fixed antenna without taking the risk of any physical intrusion into the communication path. Such links are employed by virtually all domestic telecommunication carriers.

- The use of digital (particularly packetized) formats for more and more forms of data allows the eavesdropper to analyze the intercepted traffic by computer, searching for key words in the body of the message or examining the packet headers for the addresses of the sender and receiver.

These threats, which make all but voice communication vulnerable to low budget eavesdropping operations, are being joined by rapid development of voice processing technology. At present, speaker independent word recognition is just beginning to become available on the commercial market [22, 9,10]. By the latter half of the decade, this technology will have progressed to where word recognition, speaker recognition, and possibly full voice understanding (voice typewriter) robust enough to be applied in the adverse environment of wiretapping will be commercially available. It is also possible that voice synthesis will progress to a point where authentication by speaker recognition will no longer be useful.

These threats appear at a time when security of communications is growing in importance for an ever broadening area of society. It is widely felt that international economic competition will intensify during the remainder of the century in an environment of increasing scarcity of resources and military standoff. This will give economic and commercial communications an intelligence value akin to that currently attached only to military transmissions and place civilian communication systems under substantial pressure to improve their security.

Decreasing cost of computation. It is a surprising fact that decreases in the cost of computation do not benefit the cryptosystem designer and the cryptanalyst equally. If a cryptographic method is of any value at all -- if cryptanalysis takes an effort which is more than a linear function of the effort required to produce the cryptogram -- a decrease in the cost of computation benefits the cryptographer to the detriment of the cryptanalyst. This is because the increased computing power that the system designer can afford to employ on encryption will require a more than proportional increase on the part of the cryptanalyst.

The improvement in security of modern cryptographic systems over those available at the time of World War II can be credited largely to the factor of one million reduction in the cost of computation which has occurred over the intervening period and this trend will make the construction of secure cryptosystems easier and easier as time goes on. What is and will probably remain difficult is constructing highly efficient cryptosystems -- cryptosystems which are minimal in number of components or maximal in speed.

<u>Very large scale integration</u>. At present, semiconductor technology permits the Data Encryption Standard to be implemented on a single silicon chip but will not accommodate DES as one of several components of a larger structure. By the mid-eighties, when chips with 100,000 to 1,000,000 devices will be common, cryptography will be integrated into packages performing broader communication functions. This will be aided by the development of custom LSI. The cost of electronic shielding now required in the highest grade cryptographic equipment will decline as the cryptodevices and their associated optically isolated communication paths are combined in single packages.

<u>Secure computing</u>. Development of secure operating systems, which can be trusted to process the confidential data of several mutually suspicious users simultaneously, is currently an active area of computer science. Although the role that cryptography will play in the inner workings of such

systems is yet to be established, cryptography and secure computing are destined to be deeply intertwined. Secure operating systems will play as crucial a role as cryptography in the development of secure computer networks, will simplify the design of communication security hardware, and make possible such flexible techniques as wide implementation of cryptographic algorithms in software.

If cryptography emerges as an important technique in the construction of secure computers, this will create a demand for strong cryptographic algorithms with better performance than DES. The complexity of DES is comparable to that of the most complex computer instructions (for example a double precision floating point multiply) and this complexity makes it too slow for use in the instruction stream of a fast computer. At present, the fastest implementations of DES would be adequate for internal use in computers of moderate speed (e.g., PDP-11's) but utterly unable to cope with the memory access requirements of super machines such as the Cray One.

Public Key Cryptography

At present, public key cryptosystems neither offer the performance nor command the trust of conventional systems. Public key cryptography is, however, a field only four years old and judged by this standard is doing exceptionally well. The two major approaches to constructing public key systems [19,15] come from widely separated areas of mathematics and are each good enough to have found application [21,16]. This, together with the lack of any significant theoretical limitation on the performance of public key systems, is reason for optimism that more and better examples will be forthcoming in the near future.

Analog and Voice Encryption

Analog encryption devices, primarily used for voice protection, account for a significant portion of the commercial encryption products today. Over the next fifteen years, use of these products will probably decline to an insignificant level in the U.S., due to the spreading digitization of the telephone system and the improving quality of both modems and voice compression equipment.

At present, digital encryption of voice telephony requires either a high speed modem or a complex voice compression system. Either of these is expensive, but both should decline in cost at the same general rate as other computing equipment and reach one percent of their present prices in 1990.

In the meantime, the quality of conventional analog scrambling equipment is being improved and its cost is being decreased by implementing it through digital signal processing technology. New research [24,25] also gives promise of higher security analog systems.

Changes in Cryptographic Tradition

Decline of system secrecy. The adoption of the Data Encryption Standard by the United States represented a fundamental change in cryptographic tradition whose beneficial effects on communication security may be DES's greatest contribution. Both classical [13] and modern [3] cryptographic experience has shown that systems developed in secret, except perhaps by the largest and most experienced cryptologic organizations, are prone to hidden flaws which lead to their downfall. If, on the other hand, a system is made public it will be subject to scrutiny by a wide range of critics and weaknesses are less likely to be overlooked.

An important beneficiary of this change in tradition may be the developing nations. These nations, which have far less stake in communications intelligence than the established powers, and consequently less interest in keeping good cryptographic systems out of the hands of their opponents, may choose to adopt systems, whether homegrown or imported, whose functioning is public for their next generation of communications facilities.

Availability of cryptographic expertise. Another change in cryptographic tradition and circumstances is likely to provide a more abundant supply of trained cryptographers.

In the past, very few jobs for cryptographers were available outside of government agencies and those who had held government positions felt constrained by security agreements not to take such jobs after leaving government employ. The widening interest in cryptography outside the government has lead to a normalization of relations between government and industry. Government cryptographers now express willingness to take industry jobs subject to the same constraints which would bind experts with classified experience in other fields such as laser physics or missile guidance. They have explicit information which cannot be shared with the new employer, but feel that their general expertise is not in itself restricted.

Although this would at first appear to be one of the areas most subject to government control, an attempt to tighten the rules would not be likely to succeed without widespread industry cooperation. More stringent statutary restrictions on former government employees would make affected government jobs less desirable and might therefore make it more difficult for federal agencies to recruit their own staffs.

Academic Interest in Cryptography

Academic interest in cryptography, which has been responsible for major cryptographic developments in the past five years, is likely to continue, although not necessarily at a constant level. This interest is abetted by the connection of cryptography with a number of other fields of current interest in mathematics and computer science and the appealing difficulty of constructing public key systems or cryptographic systems with other interesting properties.

The theory of computational complexity has had, and will probably continue to have, the closest connection to cryptography, since cryptography provides a potential application for a wide range of lower bound results in complexity theory. To date, the problem of establishing lower bounds for classical computational problems has proved the most difficult (as well as the most interesting) problem in complexity theory. The possibility of cryptographic application lends interest to results about lower bound problems potentially more tractable than those studied so far.

Several other areas have close structural connections with cryptography. The central problem of cryptanalysis is equivalent to the "machine identification" problem in automatic fault diagnosis, since discovering which part of a mechanism has failed is equivalent to finding the key in a cryptographic system. Cryptanalysis is also related to the problem of decoding in communication theory and to the problem of pattern recognition and both theories show promise of future contributions to cryptanalysis.

Cryptography is valuable to researchers both as a source of new problems and as a field of application for existing results. Academic interest in the subject is a natural outcome of the growth in finite and combinatorial mathematics which began during the sixties and will continue for the foreseeable future.

The Data Encryption Standard

The NBS Data Encryption Standard appears likely to prove adequate for its intended uses during the next five years. On the other hand, it appears unlikely that it can outlive the decade of the 1980's.

Although Diffie and Hellman's 1977 estimate [7] that a twenty million dollar key exhaustion machine that could break

DES in, on average, half a day now appears to have been overly optimistic in some of its details, it seems that following the same architecture and using a modified version of Advanced Micro Devices' newly announced DES chip, a fifty million dollar version with a two day average search time might be achieved by the end of 1981 [8].

The difficulty of breaking DES by exhaustive search of its keyspace will be diminished by any improvement in semiconductor technology: speed, wafer size, density, or yield, and each of these areas is under active attack. The Deputy Directorate for Research and Engineering of the Department of Definse is sponsoring a program of industry research in Very High Speed Integrated Circuits, which projects a factor of 100 improvement in speed over the next five years. The new field of "wafer scale integration," will probably allow each card in a repetitive structure such as the DES search machine to be placed on a single wafer. Density and yield are fundamental problems of semiconductor manufacture and improvements in both areas are under development throughout the industry.

In August 1976, the National Bureau of Standards held a workshop on the feasibility of building a DES key exhaustion machine [17]. The scenarios proposed by this conference made the prospect seem comfortingly remote at the time, but some now take on a more threatening aspect. In particular, the prediction of a Josephson junction machine capable of achieving Diffie and Hellman's objectives by 1990 is strongly reinforced by IBM's announcement in January 1980 of a prototype Josephson junction computer scheduled for completion in 1985.

These developments suggest that the cost of building a special purpose DES search machine will drop substantially toward the end of the decade, although the problem may not become tractable for general purpose computers till several years thereafter.

Government Regulation

It is difficult to predict the effect of a governmental attempt to regulate cryptographic research, or even to predict whether such an attempt will be made. Suggestions for government policy have ranged from increasing the funding available for cryptographic research through NSF to asking congress for a law which would impose the same kind of government domination which the Atomic Energy Act applies to all nuclear information.

At present, government policies, and the legal means for implementing these policies, are uncertain. Some government agencies, particularly the National Science Foundation, have funded and encouraged unclassified research in cryptography, while others have attempted, through the means at their disposal, to put a damper on the same work. And present indications are that both trends continue.

Speaking before the Armed Forces Communications and Electronics Association on 8 January 1981, Admiral Robert Inman, Director of NSA, announced both that his agency was beginning a program of open funding of cryptographic research in the universities and that researchers at Stanford University, formerly a center of harsh criticism of NSA influence on the Data Encryption Standard, would be among the first recipients.

During the past year, the American Council on Education, at the suggestion of NSA, formed a Public Cryptography Study Group. After several meetings, this committee has come forth with a draft proposal for voluntary prepublication review of cryptographic research papers by the federal government [1], under which researchers would be encouraged to submit papers to NSA for examination prior to publication. Earlier drafts contained provisions for some nonvoluntary measures and one member of the committee, Prof. George Davida of the Georgia Institute of Technology, has expressed deep concern that the committee's report may be used to argue for mandatory controls at a later date.

In an area not directly related to cryptography, the Export Administration Act was invoked to discourage Russian and Chinese participation in a meeting on bubble memory technology, early in 1980 [23]. In a possibly contradictory spirit, the preamble to a Federal Register announcement of proposed changes in ITAR states, "... provision has been added to make it clear that the regulation of the export of technical data does not purport to interfere with the first amendment rights of individuals [12]." The effect of such government attempts to restrain publication are hard to predict. As long as they are uncontested, they seem to serve the government's immediate interests. Informal prepublication review, in particular, provides an opportunity for NSA to discuss the consequences of publication with authors, possibly on a confidential basis, and perhaps make them more sympathetic to its point of view. Any attempt to use legal pressure against an uncooperative opponent, however, is likely to result in concerted opposition by the press and widely publicized legal proceedings such as followed the Department of Energy's attempt to stop publication of an article on fusion bombs in "The Progressive" in 1979 [18].

Even though the hearings in the Progressive case were closed, they disclosed more information and attracted more attention than the unimpeded publication of the original article could have. Were a criminal trial to result from a defendant's refusal to comply with a court restraining order, even more information could be expected to come to light.

Cryptographic secrets are among the most fragile and NSA would most likely attempt to avoid a first amendment battle over the publication of independent cryptographic research.

In most of this report, it is tacitly assumed that government influence will continue in an irregular pattern much like the present one and that federal regulation will not be an all pervasive force in public cryptography.

The Period from 1980 to 1985

The Data Encryption Standard will remain viable during this period. Products implementing DES will continue to appear and will offer more elaborate key management and other features as time goes on.

The development of standards for using DES in computer communication networks will dominate cryptographic development for the next two or three years. This, together with increasing public acceptance of cryptography, will result in a wide spectrum of DES based security products in the mid 1980's.

Cryptographic devices will continue to employ the current "LSI" technology, using one or more discreet DES chips, during the next two or three years. Later products will begin a transition to a technology in which cryptography will be placed on the same chip with, for example, a packet switch or voice compressor. These transition products may include a chip with more than one DES device (for reliability) or a microprocessor with a DES instruction.

Security systems employing public keys will continue to be built for special applications and some public key products will no doubt reach the market, probably to provide signatures in value added communication networks.

Current development projects in secure computing will begin to produce multi-level secure operating systems by the early mid-eighties. The role of cryptography in implementing such systems is as yet unclear, but whether or not secure operating systems use cryptography internally, they will be a key component in cryptographically secure communication networks and will sharply reduce the cost of implementing communication security.

The Period from 1985 to 1990

Very Large Scale Integration

By the late 1980's, Very Large Scale Integration will have a profound effect on cryptographic hardware, reducing the cost of high grade communication security equipment by an even bigger factor than the reduction in computing costs generally.

VLSI will permit circuitry that now requires cards or entire racks to be placed on single pieces of silicon. This will make the cost of incorporating DES in an integrated packet switch proportional to the increased area required to include its 5,000 devices in the whole switch's million, an overhead of less than one percent.

Integration of cryptography into larger systems will dramatically reduce the cost of radiation shielding and tamper resistance. Reduced size and smaller power dissipation coupled with internal optical isolation will permit a very high degree of shielding at very little increased cost. The same factors of size and power, coupled with developing tamper resistance technologies, will make it more difficult for an opponent to extract keying information by dismantling the equipment.

Public Key Cryptography

Prospects for development of new and more efficient public key cryptographic systems by the latter part of the eighties are quite good. Public key cryptography is more successful today than algebraic coding theory was at the age of four. The major breakthroughs in that field did not begin till the latter part of its first decade, but then progressed rapidly. The similarity of the two fields is reason for optimism that in the absence of interference public key cryptography will follow a similar course.

Increasing use of the available public key systems in the 1980's will spread awareness of both their advantages and the performance shortcomings of the early examples. The research response to this awareness will probably produce better public key systems in time for use during the first half of the nineties.

Secure Computing

Secure computing will be widespread and the now esoteric techniques used to verify the correctness of programs will be standard tools of programming. This will make available not only operating systems trusted to manage multiple levels of sensitive information but special purpose programs for encryption or cryptographic control.

The spread of secure computing will also have an effect on the design of computer hardware and special security mechanisms (some of them cryptographic) will be incorporated into computer architecture.

Voice Technology

Speaker independent word recognition products will be common and of adequate quality to be applied in the adverse environment of wiretapping. Speech generation good enough to impersonate a speaker is also possible, but full voice understanding (voice typewriter) is unlikely.

Personal Computing

Personal computing will have developed to the point where many individuals and small companies will have as much computing power as is currently available to laboratories of substantial size. This will broaden the base of research in computer science and probably lead to unanticipated results in cryptography, among other areas.

Adequacy of DES

By the late 1980's the security of DES will become marginal for many applications while remaining adequate for others. The most likely response will be for multiple encryption to become the *de facto* standard in higher security applications.

The Period from 1990 to 1995

In the early nineties, cryptography and its associated technologies will be highly developed and in extensive use throughout a largely electronic information economy. Secure computing devices containing integrated cryptographic facilities will be widespread. High bandwidth (from 9.6 kilobaud to multi megabaud) digital communications will be nearly ubiquitous.

Threats will increase at the same pace as facilities. Personal computing resources will be vast and computing techniques and facilities adequate to intercept and analyze data and voice traffic will be available even to small organizations. This mature communication security environment will provide the setting for a major overhaul of communication security practice.

By this time, the Data Encryption Standard is certain to require replacement, but what form this replacement will take is as yet uncertain. The most obvious possibilities are:

- Without any actual change in the DES itself, standards for employing DES will be revised to accommodate multiple encryption. (This has the marked disadvantage of decreasing the speed of encryption even further.)

- The DES key schedule will be revised to incorporate more key bits. (This would impose no additional speed penalty.)

- If a larger block size is considered necessary, a system with a similar internal structure, but based on a 128 bit block might be designed.

New developments in cryptographic technology provide another direction in which to look for competing candidates.

- A public key system of adequate performance may be developed and achieve general acceptance.

  Advances in complexity theory may give rise to a provably secure system.

In 1990, public key cryptography will be fifteen years old and is very likely to have made great strides beyond its present position. As current public key systems are already useable for many purposes, a 1990 public key system adequate as a general standard is a strong possibility.

It is also possible, though not probable, that by the early nineties a breakthrough in complexity theory will make possible a much higher degree of certainty in the security of cryptographic systems than is now possible. Such a breakthrough need not necessarily provide a solution to the problems which dominate complexity theory at present nor would the cryptographic system developed from it necessarily be similar to current systems.

The precise impact of such a system would depend on the details of the breakthrough and particularly on the performance of the system. If, however, the theoretical results were strong and the performance acceptable, it would probably see widespread use.

A very strong possibility is of a less theoretical nature. By the early nineties, voice and data communication networks using DES will be common throughout the federal government and these networks will exist side by side with comparable facilities for classified communications. The cost of this redundancy, coupled with a possible decline in cryptanalytic communications intelligence, may lead the government either to declassify one of its own cryptographic systems or to accept an outside system as adequate for classified use and thereby adopt a single system for all government communications.

Conclusions

Unless perturbed by outside influences, cryptography will continue to develop over the next fifteen years and assume an important position in commercial communication technology. The timescale within that frame can only be approximated because of uncertainty about the rate of market growth, particularly the federal market, the course standards development, and the possible effect of new government attempts at regulation.

The same technological developments that are making processing, storage, and communication of information the largest and most important part of our national economy, will provide opponents at home and abroad with the means to intercept or disrupt communications in our "information economy" at will. This combination will make a well developed technology for protection of information in transit or storage indispensible. For an adequate cryptographic technology to be available to serve this need, standards for compatibility of cryptographic communication systems must be developed, and research toward systems with both assured security and such new features as the digital signature must be continued.

References

[1] Draft Final Report of the American Council on Education, Public Cryptography Study Group (January 1981).

[2] H. P. Burstyn, "Slow growing encryption market to spurt in '80's," Electronic Business (January 1979), pp. 76-77.

[3] S. Lu and L. Lee, "A simple and effective public key cryptosystem," Comsat Technical Review, Vol. 9, No. 1 (Spring 1979). This paper was published without review outside Comsat and immediately exposed as a rediscovery of a system considered by Rivest, Shamir, and Adleman and rejected as weak. Their analysis appears in: R. Rivest and L. Adleman, "How to break the Lu-Lee cryptosystem," to appear, Computer Security Journal.

[4] "Data encryption standard," Federal Information Standards Publication 46, National Bureau of Standards (Jan. 15, 1977).

[5] W. Diffie and M. E. Hellman, "Multiuser cryptographic techniques," Proceedings of the National Computer Conference, New York (June 7-10, 1976), pp. 109-112.

[6] W. Diffie and M. E. Hellman, "New directions in cryptography," IEEE Trans. on Inform. Theory, IT-22, No. 6 (Nov. 1976), pp. 644-654. (See pp. 143-180, this volume.)

[7] W. Diffie and M. E. Hellman, "Exhaustive cryptanalysis of the NBS data encryption standard," Computer, Vol. 10, No. 6 (June 1977), pp. 74-84.

[8] Unpublished calculations by Diffie based on 1980 conversations with Advanced Micro Devices personnel.

[9] "NEC systems recognize and speaker's words," Electronics, 19 (June 1980), pp. 69-70.

[10] "Typewriters with ears, words with pix," Electronic Mail and Message Systems, Vol. 4, No. 18 (Sept. 15, 1980).

[11] International Resource Development, "Data and voice encryption," (March 1979), p. 62.

[12] "Revision of the international tariff in arms regulations," Federal Register, 45-FR-83970-95 (Dec. 19, 1980).

[13] D. Kahn, The Codebreakers, The Story of Secret Writing, New York: Macmillian (1967).

[14] "Unscrambling the encryption market," Quantum Science Corporation, MAPTEK Brief, Vol. 78, No. 424 (Mar. 31, 1978).

[15] R. C. Merkle and M. E. Hellman, "Hiding information and signatures in trapdoor knapsacks," IEEE Trans. on Inform. Theory, IT-24, No. 5 (Sept. 1978), pp. 525-530. (See pp. 197-215, this volume.)

[16] F. H. Myers, "A data link encryption system," National Telecommunications Conference, Washington, D.C. (Nov. 27-29, 1979).

[17] "Report of the 1976 workshop on estimation of significant advances in computer technology," National Bureau of Standards (Aug. 30-31, 1976).

[18] The article, "The H-bomb secret, how we got it - why we're telling it," by Howard Morland was finally published in The Progressive for November 1979. Most of this issue and the May 1979, "Born secret," issue of The Progressive are devoted to explaining the legal battle.

[19] R. L. Rivest, A. Shamir, and L. Adleman, "A method for obtaining digital signatures and public key cryptosystems," Communications of the ACM, Vol. 21, No. 2 (Feb. 1978), pp. 120-126. (See pp. 217-239, this volume.)

[20] B. P. Shanning, "Data encryption with public key distribution," IEEE EASCON'79, Washington, D.C. (Oct. 9-11, 1979).

[21] G. J. Simmons, "Message authentication without secrecy: a secure communications problem uniquely solvable by

asymmetric encryption techniques," IEEE EASCON'79, Washington, D.C. (Oct. 9-11, 1979), EASCON'79 Record, pp. 661-662.

[22] G. Kaplan, "Words into action I," IEEE Spectrum, Vol. 17, No. 6 (June 1980), pp. 22-25; R. Reddi, "Words into action II," IEEE Spectrum, Vol. 17, No. 6 (June 1980), pp. 26-28; Y. Kato, "Words into action III," IEEE Spectrum, Vol. 17, No. 6 (June 1980), p. 29.

[23] N. Wade, "Science meetings catch U.S. - Soviet chill," Science (Mar. 7, 1980), p. 1056.

[24] A. D. Wyner, "An analog scrambling scheme which does not expand bandwidth part I: discrete time," IEEE Trans. on Inform. Theory, IT-25, No. 3 (May 1979), pp. 261-274.

[25] A. D. Wyner, "An analog scrambling scheme which does not expand bandwidth, part II: continuous time," IEEE Trans. on Inform. Theory, IT-25, No. 4 (July 1979), pp. 415-424.

Author Index

Subject Index

9780367286880